Coming to Terms
with John F. Kennedy

Coming to Terms with John F. Kennedy

Stephen F. Knott

 University Press of Kansas

Published by the University Press of Kansas (Lawrence, Kansas 66045), which was
organized by the Kansas Board of Regents and is operated and funded by Emporia
State University, Fort Hays State University, Kansas State University, Pittsburg State
University, the University of Kansas, and Wichita State University.

Library of Congress Cataloging-in-Publication Data

Names: Knott, Stephen F., author.
Title: Coming to terms with John F. Kennedy / Stephen F. Knott.
Description: Lawrence, Kansas : University Press of Kansas, 2022. |
   Includes bibliographical references and index.
Identifiers: LCCN 2021062299
   ISBN 9780700633654 (cloth)
   ISBN 9780700633661 (ebook)
Subjects: LCSH: Kennedy, John F. (John Fitzgerald), 1917–1963. | United
   States—History—1953–1961. | Presidents—United States—Biography.
Classification: LCC E842 .K56 2022 | DDC 973.922092 [B]—dc23
LC record available at https://lccn.loc.gov/2021062299.

British Library Cataloguing-in-Publication Data is available.

Printed in the United States of America

10 9 8 7 6 5 4 3 2 1

The paper used in this publication is acid free and meets the minimum requirements of
the American National Standard for Permanence of Paper for Printed Library Materials
Z39.48-1992.

For Maura Porter and Bill Van Riper
who kept the faith

And for David and Brian Knott
and Travis Scarboro

As every past generation has had to disenthrall itself from an inheritance of truisms and stereotypes, so in our own time we must move on from the reassuring repetition of stale phrases to a new, difficult, but essential confrontation with reality.

For the great enemy of truth is very often not the lie—deliberate, contrived and dishonest—but the myth—persistent, persuasive, and unrealistic. Too often we hold fast to the clichés of our forebears. We subject all facts to a prefabricated set of interpretations. We enjoy the comfort of opinion without the discomfort of thought.

Mythology distracts us everywhere. . . .

John F. Kennedy, June 11, 1962

CONTENTS

ACKNOWLEDGMENTS

I am deeply indebted to my friends Maura Porter and Bill Van Riper for their valuable insights, and to my editor, David Congdon, for his indispensable advice and encouragement. I also wish to thank my peer reviewers Patrick Lacroix and another scholar who prefers to remain anonymous. These scholars were remarkably generous in taking time out of their busy schedules and sharing their extraordinary knowledge of the Kennedy presidency. Their contributions dramatically improved this book.

I am also grateful to Colin Tripp, Erica Nicholson, and Evan Hershman, for their meticulous attention to detail. I would also like to thank John Dennehy, Arthur J. Donoghue, Rich Keyes, and Lisa Fruitt, all of whom were colleagues at the John F. Kennedy Library and became lifelong friends. Additionally, I am grateful for the friendship and support of Joe Doherty, Brian Walsh, Frank Colpoys, Jim Moloy, Rich Wade, and Gregg Lysko. My wife, Maryanne, and my daughter, Maura, were, as always, at the heart of this endeavor, as was my granddaughter, Lily. My prayer is that Lily will journey through the twenty-first century in a nation that remains a beacon of hope and promise.

I have grappled with John F. Kennedy's legacy all my life. He was the first president I remember, and his death was the first occasion in my life when I saw my mother cry. When I was five years old, I would listen to Jimmy Dean sing "PT-109," a top-ten hit in 1962, on my parents' massive console stereo. The song was an over-the-top tribute to JFK and the generation, including my father, that fought the "good war" against the "Japs," as the song intoned. My Dad and his fellow veterans had vanquished the brazen enemy and were now led by one of their own, "a mighty good man," according to Jimmy Dean.[1]

My mother's devotion to all things Kennedy was rooted in her Irish-Catholic heritage. She had fought to establish a Catholic parish in our small New England town in the face of some residual anti-Catholicism found among the old-line Yankee Protestants. Kennedy's Catholic faith and Irish heritage were all that was needed to win her allegiance. By breaking the "Protestants only" hold on the American presidency, John F. Kennedy became, as far as my mother was concerned, a candidate for sainthood.

This faith-based, ethnic allegiance had its downside, as I witnessed up close and personal in 1969. That summer, I looked over my mother's shoulder as she wrote a letter of support for Senator Edward Kennedy (D-MA) after the death of Mary Jo Kopechne at Chappaquiddick. The doings on that remote island off of Cape Cod remained a somewhat off-limit topic of conversation in our home, although it caused frequent dustups between my mother and her Republican friends.

The following year, I went door to door campaigning for Kenneth O'Donnell, a member of JFK's "Irish Mafia," who was running for governor of Massachusetts. My bedroom at home was something of a shrine to Camelot, decorated with photos and memorabilia of the thirty-fifth president. I went on to serve as a college coordinator for Edward Kennedy's campaign for the Senate in 1976, and my first job out of college was at the John F. Kennedy Library in Boston, where I was hired in 1979. My mother could not have been prouder of that achievement, even though I was basically a glorified tour guide at the museum. It was, as the Kennedy Library museum curator and Irish Mafia member Dave Powers was fond of saying, like dying and going to heaven.

Dave Powers's office was two doors from mine, and listening to Powers regale me with stories about this skinny young PT boat veteran who recruited him at his Charlestown tenement in 1946 made me feel like I had become a part of "we happy few, we band of brothers." It was Powers who introduced me to Jacqueline Kennedy Onassis, prompting the one and only time in my life when I became completely tongue-tied. In my mother's mind, this introduction was the highlight of my life.

During the almost six years I worked at the Kennedy Library, I frequently went into the archives, where an archivist would let me peruse material, including tape recordings, that was still closed to researchers. I was given access to "closed" materials that a hyper-protective family denied to most scholars save a favored few, including Arthur Schlesinger Jr. and Doris Kearns Goodwin.

Ironically, just as I reached the mountaintop, my faith began to wane. During my time at the Kennedy Library, I saw things that soured me on the Kennedys, including a certain arrogance on the part of some members of the family, and a propensity of Kennedy groupies to prostrate themselves for a brush with American "royalty." One longtime groupie's claim to fame was her role as a babysitter for Robert Kennedy's grandchildren, and she could not have been prouder. I was also repelled by the parade of extramarital affairs within the Kennedy circle, which were too numerous to count; it was as if it were a sign that you had made it to honorary Kennedy status if you had someone on the side. Throughout the 1980s and 1990s, the bad behavior of far too many presidential nephews was off the charts, not to mention the behavior of Senator Edward Kennedy. It also became clear to me that members of the Kennedy family saw the library as a stylish backdrop for photo ops promoting the latest family endeavor, not as a treasured historical resource. One of my most deflating experiences was hearing a longtime Kennedy aide express his surprise that visitors to the library were "still believing that crap"—the introductory film and exhibits at the library.

I left all this behind in 1987 after becoming a Reagan Democrat, eventually moving to Colorado to teach but also to escape Massachusetts and the dead weight of Kennedy-mania. But almost twenty years after leaving the Kennedy Library, fate, or something, brought me back to Kennedy-land when, at the University of Virginia's Miller Center of Public Affairs, I became involved with and directed for a time the Edward M. Kennedy Oral History Project. Once again, I saw up close and personal the family's propensity for trying to spin history, and again witnessed the phenomenon of people with stars in their eyes hoping to get an invitation to Hyannisport or to "the senator's" hideaway office in the United States Capitol. This experience validated all that I had come to believe during the previous decades about the now somewhat tottering Kennedy myth: that it was all spin, aided and abetted by toadies, ideologically biased scholars, and a sympathetic news media.

And yet . . . amid the debacle of the Trump presidency, with its blatant appeals to the worst in us, and with so many of those whom I viewed as intellectual influences either remaining silent or overtly endorsing Trumpism, I reconsidered my move to the Right and began rebuilding some of the intellectual bridges I had burned.

Let me further explain my intellectual transformation. I start from the premise that the American republic, despite its flaws, is worth preserving. I continue to be a champion of America's political institutions, particularly the office of the presidency, whose overall balance sheet was, until recently, a net positive in terms of its contributions to a healthy political order. Yet growing up in the latter half of the twentieth century, it was clear to me that many on the American Left found very little in the American system worthy of preservation. I recoiled from what I considered to be simplistic populist appeals framed with the battle cry of "us versus them"—that somewhere there was an elite cabal at work busily plotting against the common man. This anti-American, anti-institutional populism was just not for me. Additionally, I consider demagogic populist appeals as anti-intellectual, as rooted in passion and emotion rather than in reason, although they tend to be remarkably effective come election day.

At times, certainly on the Far Left, it was widely accepted that this oligarchic, corrupt society needed to be radically changed, perhaps even overthrown. This belief was fueled by conspiracy theories involving a murky "Deep State" undermining the interests of the American people and of world peace. During the Vietnam War, I often heard that America was involved in the conflict to acquire oil reserves in the South China Sea, or to line the pockets of weapons manufacturers. Time and again the worst possible interpretation of American actions was the option of first resort for those on the Left: for instance, that George W. Bush invaded Iraq in 2003 due to the connivance of various Texas oil barons or of Dick Cheney and his Halliburton cronies. This was of a piece with the view that the United States was equivalent to, if not worse than, the most odious authoritarian regimes of the day.

Today I see that same resort to conspiracy theories among Donald Trump's followers. Theories that were once the province of the Left and reflect the same disdain for the American political order and its institutions, including the American military, the FBI, the CIA, and the State Department, are at the core of Trumpism. During my time at the Naval War College, I had the privilege of teaching students from all of these "Deep State" entities, and routinely found them to be devoted public servants. They are not the enemy of the people.

Trump also embraced other tenets of the 1960s Left, including the idea that the United States and Russia are morally equivalent. Trump noted that Vladimir Putin displayed better leadership qualities than Barack Obama, accepted Putin's word over the word of his own law enforcement agencies regarding Russian interference in the 2016 election, and claimed that the United States was really no better than Putin's regime in terms of its conduct of foreign policy.[2]

The intelligent conservatism I admired, as opposed to the John Bircher or Trumpist variety, promoted the rule of law and a kind of thoughtful patriotism, and an aversion to conspiracy theories. Too many conservatives abandoned these principles and have become full-blown Trumpists, even after Trump promoted the insurrection of January 6, 2021, and attempted to bully state election officials into overturning election results. His efforts to extort the government of Ukraine by withholding military aid in exchange for damaging information on his potential opponent in 2020 is unparalleled in American history. Additionally, many of Trump's supporters believe that the white race is being replaced, which is, needless to say, just a few steps removed from the notion of white supremacy, as we saw on full display during the white supremacist rally in Charlottesville, Virginia in 2017.

Trump is the epitome of a demagogue, whose time in office was spent circulating conspiracy theories and degrading the norms of civility that permit a republic to function. Trump exploited the lowest public passions and rejected expertise almost instinctively, surrounding himself with untutored, anti-intellectual ideologues. Trump and Trumpism are not things I want to be remotely connected with; in fact, I will spend the remaining years of my life trying to rebuff this malignant movement—thus my decision to revisit my own thinking, my own past, which was tangentially but in an odd way firmly connected to John F. Kennedy.

I began to see that whatever his personal flaws, Kennedy's lofty rhetoric appealed to what is best in America, without invoking the snarling nativism of his least illustrious successor. Sixty years later, the racial discord that characterized the Kennedy years was still very much with us, aggravated by Trump's demagogic appeals to white resentment toward minorities of all kinds. Trump destroyed what little was left of the "party of Lincoln," while elements of that agenda had been embraced, belatedly, by President Kennedy, and continued by his Democratic Party successors, most notably his vice president, Lyndon Johnson.

John F. Kennedy saw the United States as a land of hope and promise, not a land in the grips of "carnage" whose salvation lies in a cramped nationalism rooted in race and reaction. Trump never grasped the importance of the American experiment as an idea, not a piece of walled-off turf. President Kennedy also celebrated achievements in the arts and letters and would have abhorred the demagoguery and the anti-intellectualism at the core of Trumpism.

I began this project hoping to find the real President Kennedy, not the one I worshipped in my youth, nor the one that I and my conservative colleagues disparaged habitually, and not the one whose principles and practices were distorted by ideologues of all stripes. I also wanted to separate him from some of the negative connotations surrounding the Kennedys writ large. For better or for worse, succeeding generations of Kennedys rode on JFK's coattails, hoping some of his "magic" might rub off on them. But the reverse has happened as well—his genuine achievements, his real record, have been obscured by their actions.

Kennedy and the brief era in which he governed are part of a lost world, possibly irretrievable, when Americans believed in themselves and in their nation. I am not referring to a mythical Camelot, but to a time when polls revealed Americans trusted their government and believed in their nation's purpose. Yet in my lifetime, I witnessed that hope and optimism evaporate. Twenty-first century Americans have much to learn from this era and from this president in our jaded, divisive times, when reality itself is up for debate. That is the reason I wrote this book, and why I decided to reexamine the first president I can remember.

The passage of sixty years has given me a broader view of Kennedy's presidency and allowed me to see how both the Left and the Right in America distorted his record for their own purposes. Kennedy's conservative critics have claimed for decades that far too much attention has been paid to the "New Frontier," that it was merely a stylish interlude of little gravity, that JFK was vastly overrated due to the propagation of the Camelot myth by various court historians and the mainstream media. It is true that court historians and media sympathizers crafted a mythical JFK, but an equally misguided account emerged on the Right in response to this idolatry. William F. Buckley Jr. observed that "nothing that Mr. Kennedy did in the way of public policy was either singular or enduring in effect," a charge echoed by one of Buckley's acolytes, Jonah Goldberg, who claimed Kennedy's generally positive reputation represented "one of the longest-lived triumphs of style over substance" in American history.[3]

At the same time, Kennedy's liberal critics argue that he was feckless when it came to civil rights (a "bystander" in the words of author Nick Bryant; "a profile in antiracist caution instead of courage," according to Georgetown history professor Michael Kazin) and reckless when it came to the Cold War.[4] Both perspectives are misguided. In the last year of his life, John F. Kennedy found his voice on civil rights and invoked both the Jewish-Christian tradition and the nation's founding principles in a clarion call for equal justice under the law. His predecessor, Dwight Eisenhower, while enforcing court orders to desegregate American society, never threw the weight of his personal stature or of his office behind this cause. Many of these commentators are also critical of Kennedy's punitive policies toward Cuba. Add to the issue of Cuba the notion that Kennedy was a "reckless" Cold War warrior who drove the world to the brink of an apocalypse, and you have a Kennedy whose image is as distorted as the one portrayed in the Camelot myth.

This brings us to another lesson to be drawn from the historiographical saga surrounding John F. Kennedy, but one that is unlikely to be heeded by authors and publishers anxious to be first: initial impressions are almost always wrong. To write with certainty about any American presidency within twenty years is an invitation to get things wrong. Published accounts of Harry Truman's presidency written in the 1950s and 1960s, or accounts of Dwight Eisenhower's presidency in the 1960s and 1970s, tended to be caricatures of the real president. The same held for Kennedy, who was canonized in the 1960s and early 1970s, and then became a figure out of *Dr. Strangelove* for a time. It often takes a minimum of twenty years to get a fair and balanced assessment of a presidency, free from the emotions of partisanship, and long enough for policies to take root and mature. In JFK's case, twenty years turned out not to be long enough, due to the machinations of the Kennedy family to keep the name politically viable, and due to ideologues of all persuasions who linked their principles to the martyred president, often distorting everything the latter stood for as president.

Even at the height of my Kennedy fandom, I was put off by the family's practice of playing favorites and keeping materials quarantined past the point where any genuine public good was served. The family repeatedly hindered those scholars who might deign to tell an unadulterated version of the Kennedy presidency. Even in my most worshipful phase, I recognized that history was far too important to be left in the hands of relatives and acquaintances.

This has done considerable damage to Kennedy's place in history, and to the American body politic. Almost sixty years have passed since the abrupt end of Kennedy's presidency, which is well past the time to abandon the myths of the idolaters and of those who revile him. One of John F. Kennedy's more underrated public addresses was delivered at Yale University in 1962, where he noted that "the great enemy of truth is very often not the lie—deliberate, contrived and dishonest—but the myth—persistent, persuasive, and unrealistic." "Mythology distracts us everywhere," he added; "every past generation has had to disenthrall itself from an inheritance of truisms and stereotypes." And while Kennedy was speaking of economics, the same holds true when it comes to his legacy, that "too often we hold fast to the clichés of our forebears."

Despite the existence of over forty thousand books dealing with the man and his era, I believe I have something new to say about this brief but important presidency.[5] My book contends that Kennedy's presidency, for better or for worse, mattered, and mattered deeply, as I will explain.

As someone who has written approvingly of Ronald Reagan and George W. Bush, I can also safely say that my interpretation differs from the Kennedy idolaters. (Much to my mother's despair, she kept asking me when I would write a book about a "good president, like John F. Kennedy.") But my interpretation also differs with those who believe JFK was simply good teeth and good hair and would be long forgotten were it not for Lee Harvey Oswald.

I will offer a more nuanced portrait of the thirty-fifth president by look-ing at Kennedy through the lens of five critical issues: his interpretation of presidential power, his approach to civil rights, and his foreign policy toward Cuba, the Soviet Union, and Vietnam. I will also examine his assassination and the evolving interpretations of his presidency, both highly politicized subject matters. In each of these areas, I will discuss the misinterpretations advanced by ideologues on both the Left and the Right, as well as from Ken-nedy's idolaters, and offer my own perspective on these issues.

Finally, as we are now in the midst of renewed great-power competition, this book will provide both historical context and offer lessons about avert-ing, as President Kennedy put it, "the final failure" of a cataclysmic conflict between the world's nuclear powers. And as race and racism continues to be an unfortunate fact of American life, Kennedy's politically courageous stance in the final months of his life provides fragments of hope regarding the ul-timate outcome of that "long, twilight struggle." It is also my hope that one of the themes of this book, my willingness to continually reexamine my own political beliefs, might encourage others to go through a similar process. This seems especially important in a time when partisanship threatens to tear the American republic apart and when compromise and moderation are seen as evidence of ideological treason.[6] One of John F. Kennedy's strengths was his aversion to ideologues and ideology itself. He understood that a house divided along ideological lines and averse to compromise would not long stand. And he would echo Abraham Lincoln's call to disenthrall ourselves of these odious practices and to think anew.

Refounding the Presidency

My interest in the American presidency began with a youthful fascination with John F. Kennedy. I accepted, without reservation, the legendary president depicted by Arthur Schlesinger Jr. and Ted Sorensen. For me, the nation's thirty-fifth president was *the* personification of the model chief executive. I held on to this belief for quite some time, but eventually I came to appreciate the dangers of a devotion to political figures based on their personal charisma. Most importantly, I began to see that certain aspects of this "model" Kennedy presidency actually harmed the office over time.

At the time of this writing, forty-five individuals have served as president of the United States, but only a handful of those men left a lasting mark on the executive office. John F. Kennedy was one of those men. Kennedy was an instrumental figure on the road to "personalizing" the presidency, elevating the office and the notion of "presidential government" to a position of prominence that was never intended in a system of separated powers. This prominence has not always served the office or the nation well since it became a permanent feature of American politics in the early twentieth century.

Despite serving in office for less than three years, Kennedy's "brief, shining moment" deserves to be studied not because it any way resembled a mythical Camelot, which was entirely a creation of Jacqueline Kennedy's imagination, but because Kennedy reshaped the office in a way equaled only by three other twentieth century presidents: Theodore Roosevelt, Woodrow Wilson, and Franklin Roosevelt. These men believed in an unbounded presidency, one whose inhabitant could be, as Wilson put it, as "big a man as he can." In this sense, Kennedy contributed to the decline of the office by distorting its intentions and its capabilities.

The notion of the presidency as the center of action and of presidential power as resting on the personal qualities of the president was central to Kennedy's understanding of the office. The hope was that a presidency-centric government, what some called "presidential government," would circumvent the archaic checks and balances that impeded government effectiveness and prevented coherent, visionary leadership. The architects of "presidential government" believed that the founders' presidency was part of a system designed for "deadlock" and was ripe for replacement. Columbia professor Richard Neustadt, who influenced Kennedy's view of the presidency, claimed that "a president's success in maximizing power for himself serves objectives far beyond his own . . . what is good for the country is good for the president, and vice versa."[1]

Untethered from the Constitution, in the absence of well-defined boundaries, it was perhaps inevitable that this conception of presidential power would lead to abuses of the kind that most glaringly appeared under Richard Nixon. "The imperial presidency," or "presidential government," was not of Kennedy's making alone, but he was a significant contributor to its development. Modern American presidents, Kennedy included, dismissed a concern held by some of their founding predecessors that the more you personalize the presidency and the more you inflate the presidential portfolio, the more you diminish it. Boundaries that existed prior to the twentieth century protected but also energized the office; without these boundaries, the presidency was placed in a remarkably vulnerable position.

Inflated expectations prompted by the promise of "presidential government" were inevitably followed by disappointment and increased cynicism regarding the office and the American government writ large. The failures of "presidential government" are too large to catalog in their entirety, but they include a "war on drugs" that is still being fought, and lost, half a century after it was first launched; a "war on poverty" whose proponents argued would eliminate poverty in the United States by 1975; a "global war on terror" that sought to democratize the Middle East; and a president, Barack Obama, who noted at the time of his nomination that "this was the moment . . . when the rise of the oceans began to slow and the planet began to heal."[2] Again, these are just a few examples of a presidency that promises too much of itself and of the entire American government. John F. Kennedy's soaring inaugural address and other far-reaching pronouncements, including the idea that "man can be as big as he wants," were significant milestones on the road to this overcommitted, unsustainable presidency. This was the most egregious, lasting failure of the Kennedy presidency.

Building on the Wilsonian Template

Kennedy set the standard that almost all his successors would follow until the presidency of Donald Trump. That standard put a premium on the personal qualities of the president as seen through the lens of the electronic media. Kennedy's mastery of television allowed him to bond with the American public in an unprecedented manner, even more so than Franklin Roosevelt (due to the limitations of radio). Political scientist Larry Sabato, while excessively celebrating Kennedy's virtues, was nonetheless correct to describe the period from 1963 to the Obama presidency as "the Kennedy Half-Century." This was an era that witnessed nine American presidents grapple with the ghost of John F. Kennedy: invoking his name and his legend on behalf of their agenda and struggling to capture elements of his style that led the American people, even to this day, to celebrate Kennedy as one of the greatest American presidents in the nation's history.[3]

I have argued elsewhere that Kennedy does not deserve the ranking of one of the greatest presidents ever, but he does deserve to be ranked as a remarkably significant president, behind luminaries such as Washington, Lincoln, and Franklin Roosevelt.[4] Kennedy converted the personalized, charismatic presidency that Woodrow Wilson envisioned into a reality, and in so doing cemented his place among the "near-greats." For most Americans, certainly most Americans who identify as politically progressive, there is no turning back from the Kennedy model of dynamic leadership, of media mastery, of connecting with and inspiring the American people. One can pejoratively label this as "style" or "fluff," but for better or worse, and some of it has been for worse, it is here to stay.

Those who dismiss Kennedy as all style and no substance are wrong to claim that he lacked substance, but they are equally misguided when they denigrate the importance of presidential style, for it matters how a president presents himself to his fellow citizens and to the rest of the world. As

George Washington approached his first inauguration, and for months afterwards, he consulted with Alexander Hamilton and others for advice on how he should conduct himself, how accessible he should be, and how much distance and detachment were appropriate for a republican chief executive. Questions regarding the president's title and, as Washington put it in a letter to Hamilton, issues concerning "the etiquette proper to be observed by the President," absorbed a remarkable amount of Washington's attention. Washington's style drew the ire of Thomas Jefferson, who upon winning the presidency did away with Washington's gilded coach and his stable of fancy white horses and stopped the practice of holding weekly "levees," which were highly scripted affairs designed to project both accessibility and dignity.[5] John F. Kennedy was in good company, for style mattered to George Washington and to Thomas Jefferson, as it does for every effective president.

Kennedy believed that Americans wanted to look up to their president and to honor their nation's achievements. His unabashedly patriotic rhetoric offers a partial explanation as to why his memory resonates with the American people decades beyond his death. But the fact that Americans felt they *knew* President Kennedy offers the best explanation for the resilience of his memory. The assassination of Abraham Lincoln generated a similar phenomenon, but remarkably, Kennedy's bond with the people was stronger than Lincoln's. Kennedy's loss was personal, for he had appeared in their living rooms on television. Anyone who wishes to see first-hand the extent to which Americans felt they knew President Kennedy and poured out their personal reactions to his assassination need only consult Ellen Fitzpatrick's *Letters to Jackie: Condolences from a Grieving Nation* (2010).[6]

So many ironies abound regarding those personal bonds that Kennedy forged with the American people, for in many ways he was a remarkably private man, an "elusive" man, in the words of Christopher Matthews, and as the entire world now knows, that private man led a life much at odds with some aspects of his public image.[7] But as with Woodrow Wilson and the two Roosevelts, Kennedy understood that establishing this bond was a source of power in a republic. Kennedy displayed a mastery of public relations that he derived partly from his father, Joseph P. Kennedy, who was a successful Hollywood producer, among other things, and who once observed that "image is reality."[8] As early as 1942, Joe Kennedy began searching for radio stations to purchase in Massachusetts for his two sons (Joseph P. Kennedy Jr. and John) who would someday be running for office in Massachusetts.[9]

The development of the new technology of television was an ideal medium for John F. Kennedy, and he understood that television completely changed every aspect of American politics and governance. Kennedy's media savvy stemmed partly from his own interest in journalism, a career he considered pursuing at one point after World War II. Ted Sorensen noted in his biography *Kennedy* that during the 1960 campaign, the candidate was unusually accessible to reporters and that "he knowingly timed his major campaign releases to meet their a.m. and p.m. deadlines." This sensitivity to the needs of reporters, along with his accessibility, benefitted him at the expense of Vice President Nixon, who ran a more buttoned-down campaign and struggled at times to hide his contempt for reporters.

This is not to say that there were not tensions between the Kennedy White House and the media, as there are during most presidencies. Kennedy complained about, and retaliated against, the media both during his campaign and while in office. In an otherwise hagiographic account of the thirty-fifth President, Sorensen was remarkably candid about Kennedy's mixed feelings toward the fourth estate. Kennedy displayed a "curious dichotomy" toward the media, for "he both assisted and resented the press corps as they dogged his every footstep. . . . He had an inexhaustible capacity to take displeasure from what he read . . . and an equally inexhaustible capacity to keep on reading more than anyone else in Washington." Sorensen added that "few, if any, Presidents could have been more objective about their own faults or objected more to seeing them in print." Kennedy was remarkably frank and "uncommonly candid" both in public and in private, but few presidents, Sorensen noted, were "so skillful in evading or even misleading the press whenever secrecy was required."[10]

In addition to his "inexhaustible capacity" to read every newspaper and periodical he could acquire, Kennedy devoured biographies and history, along with Ian Fleming's James Bond series. His interest in biography stemmed from the fact that, as he told his friend Benjamin Bradlee, biography answers the question, "What's he like?"[11] Kennedy provided enough fodder to the press and the public to keep them engaged, but never enough to fully answer the question, "What's he like?"

His administration was accused, oddly enough by Kennedy's own Pentagon press secretary, of attempting to "manage" the media. This was in accord with his circumscribed interpretation of freedom of the press, for Kennedy believed the media had a responsibility to act in the interest of national security. Speaking ten days after the Bay of Pigs debacle in April 1961, Kennedy argued that both the press and the presidency shared "common responsibilities in the face of a common danger." He asked the media to "recognize the nature of our country's peril" from a ruthless opponent, international communism, which did not have to deal with a free press, and urged the media to impose "the self-discipline of combat conditions." He did not threaten government sanctions of any type, nor the creation of an Office of War Information, but wanted the media to police itself. Prior to publishing a story, the president believed that every newspaper should ask, "Is it in the interest of the national security?"[12]

Kennedy was often angry at the media for their "irresponsible" reporting, even though this was an era when patriotism and journalistic self-restraint acted as a check on no-holds-barred reporting. Media self-restraint was true not only regarding national security matters, but also when it came to matters dealing with Kennedy's health and his reckless pursuit of sex. Much of what is known today about Kennedy's serial adultery was known at the time by some members of the media who abided by a code which deemed "personal" foibles off-limits. Additionally, while Kennedy's Addison's disease was raised during the 1960 campaign by Lyndon Johnson, and promptly denied, little probing was done regarding Kennedy's other myriad ailments that he dealt with by consuming a cocktail of drugs. Kennedy's health issues were successfully covered up, assisted by a public relations campaign involving the release of photographs of touch football games or sailing expeditions off the coast of Cape Cod. The promotion of the President's Council on Physical Fitness or stunts such as fifty-mile hikes, which many New Frontiersman undertook, but not the president, added to the image of a youthful president who celebrated the vigorous life. But again, delving into health matters was considered bad form by a media that, less than twenty years earlier, ignored the fact that Franklin Roosevelt was dying while running for a fourth term in office.

While Kennedy did not always see the press as an ally, he clearly benefitted from an ethos of the World War II generation which deferred to leadership in a time of war, be it hot or cold. This generation, or at least almost all the male journalists of that generation, erected a high wall of separation between the public and the private. Journalist Ben Bradlee summed up this attitude best by noting that "my rule used to be if private behavior didn't interfere with public business, then it stayed private."[13]

Kennedy's good relationship with the press drove Richard Nixon to distraction, and to this day, allegations that the media was "in the tank" for Kennedy animate much of the conservative criticism of the mainstream media. But while beat reporters tended to be charmed by Kennedy, Nixon was the overwhelming favorite among publishers and editors, and according to some estimates, Nixon won well over three to four times more newspaper endorsements for his presidential campaign than Kennedy. A paltry 16 percent of the nation's newspapers endorsed Kennedy for president in 1960.[14] As a consequence, Kennedy decided to hold live televised press conferences to circumvent the editorial slant of some hostile print outlets.

Conservative critics are right to note that Kennedy developed close relationships with the media which by today's standards would be considered inappropriate. He had a warm rapport with Ben Bradlee of *Newsweek,* Sander Vanocur of *NBC News,* humorist Art Buchwald, author George Plimpton, presidential chronicler Theodore White, journalist Tom Braden, and Philip Graham, publisher of the *Washington Post,* among others. Bradlee, who would later expose Richard Nixon's misdeeds while serving as editor of the *Washington Post,* denied that he was aware of Kennedy's philandering, even though his sister-in-law was sleeping with the president. To make matters worse, Bradlee was so infatuated with Kennedy that he wrote a strategy memorandum for the presidential candidate in 1959 providing intelligence on Lyndon Johnson's campaign and warning Kennedy to be on guard against Johnson's maneuvering at the 1960 Democratic National Convention.[15]

But some of the credit for Kennedy's good relationship with the press and the public was due to the political skills of Kennedy himself, not simply the result of a supine press. He was an attractive figure, a man capable of great charm, and he, like all skilled leaders, put this to use. To this day, almost sixty years removed from his death, those who knew him, or even had a brief encounter with him, talk about his magnetism. Kennedy managed to walk that remarkably fine line between republican accessibility with the citizenry and maintaining the distance that fosters respect and legitimates authority. People looked up to Kennedy but felt he was on their side at the same time. Striking that balance is no easy task.

Many of the same conservative critics who accuse the press of rolling over for Kennedy argue that his success was due to his telegenic qualities. These critics tend to neglect the fact that similar accusations were made against Ronald Reagan. Superficial Hollywood glamour and an ability to read other people's line's—Ted Sorensen's in Kennedy's case, Peggy Noonan's in

Reagan's—so this narrative goes, explains their success. Both men bought their way to power, their opponents argued, with money provided by Joseph P. Kennedy throughout his son's pursuit of public office, or in Reagan's case through the largesse provided by a group of California millionaires in his gubernatorial and presidential races. This narrative is woefully incomplete, in that both men were remarkably skilled politicians with a message that resonated, and both men were masters of the new technology of television and rode it all the way to 1600 Pennsylvania Avenue. Most importantly, both men were men of substance (with Kennedy holding the lead in native smarts), as much as it pains ideologues on both sides of the partisan divide to concede this point.

John F. Kennedy's political skills faced their greatest test in 1960 when he secured the Democratic Party's nomination for president even though he was not the choice of party leaders that year. The junior senator from Massachusetts really had no other option if he were to successfully run for president in 1960 than to circumvent the "establishment." Kennedy had to prove he could win using the system Woodrow Wilson and other progressives had created to bypass the party hierarchy. Enormous television ad buys helped Kennedy do precisely that in primaries from New Hampshire to Oregon. Backed by the wealth of the candidate's father, the Kennedy campaign was able to buy large amounts of television advertising and to target those buys to specific voting groups. Jacqueline Kennedy, while pregnant for much of the 1960 campaign, did her part by recording a television ad in Spanish for her husband aimed at Hispanic voters. The campaign also used television to great effect to beat back allegations in the pivotal West Virginia primary that Kennedy's Catholicism should disqualify him from the White House. His triumph in that overwhelmingly Protestant state came close to giving him a lock on the Democratic Party's nomination.[16]

The Kennedy campaign relied heavily on polling to craft their advertising buys, which is routine today, but was not in 1960. The campaign also went negative, using television ads attacking Richard Nixon by showing a clip of President Eisenhower being asked at a press conference if he had adopted any of Nixon's ideas while the latter served as vice president. The president responded, "If you give me a week, I might think of one. I don't remember."[17]

Negative ads were used in 1952 in the race between Eisenhower and Adlai Stevenson, but this ad directed against Nixon was particularly effective, and damaged his claim that he had more governing experience than Kennedy. As historian Robert Dallek has observed, Kennedy's campaign in 1960 "created a new template" that all presidential candidates have followed since then, the only variation being the addition of social media platforms to supplement television and radio. Despite this variation, as Dallek notes, "what they are doing . . . is taking a page from Kennedy's book."[18]

The Kennedy campaign also allowed film producer Robert Drew, considered to be the father of American cinema verité, unprecedented access to the candidate during the critical primary in Wisconsin where Kennedy squared off against Senator Hubert Humphrey of Minnesota. The finished product, *Primary,* is considered a classic in documentary filmmaking and was the result of Kennedy's grasp of the importance of film. Drew noted that both he and the candidate "had an intellectual understanding from the start . . . Kennedy appreciated the fact that I was trying to improvise a new form of film journalism. I don't think Senator Humphrey did."[19]

Kennedy was well plugged into Hollywood both through his father and through his brother-in-law Peter Lawford, the British-born actor who married Kennedy's sister Patricia in 1954. A member of Frank Sinatra's "Rat Pack," Lawford helped recruit Kennedy into the Sinatra circle, and vice versa. Sinatra produced Kennedy's campaign song for 1960, a revised version of his hit record "High Hopes" that read in part, "Everyone wants to back Jack, Jack is on the right track, 'Cause he's got high hopes."[20] Suffice it to say that Kennedy's campaign song had the edge over Nixon's "Click with Dick," which offered the following line as an enticement to vote for the vice president: "Come on and click with Dick, the one that none can lick."[21]

Kennedy also began the dubious practice of presidential candidates appearing on television entertainment shows. On June 16, 1960, he gave an interview to Jack Parr on his nationally broadcast show, *Tonight Starring Jack Parr.* Parr noted afterwards that his audience was impressed with Kennedy, for "they had never before seen such a young, attractive senator." The bulk of the conversation between Parr and the candidate focused on why someone with Kennedy's wealth would enter the political arena, and how he intended to confront communism. Asked to describe any humorous events that occurred on the campaign trail, the senator noted that he had been made "an honorary Indian" and he now cheered for "our side" while watching shows on television.

Those who assume that Kennedy's success as a candidate was solely the result of his mastery of television sometimes exaggerate their case. For instance, Ron Simon of the Paley Center for Media observed, "Kennedy preferred to press the electronic flesh," rather than engage in the time-consuming and draining physical interaction on the campaign trail.[22] But this is overdrawn, for Kennedy campaigned at a frenetic pace, interacting with the public at countless events, despite the fact that this style of campaigning came with some risk to his own health.[23] In 1960, he engaged in door-to-door campaigning in places like West Virginia, where the influence of television was minimal. More importantly, the candidate encountered poverty of a type he had never seen before and was moved by this experience. He was especially moved by the situation in McDowell County, West Virginia, and his first executive order was to create something akin to the food stamp program, with residents of McDowell County the first recipients.[24] Kennedy's hands were frequently swollen, in West Virginia and elsewhere, from his interactions with overeager voters.

That "Religious Thing"

There was one issue in 1960 that Kennedy could not charm his way out of, and that was his Catholic faith. No Catholic had ever been elected president, and many Americans assumed that Kennedy would place the interests of the Vatican ahead of those of the United States. The Reverend Norman Vincent Peale, a popular radio and television preacher and the author of *The Power of Positive Thinking,* had nothing positive to say about the prospect of a Catholic president, which was somewhat typical of many Protestant ministers. "Faced with election of a Catholic," the self-help guru observed, "our culture is at stake." (In 1956, Democratic Party nominee Adlai Stevenson, upon hearing of Peale's endorsement of Dwight Eisenhower, noted, "I find the Apostle Paul appealing and the Apostle Peale appalling.")

The Reverend Billy Graham also joined the effort to stop Kennedy, all the while keeping Richard Nixon apprised of his efforts. Stung by the attacks on Norman Vincent Peale, Graham opted to work covertly on Nixon's behalf, telling the vice president that he would avoid openly supporting him, but "privately I intend to do all in my power to help you get elected."[25] Rumors swirled throughout the Bible Belt that Kennedy planned to hang rosary beads made from bowling balls from the Statue of Liberty and would install a hotline between the White House and the Vatican. As Shaun Casey has observed, the argument of Peale and Graham and countless other Protestant clergymen was that "if Kennedy was elected President, he'd criminalize birth control, he'd cut off foreign aid that helped countries invest in birth control, and he'd funnel tax money to Catholic parochial schools."[26] Historian Arthur Schlesinger Sr. noted that discrimination against Catholics "was the deepest bias in the history of the American people."[27] While other groups may have a just claim for that "honor," Catholicism was definitely near the top of the list. And anti-Catholicism was not confined to evangelical Protestantism; as Arthur Schlesinger Jr. told Kennedy, "Some liberals, I am ashamed to say, are secret anti-Catholics."[28]

Kennedy decided to try and put the question of "dual loyalty" to rest with a risky appearance before the Greater Houston Ministerial Association on September 12, 1960. Both Lyndon Johnson and Speaker of the House Sam Rayburn urged Kennedy not to appear before the Houston ministers' association. Kennedy rejected their advice and gave a spirited address, although one troublesome to traditional Catholics, refuting allegations that he would obey the pope and not the Constitution of the United States. "Contrary to common newspaper usage, I am not the Catholic candidate for President. I am the Democratic Party's candidate for President, who happens also to be a Catholic. I do not speak for my church on public matters, and the church does not speak for me." Once again, Kennedy used television to amplify his message, using his address to the ministers to deal with the "religious thing," as he called it. Kennedy's speech was broadcast throughout the state of Texas by nineteen local television stations, while the campaign's own film crew taped the event and produced half-hour, five-minute, and one-minute advertisements for broadcast throughout the nation. Many of these ads aired outside the South, in urban areas with a substantial Catholic population, sparking a certain zeal for the candidate among his religious brethren.[29]

Hostility to Kennedy's Catholicism did not subside after he won the election. Billy Graham's father-in-law, L. Nelson Bell, wrote to Richard Nixon prior to Kennedy's inauguration, claiming that the latter's victory was comparable to "the death of a loved one." The United States, as Bell knew it, was dead. A "completely integrated and planned attempt" now loomed, designed to allow for a "take over [of] our nation for the Roman Catholic Church." Bell added, "You, Dick, stood for things which have made America great, while Mr. Kennedy appealed to the most venal elements" in American society.[30]

It is somewhat remarkable that there was a sixty-year gap between the election of the first Catholic president and the second, Joseph Biden. Equally remarkable is the fact that the only Catholic vice president in the nation's history is the same person, Joe Biden, who broke the Protestant hold on that office in 2008. Biden's achievement was overshadowed by a more impressive triumph that year, the election of the first Black president.

President Biden's religion did not seem to be a major issue in 2020, except among, in a remarkable twist of history, his fellow Catholics. According to an analysis by the Pew Research Center, President Trump narrowly carried Catholic voters in 2020 by 50 percent to 49 percent over Biden.[31] This could be seen as a positive development in that a slim majority of Catholics voted on the issues, perhaps, not on the basis of elevating "one of their own." On the other hand, many Catholics would claim that Biden was not "one of their own" due to his support for abortion rights and gay marriage. He was, in the minds of these Catholics, an apostate who should be denied the sacrament of Holy Communion.

"The Vital Center of Action"

Unlike many of those who seek the presidency, John F. Kennedy thought deeply about executive power in the American republic. His thinking was firmly embedded in the progressive political thought of Theodore Roosevelt and Woodrow Wilson, whose conception of executive power could be best summarized as a belief in presidential primacy, with a chief executive with near unlimited power presiding over a federal government equally unbound. The progressive presidency emphasized efficiency and energy and tended to view checks and balances as an impediment to be overcome by presidential leadership. The chief executive served as the voice of the people, the one nationally elected figure who could fully grasp the whole. Progressive politicians and their brethren in the academic world viewed the Constitution as a quaint document written in horse-and-buggy days, an outmoded form of government designed for deadlock and incapable of dealing with the complexity of the twentieth century. Constitutions, like living organisms, must evolve with the times, and it was the job of the president to assist in that process of evolution, partly through educating the public of the necessity for change. Scientific advances had changed the face of the world, including our understanding of politics and government, both of which were now subject to quantifiable examination, allowing Americans to create a better society, a great society. President Kennedy embraced this doctrine, noting, "Man can be as big as he wants. No problem of human destiny is beyond human beings. Man's reason and spirit have often solved the seemingly unsolvable— and we believe they can do it again."[32]

By detaching the presidency, and to some extent the entire federal government, from the Constitution, the proponents of an activist presidency helped to personalize the office. In other words, according to its intellectual founder, Woodrow Wilson, the president must be as big a man as he can, using all the talents at his disposal to forge a bond with the masses and lead the latter into the promised land. The president's charismatic qualities are critical to his success, which means his personality is the cornerstone of the Wilsonian presidency. This is, as Garry Wills described it, "rule by dazzlement."[33] In this sense, John F. Kennedy was the perfect candidate, the perfect president, to fulfill the Wilsonian vision.

Kennedy absorbed much of his belief in unbridled executive power from his father, who was a prominent New Deal Democrat who held several important positions during Franklin Roosevelt's presidency. But the progressive conception of the presidency was also a cherished belief among prominent political scientists and historians who served as a type of intellectual brain trust for the Democratic Party. Arthur Schlesinger Jr., James McGregor Burns, Richard Neustadt, and Henry Steele Commager, among others, built the theoretical foundation for this activist, personalized presidency.

Apart from Henry Steele Commager, all these men were part of an extended Kennedy circle. Schlesinger served as a link between Kennedy and the "liberals" as well as a speechwriter for Kennedy, while Burns, the author of what amounted to a campaign biography of Kennedy, was given special access to the candidate and his staff in 1959. Richard Neustadt served as an advisor to the celebrated Kennedy transition (seen as something of a "model" transition) and a "consultant and troubleshooter" during Kennedy's presidency.[34] These scholar-activists were determined to revitalize an office they believed had become moribund during the Eisenhower years. Schlesinger was the proponent, as was his father, of a somewhat suspect theory that American history unfolded in cycles, with periods of selfish pragmatism followed by periods of idealism and innovation. Kennedy seemed to buy into the idea that in 1960 the nation stood "on the threshold of a new political era" characterized by idealism and requiring "vigorous public leadership."[35]

While Schlesinger became a special assistant to the president, Richard Neustadt, from his academic perch at Columbia University, was arguably more influential in terms of shaping Kennedy's conception of presidential power. Neustadt's book, *Presidential Power: The Politics of Leadership* (1960), was read by Kennedy and members of his inner circle and became something of a Bible for those convinced that the president should be as big a man as he wanted to be. "This is not a book about the presidency as an organization, or as legal powers, or as precedents," Neustadt wrote, for "the probabilities of power do not derive from the literary theory of the Constitution." Neustadt was focused on the question of presidential effectiveness, in other words, "how to be on top in fact as well as name."[36] Neustadt was preparing to join Kennedy's staff when the president was assassinated.

Richard Neustadt's blueprint guided a new president eager to break the institutional shackles he inherited from Eisenhower, with its excessive reliance on cabinet government and its military-style chain of command. In the eyes of New Frontiersmen, Ike was the personification of executive inaction and a prisoner of an antiquated staff system. Cabinet government had to go, as Ted Sorensen observed with some delight, noting that "no decisions of importance were made" at Kennedy's cabinet meetings, and "few subjects of importance, particularly in foreign affairs, were ever seriously discussed." Cabinet meetings were, as the president put it, "a waste of time."[37] In Kennedy's view, Eisenhower's institutionalized presidency had constrained the president to the point where he was unable to act. Eisenhower's weekly cabinet meetings were abolished, and his sharing of power with a strong chief of staff, Sherman Adams, and a revised National Security Council that guided much of the president's agenda, were all scrapped. Kennedy believed that Eisenhower had neutered himself and become a "slave of organization."[38]

Upon assuming the presidency, Kennedy reduced his cabinet to irrelevancy, did not appoint a chief of staff, cut the size of his entire White House staff, and became something of his own secretary of state. Sorensen noted that Kennedy "abolished the pyramid structure of the White House staff" and "paid little attention to organization charts and chains of command which diluted and distributed his authority." As Alan Brinkley observed, Kennedy, along with almost every president since his time, "considered most federal employees narrow-minded bureaucrats who stood in the way of progress."[39]

Kennedy's presidency would cut through this moribund bureaucracy and invigorate the process using outside channels and an ad hoc approach to problem solving, all designed to jolt the system into action. John F. Kennedy was determined not only to get the country moving again but to get the presidency moving as well. "You are the only person you can count on," Richard Neustadt told Kennedy in a transition memo written in October 1960, "to be thinking about what helps you."[40] This advice undoubtedly reinforced the inclinations of a president-elect who was determined to center all policy, politics, and personnel decisions on one man, "the leader of the free world."

Kennedy publicly outlined his vision for the presidency in an address at the National Press Club on January 14, 1960, where he claimed that the "central issue" of the election was "the presidency itself." The history of the American nation, "its brightest and its bleakest pages" had been written by the nation's presidents. Both the times and the people demanded "a vigorous proponent of the national interest. . . . They demand a man capable of acting as the Commander-in-Chief of the Grand Alliance." It was essential at the dawn of a new decade that the chief executive act as a vigorous proponent "in every sense of the word. He must be prepared to exercise the fullest powers of his office—all that are specified and some that are not." Kennedy believed the parameters of presidential power were defined by what the times demanded, and the president must move in concert with his time, not reduce himself to the status of an administrator, even if the Constitution and precedent indicated otherwise. Kennedy noted that, uniquely among the branches of government, the president had a "national constituency," thus leading him to embrace Woodrow Wilson's famous aphorism, "The president is at liberty, both in law and conscience, to be as big a man as he can." But Woodrow Wilson "discovered that to be a big man in the White House inevitably brings cries of dictatorship," Kennedy observed, but "so did Lincoln and Jackson and the two Roosevelts. And so may the next occupant of that office, if he is the man the times demand. But how much better it would be, in the turbulent sixties, to have a Roosevelt or a Wilson than to have another James Buchanan, cringing in the White House, afraid to move."[41]

The American president, he went on to note, is at "the vital center of action in our whole scheme of government," which had been true for the most part in the twentieth century but was not true from 1789 to 1901. The chief executive was also "not only the center of political leadership," he "must be the center of moral leadership—a 'bully pulpit,' as Theodore Roosevelt described it. For only the President represents the national interest. And upon him alone converge all the needs and aspirations of all parts of the country, all departments of the government, all nations of the world." It was going to be the job of the president in the 1960s to "summon his national constituency to its finest hour," meaning that he would demand of the American people sacrifices designed to overcome "the soft national will" that had set in during the 1950s.[42] That September, Kennedy expanded on his National Press Club remarks by noting that the nation's standing in the world depended on "presidential prestige," that forward thinking on domestic matters hinged on "presidential leadership." He added that the nation would stagnate "if the President does not move."[43]

"This Is War"

President Kennedy's concept of a chief executive who served as "the vital center of action" was particularly evident in April 1962 when he confronted the major steel companies who violated an agreement the president believed he had brokered between the steel industry and the United Steel Workers. The "Eisenhower recession" had ended by 1962, but the administration feared that inflation would undermine the American economy. The president had called on labor and management to "apply the test of the public interest" to their wage and pricing decisions.[44] The steelworkers' contract was set to expire in 1962, and Kennedy invited Roger Blough, head of U.S. Steel, the nation's largest steel manufacturer, and David McDonald, head of the United Steelworkers, to a White House meeting to urge the two parties to reach a non-inflationary agreement. Kennedy proposed a modest pay increase for the steelworkers, one that would allow the companies to pay higher wages while keeping prices frozen. Believing that he had forged a compromise between the steel industry and the union, Kennedy praised both sides for demonstrating "industrial statesmanship of the highest order."[45]

On April 10, 1962, Roger Blough handed Kennedy a press release announcing that his corporation was raising prices beyond what Kennedy believed had been agreed upon. Kennedy was convinced that U.S. Steel had double-crossed him and, in keeping with a tradition begun with Teddy

Roosevelt and Woodrow Wilson and accelerated under Franklin Roosevelt, he used all the federal power at his disposal to force "big business" to alter decisions he believed were contrary to the common good.

Kennedy was furious at Blough's betrayal, viewing this as a slight against him and against a key element of the president's base, organized labor. He informed members of his staff that "this is war," and told David McDonald, "You've been screwed and I've been screwed." To his friend Ben Bradlee, he added, "They fucked us and we've got to try to fuck them." The next day at a press conference, he demanded the steel companies cancel the increases and accused them of engaging in an "irresponsible defiance of the public interest." Their "pursuit of private power and profit exceeds their sense of public responsibility."[46] Kennedy concluded his opening statement by recalling his inaugural address: "Some time ago I asked each American to consider what he would do for his country, and I asked the steel companies. In the last twenty-four hours we had their answer."[47]

The administration used lawful and unlawful means to force the steel companies to rescind their price increase, including a coordinated public relations campaign to portray the decision as unpatriotic at a time when Americans were dying in South Vietnam, where, as the president noted at his fiery press conference, "four [Americans] were killed in the last two days."[48] Defense Secretary Robert McNamara shifted contracts for submarine plating to smaller companies that had balked at the price increase, while Robert Kennedy's Justice Department engaged in a vigorous examination of the practices of steel executives, including their expense accounts, and convened a grand jury to examine any potential antitrust violations. "We were going for broke," the attorney general later observed. "I told the FBI to interview them all [the steel executives]—march into their offices the next day. . . . I agree it was a tough way to operate. But under the circumstances we couldn't afford to lose." The FBI roused reporters out of bed in the middle of the night to confirm reports that the president of Bethlehem Steel had reversed his position on holding the line on prices until U.S. Steel had announced an increase.[49]

Kennedy's friend and fellow PT boat commander Paul "Red" Fay recorded the president musing about the pressure applied and asking, "Do you know what you're doing when you start bucking the power of the President of the United States? . . . I don't think US Steel or any other of the major steel companies wants to have Internal Revenue agents checking all the expense accounts of their top executives. Do you want the government to go back to hotel bills the time you were in Schenectady to find out who was with you? Hotel bills . . . nightclub expenses?" According to Ben Bradlee, the president had an exchange with a steel executive who complained "that all the telephone calls of the steel executives in all the country are being tapped . . . why is it that the income tax returns of all the steel executives in the country are being scrutinized?" Kennedy replied, "And I told him that the Attorney General would never do such a thing." But the steel executive was right, as the President conceded to Bradlee, and some of those wiretap transcripts ended up being read by the president.[50]

Kennedy's war with the steel barons involved a ruthless use of federal power against the private sector, but it was widely hailed by progressives. For Arthur Schlesinger Jr., Kennedy's showdown with big steel conjured up fond memories of Andrew Jackson's war against Nicholas Biddle's Bank of the United States. Schlesinger observed that Kennedy had "no direct authority available against the steel companies. Instead, he mobilized every fragment of quasi-authority he could find and, by a bravura public performance, converted weakness into strength."[51] Kennedy's actions represented a fulfillment of the progressive dream of using the bully pulpit along with the full weight of the law, and then some, against the malefactors of great wealth. By April 12, the steel war had ended, with all the major steel companies rescinding their price increases by that date.

Kennedy's handling of the seventy-two-hour "steel crisis" won him the plaudits of a majority of Americans, with 73 percent of Americans expressing a favorable opinion after he forced "big steel" to roll back prices. Republicans and businessmen were less impressed, viewing the administration's actions as a heavy-handed use of government power applied to the private sector. Kennedy's actions, even if motivated by a commitment to defending the public interest, set a dangerous precedent. His administration's actions were, in fact, an abuse of power. If there were antitrust violations involving "big steel," the Justice Department could have pursued several legal remedies. But instead, the Kennedy administration chose a course of action that had all the hallmarks of Richard Nixon's presidency, with Internal Revenue Service audits and electronic surveillance designed to "screw" their enemies. As Donald Trump's presidency revealed, targeting private industries and media outlets opposed to presidential preferences remains an irresistible temptation for those dismissive of constitutional limits and the rule of law.

Master of the Medium

It was during the first televised presidential debate ever held that John F. Kennedy's media prowess proved most effective. Kennedy spent much of his debate prep working on his tan and paying a pre-debate visit to the studio to determine what color suit would be most appropriate, and simply getting the lay of land regarding things like camera placement and room temperature. Nixon paid no such visit and paid a price for it. As Ron Simon noted, echoing the words of Sun Tzu, "Every debate is won before it is ever fought."[52] Over the course of the four debates, Nixon's performance improved, but the damage was done during that first, and most watched, debate. The audience that viewed the first debate was one of the biggest in the history of the medium, some seventy million people, who represented three-quarters of the nation's adults.[53] Nixon look haggard and ill at ease, a man who was not comfortable in his own skin, which was in fact the case. Nixon had been hospitalized recently for a knee infection, had lost weight, and had engaged in a frenzy of campaign activities in the days leading up to the debate. He also wore a gray suit that blended into the background, and his lack of makeup highlighted his gaunt appearance and an ominous five o'clock shadow. Kennedy looked at the camera, to the audience, as he spoke, while Nixon looked at Kennedy while he spoke. Nixon also perspired throughout while his eyes tended to dart about, giving him the look of a suspect in a police lineup. One survey indicated that approximately four million people based their vote on the outcome of the debates, and that group broke three to one for Kennedy. At the conclusion of the fourth and final debate, the Gallup Poll showed Kennedy leading Nixon by 51 percent to 45, which represented a reversal of a poll taken that summer showing Nixon leading by six points.[54]

Ironically, Kennedy rode into the White House using a medium that he had praised and learned to master, but at the same time he had misgivings about this new technological wonder. While he helped usher in the era of TV-saturated politics, he understood that television had the ability to alter reality and dramatically inflate the cost of political campaigns. He feared that the cost of advertising on television might lead candidates to become captives of the special interests bankrolling their campaigns. "A solution must be found," he wrote in *TV Guide* in November 1959, "to this problem of TV costs" if candidates for office and all political parties "are to have equal access to this essential . . . medium."[55]

There was another equally serious problem, in that a successful television candidate may not always "deserve it," for television was a medium "which lends itself to manipulation, exploitation and gimmicks. It can be abused by demagogues, by appeals to emotion and prejudice and ignorance," Kennedy observed. He warned of the rise of candidates who packaged their message as a result of the data acquired from focus groups and noted that campaigns can be "taken over by the 'public relations experts' . . . who tell the candidate what to say, what to stand for, and what 'kind of person' to be."[56]

As he transitioned into the presidency, evidence of Kennedy's mastery of television was on display in his nationally broadcast press conferences, which he held on average every sixteen days. Woodrow Wilson held the first presidential press conference on March 15, 1913, as part of his broader design to create a presidency that shaped public opinion and circumvented the laborious dead weight of the print media or the other branches of government. As Wilson's biographer John Milton Cooper noted, Wilson was a professor and considered the essence of leadership to be "educating the public."[57] President Kennedy's average audience was eighteen million Americans, although by the end of 1961, ninety percent of the American public had seen at least one of his first three press conferences.[58] These staggering numbers exceeded Woodrow Wilson's wildest dreams, as the new medium of television allowed the president to speak directly to millions of Americans. As Wilson succinctly put it, "the forming of the masses is the whole art and mastery of politics." For Wilson, it was the role of a leader to "impel them [the people] to great political achievements."[59]

Dwight Eisenhower was the first president to hold televised press conferences, but they were subject to editing and never aired live. Despite their crafted nature, Ike's comments often consisted of a string of non-sequiturs and metaphysical meanderings. Eisenhower also tended to deflect questions about controversial matters by proclaiming, "I'll have to look that up." What was not fully understood at the time was that Eisenhower's flummoxed performances were contrived, as Ike refused to show his cards and always sought to leave his options open.[60] Kennedy's press conferences differed in every conceivable manner from those of his predecessor, and while he was dealing with a press that was generally compliant and at times swooning over him, there was more at work here, for Kennedy displayed a quick wit and something of a photographic memory when it came to discussing both domestic and international affairs. Kennedy wasted no time in launching these live press conferences—five days after his inauguration, he held his first conference in the State Department auditorium, a large venue capable of accommodating all the reporters who had requested credentials to attend. Kennedy studied his performance at these events, watching recordings of his press conferences and seeking advice from media professionals, such as director Franklin Schaffner (who would go on to direct *Planet of the Apes* and *Patton*) and producer Frederick Coe (who produced *The Miracle Worker*). Kennedy was his own toughest critic when it came to his television appearances, as can be seen in outtakes from an interview he did with Chet Huntley and David Brinkley of *NBC News* on September 9, 1963, where he asked for a second take for some of his answers. "There's one or two places [that] were a little ragged . . . South Vietnam was a little more verbose than it needed to be." Huntley and Brinkley obliged.[61]

Franklin Roosevelt had done this with radio, but television, with its "see it now" moving images, represented a quantum leap in allowing a chief executive to forge that bond. Simply put, Kennedy thrived in this unfiltered and live environment. As his press secretary Pierre Salinger put it, "The fact of the matter is that the time when President Kennedy started televised press conferences there were only three or four newspapers in the entire United States that carried a full transcript of a presidential press conference. Therefore, what people read was a distillation, of the press conference, what they wanted to distill out of it. We thought that they should have the opportunity to see it in full."[62]

The "pen and pencil press" hated the fact that Kennedy televised his press conferences live, precisely because they would no longer be able to act as the semiofficial scribes and interpreters regarding the president's public statements. As Salinger put it, "We had to have a weapon by which we could go over the American press's head to the American people."[63] For this reason and others, many old-school journalists recoiled at the phenomenon of the televised press conference. One reporter bitterly noted that "we were props in a show. We should have joined Actors Equity," while another remembered Kennedy looking "right over our heads, right into the camera," not at the reporters asking the questions. Nonetheless, this same reporter conceded, "This was a man who was extraordinarily professional."[64]

Kennedy's appreciation for the power of images was not limited to the new electronic media, for traditional still photography remained a powerful marketing tool. Kennedy understood the interest the public held in his young and attractive family, and in his extended family as well, none of whom were camera shy. Two popular periodicals of the era, *Life* and *Look*, both noted for their excellence in photojournalism, were more than happy to oblige. Media critic Daniel Okrent described *Life* magazine as "*People* magazine before there was a *People* magazine . . . It was *60 Minutes* and *The Today Show* and the [network] evening news all rolled into one."[65]

Life's issues between 1960 and 1963, and beyond, were filled with photographs of the smiling family playing touch football in Hyannisport or sailing off Cape Cod, or "John-John" peering out from a trap door in the president's desk, or the Kennedy children and the First Lady riding a sleigh on the White House lawn after a snowstorm in Washington. *Look* photographer Stanley Tretick snapped the iconic shots of John F. Kennedy Jr. under the President's desk, prompting Kennedy to remark, "You can't miss with these, can you Stan?"[66] In keeping with his appreciation of the power of imagery, President Kennedy created the position of Official White House Photographer. Cecil Stoughton, a captain in the Army Signal Corps, held that position during the Kennedy years. Stoughton was selected by Kennedy's military aide, Army Major General Chester Clifton, who apparently told President Kennedy that, as Stoughton put it, "he was going to be 'in the public eye' and needed a photographer in-house (one they could 'control') to release photographs to the press." Stoughton recalled years later, "Prior to JFK, we had Eisenhower, and there was no need for a photographer. He was about 63 years old, and he didn't have the charm and charisma of President Kennedy and he didn't have a family that engaged the American public." Stoughton had an office in the basement of the White House, and was on call to Evelyn Lincoln, Kennedy's secretary, who would press a button summoning him to the Oval Office. Stoughton would sprint upstairs knowing that the president would be "waiting for me."

Some of the more moving photographs of the president with his children were taken while the First Lady was traveling, including a famous shot of Kennedy clapping while Caroline and John danced in the Oval Office. Jacqueline Kennedy was more concerned with protecting her children's privacy than with promoting the president's public image. But during his time in the Kennedy White House, Cecil Stoughton took over eight thousand photographs, and as a photography editor at *Life* later noted, "When these pictures were published around the world, they helped create the aura that later came to be called Camelot." As the British newspaper *The Guardian* noted at the time of

Stoughton's death, "This proved to be the start of the practice of marketing international heads of state as family men."[67] Arguably this practice, at least in the American context, began much earlier, with Kennedy's competitor for the title of youngest president, Theodore Roosevelt, who exposed his family to a level of media scrutiny unheard of before his time. But Kennedy elevated the exposure of the presidential family, of the personal side of the presidency, into an art form.

The Mythologized Presidency

The Kennedy presidency represented Wilsonianism at its apex in terms of adopting the notion that the presidency should be as big as its occupant wished and that bonding with the public was the key to effective governance. Kennedy propelled the presidency down an unsustainable path that ultimately led to an erosion of the public's confidence in the executive branch and in the entire federal government. But all that lay ahead; during the Kennedy years, most Americans believed in their government and in their nation's greatness. This greatness had been established through victory in a two-front world war and in the remarkable success of American economic power (the United States had a larger gross national product than the rest of the world combined in the late 1940s). The notion that America could accomplish anything was gospel among those who became known as the "greatest generation."

Kennedy's belief in America's exceptional place in the world permeated all his major speeches, including his rightly celebrated inaugural address. The nation would "pay any price, bear any burden" to "assure the survival and the success of liberty" around the globe and was committed to a "long, twilight struggle" against "tyranny, poverty, disease, and war itself." And in one of his most far-reaching speeches, a commencement address at American University on June 10, 1963, Kennedy captured the essence of American exceptionalism and of the nation's love affair with progress. While making an impassioned appeal for peace and for a reexamination of the underlying sources of the Cold War and of the nature of the Soviet Union, Kennedy noted that "our problems are manmade. Therefore, they can be solved by man. And man can be as big as he wants. No problem of human destiny is beyond human beings. Man's reason and spirit have often solved the seemingly unsolvable and we believe they can do it again."[68]

John F. Kennedy personified this "can do" American spirit, and perhaps more than any other modern president, he created a mythology about the office that emphasized its near-superhuman burdens. Pulitzer Prize–winning novelist Norman Mailer described Kennedy as "Superman" in a glowing account written for *Esquire* magazine in 1960 designed to help JFK win the presidency. Mailer believed Kennedy could revive the American imagination and unleash its "existential" creativity, both of which had lapsed into a coma after eight years of Eisenhower-induced conformity. Kennedy was the man, the only man, in a field of tired machine pols, who could tap into the nation's "pioneer lust for the unexpected and the incalculable."[69] Kennedy was not responsible for Mailer's hyperbole, but he embraced the notion of a heroic presidency, a crucible of leadership where "all the needs and aspirations" of his fellow countrymen as well as citizens of the earth "converge[d]."

While Kennedy seemed to enjoy his time as president, he also fostered the image of the solitary man of extraordinary talent burdened with the weight of the world. The famous George Tames photo of Kennedy hunched over while framed by windows in the Oval Office captured the essence of this mythology. Kennedy was apparently reading a newspaper when Tames snapped this famous photograph which took on a life of its own, even acquiring a title, "The Loneliest Job."[70] Kennedy arguably choreographed this imagery, having suggested in his National Press Club Speech in 1960 that "the President is alone, at the top," but he deals with this loneliness with a monk-like determination to save the world. While he is "acting alone," he is "always acting, moving, in the interest of the American people and of all nations of the world."

Action was the coin of the Kennedy realm, and perhaps it was no accident that the Kennedy administration seemed to lurch from one crisis to another. In his biography *Kennedy,* Ted Sorensen giddily recounts the number of crises President Kennedy confronted while in office. Sorensen's delight is indicative of the fact that charismatic leadership thrives on crisis. As Kennedy observed in 1960 in a not-so-veiled swipe at Dwight Eisenhower, the president "must originate action as well as study groups." The president is the world's constable, for "if a brushfire threatens some part of the globe— he alone can act, without waiting for the Congress."[71] This was arguably the most explicit definition of what Arthur Schlesinger Jr. would later call the "imperial presidency."

John F. Kennedy's expansive concept of the presidency became the standard by which his successors would be measured. Kennedy's tragic assassination contributed to making him seem larger than life and ensured that his conception of the presidency became embedded in the American mind. We live in a nation that remains transfixed by the Kennedy presidential model, even after the disastrous experience of the Trump presidency. Kennedy did not design this model, but he embraced it with vigor. He was remarkably successful at building a bond with the American people that exceeded the dreams of the model's creators, all of whom underestimated its potential dangers.

2

The Hundred Years' War

I moved to Boston on October 1, 1979, to take a position at the soon-to-open John F. Kennedy Library. Each day, as I sat in my office at the library, I could look out the window and see a motorcade of school buses surrounded by a massive police escort. These buses transported Black school children from predominantly Black Roxbury and Dorchester into South Boston. Once there, the school children would be met with rocks, bottles, and assorted racial epithets. By the time I arrived at the library, this had been going on since 1974, due to a court order handed down by Judge W. Arthur Garrity, a longtime protégé of John and Robert Kennedy. By 1979, Garrity was being guarded around the clock by US marshals due to repeated threats on his life. When I would occasionally be involved in outreach to the South Boston community, I would be lectured by residents who argued that President Kennedy and his brothers had betrayed them and endangered the lives of their children.

John F. Kennedy assumed office one hundred years after Abraham Lincoln was inaugurated. While slavery in the United States was abolished in 1865, a system of separate and unequal treatment of Black Americans remained the norm in 1961. While some progress had been made in terms of integrating the military and securing on paper the notion of segregation being inherently unequal, the American South and much of the North had managed to substitute a "Jim Crow" regime which effectively marginalized an entire race of American citizens.

During his tenure as a member of the House of Representatives and later as a senator from Massachusetts, John F. Kennedy voted for civil rights initiatives but never embraced the issue with the passion of a Hubert Humphrey or a Paul Douglas. Senator Kennedy represented a state that was overwhelmingly composed of white voters, with the mid-twentieth century Black population of Massachusetts coming in at well under 10 percent.[1] A substantial portion of his Massachusetts base was hostile to the Black minority in their midst, as the world would witness just a few years after Kennedy's murder during the busing crisis in Boston of the 1970s. As he admitted, Kennedy did not have a lot of contact with Black Americans, a consequence of his status as a trust fund baby who served in a segregated navy in World War II.

However, the conventional narrative overstates Kennedy's indifference to civil rights, at least during his tenure in the House of Representatives. He courted Black voters in his 1946 race for Massachusetts' eleventh congressional district seat, highlighting the service of Black soldiers during World War II at a time when many white voters questioned their commitment to fight. After winning his congressional seat, Kennedy voted for the abolition of the poll tax, supported home rule for the District of Columbia, backed legislation designed to remove discriminatory practices in the Selective Service process, and fought to ban employment discrimination in the capital. In his race against Senator Henry Cabot Lodge Jr. (R-MA) in 1952, Kennedy vigorously wooed the Black vote in Massachusetts and criticized Lodge for his opposition to rules changes that would weaken the filibuster, the favorite technique employed by Southern Democrats to kill civil rights legislation.[2]

As with other white politicians hoping to win political power, Kennedy trimmed his progressive stance on racial issues as he turned his attention to the national arena. As a New Englander with presidential ambitions, Kennedy belonged to a political party that had governed until relatively recently as the party of segregation and outright race-baiting. This had begun to change under Franklin Roosevelt, who haltingly pushed his party and the nation toward equal justice under the law, but FDR's actions fell far short of what many liberals in his own party, including his wife, supported. Roosevelt's successor, Harry S. Truman, had proposed several important civil rights initiatives at great political cost. But for Senator Kennedy, as his alter ego Theodore Sorensen would later observe, "civil rights was not a high priority."

Kennedy was "slow to recognize the moral imperative underlying the need for change," Sorensen noted ruefully during the 1960 race for president. He added that civil rights "was not central to the campaign," although the arrest of Martin Luther King, and other events from the campaign trail, opened his eyes to the importance of the issue.[3] Civil rights was treated by some of Kennedy's political advisers as an issue capable of fracturing what remained of the New Deal coalition. In their view, Kennedy presided over a party that contained a segregationist base they could not afford to alienate. But no honest account of his presidency can ignore the fact that he belatedly threw the full weight of his office behind one of the most comprehensive civil rights bills ever proposed by an American president.

Southern Strategy

Conventional wisdom holds that President Kennedy did not wish to alienate powerful Southern committee chairmen in Congress by pressing for civil-rights legislation, which was undoubtedly true. But perhaps there was another element at work animating Kennedy's early lukewarm approach to civil rights. It was, oddly enough, rooted in a faulty interpretation of history. Kennedy was interested in American history, and in his interpretation the post–Civil War Reconstruction era had been a disaster. The lesson Kennedy took from this "tragic era" was to avoid the heavy-handed use of federal power in the service of civil rights for Black Americans.

Kennedy's views were in accord with the dominant thinking of mid-twentieth century scholars and with the thinking of most Democrats of that time. Claude Bowers, a prominent party operative and part-time popular historian, had made a career out of propagating an overtly racist view of Reconstruction. Bowers's bestseller *The Tragic Era* contained passages such as "then came the scum of Northern society . . . inflaming the negroes' egotism, and soon the lustful assaults began. Rape is the foul daughter of Reconstruction. . . . It was not until the original Klan began to ride that white women felt some sense of security."[4] Bowers's account of the horrors of Reconstruction had impressed Franklin Roosevelt, who sang Bowers's praises in book reviews and in private correspondence and rewarded him with ambassadorships. Roosevelt was a northern patrician politician anxious to allay the fears of the party's Southern base, and both FDR and JFK understood that the road to the presidency for a Democrat ran through Dixie. "I'll be singing 'Dixie' for the rest of my life," Kennedy told a reporter after he almost became the

Democratic Party's vice-presidential nominee in 1956, thanks to Southern support.[5]

No conclusive evidence exists demonstrating that Kennedy was influenced by Bowers, but one of his Massachusetts constituents, Blanche Ames, whose father had served as a Reconstruction governor of Mississippi and was a fierce champion of equal rights, was convinced that Kennedy had read Bowers and had embraced his view of Reconstruction. She let Kennedy know of her contempt for his position on multiple occasions, accusing him of "slanderous misstatements" regarding Reconstruction and her father's role in overseeing that program in Mississippi. Ames wrote a biography in defense of her father's reputation where she rightly observed that Kennedy was circulating "untruths" propagated by the "Dunning School of historians and their modern followers."[6] Ames wrote to Kennedy so often that the president asked her grandson, the writer George Plimpton, to see if her could get her to "cease and desist." Her letters were disrupting the daily work of government, Kennedy jokingly told Plimpton.[7]

Blanche Ames was right to conclude that somewhere along the way, either at Harvard or elsewhere, Kennedy was exposed to the thinking of what was known as the "Dunning School" at Columbia University. This group of scholars believed that policies to bring the post–Civil War South into line with the principles of the Declaration of Independence were carried out in a tyrannical manner by northern Republicans who were indifferent to the "rapacious" practices of the newly freed slaves. Some members of this school were prone to praise organizations like the Ku Klux Klan, while many considered the attempted impeachment of Andrew Johnson by the "Radical Republicans" to be a symptom of the tyrannical overreach of the architects of the Thirteenth, Fourteenth, and Fifteenth Amendments to the Constitution.

The Dunning School's influence can be seen in Kennedy's Pulitzer Prize–winning book *Profiles in Courage* (1956), a book coauthored with Ted Sorensen.[8] It was this book that so upset Blanche Ames and led her to begin her letter-writing campaign that lasted into Kennedy's presidency. Kennedy viewed Andrew Johnson as the "courageous" if "untactful" victim of a congressional witch-hunt led by "extremists" determined to neuter the presidency. Johnson had "committed himself to the policies of the great emancipator [Lincoln]," and while he was a rough-hewn man, he was determined not to treat the South as "conquered provinces" but to allow it to "resume its place in the Union with as little delay and controversy as possible."

Impeaching Johnson "was the one final step" that was "necessary before they [the Radical Republicans] could crush their despised foe." Their "vengeance" knew no bounds, and only the courageous stand of Republican Edmund Ross from Kansas prevented this coup d'etat from happening.[9]

This was all fiction, but it was accepted as gospel by mid-twentieth century Democrats. Andrew Johnson was overtly racist in outlook and as raw a demagogue as Donald Trump, and was a dangerous, delusional man who was rightly impeached (he was inclined to compare his political travails to Jesus Christ's crucifixion). His removal from office might have led to the imposition of policies that would have hastened the achievement of equal rights under the law for countless numbers of freed slaves.

Another chapter in *Profiles in Courage* offered a glowing account of Senator Lucius Q. C. Lamar of Mississippi for his alleged moderation while serving in the United States Senate after the Civil War. But there was nothing moderate about Lucius Lamar, who believed in, as he put it, "the supremacy of the unconquered and unconquerable Saxon race." Lamar defended Klan members in court and campaigned openly for public office with a "Grand Dragon" from the Klan at his side. He was a leader in the effort to "defy the federal laws" and overthrow the Reconstruction government in the Magnolia State.[10]

A special inaugural edition of *Profiles in Courage* featured an introduction by Allan Nevins, who had formed the group "Professors for Kennedy" in the run-up to the election of 1960. Nevins was a close friend of Claude Bowers and was influenced by the Dunning School's perspective on Reconstruction. Reconstruction, according to the leader of "Professors for Kennedy," was an era of "corruption, incompetence, and extravagance," an era filled with "maladies" from "carpetbagger and Negro rule."[11] Kennedy's motive for adopting the Dunning School's flawed account of the Civil War and Reconstruction in *Profiles in Courage* is difficult to determine with certainty. He could have arrived at this honestly, since that account was gospel among many mid-twentieth century white Americans, or he could just as easily have been fueled by a desire to win the White House by singing "Dixie." As with many political figures, it was likely a mix of principle (albeit flawed) and pragmatism.

Regardless of his motive, in a nation where the "War Between the States" was still being fought in a sense, Kennedy's position allayed any fears of Southern Democratic voters who remained faithful to the mythology of "the Lost Cause." Robert Kennedy would later observe that it took the violent confrontation at the University of Mississippi in September and October 1962 to alter the president's view of Reconstruction, along with the visit of historian David Donald to the White House, who presented the "Radical Republicans" in a more favorable light, including one of Kennedy's senatorial predecessors from Massachusetts, Charles Sumner.

Arthur Schlesinger Jr. also contributed to Kennedy's reeducation by recommending the works of historian C. Vann Woodward, who held a far more sympathetic view of the Radical Republicans than members of the Dunning School. Kennedy told Schlesinger, "I don't understand the South . . . I'm coming to believe that Thaddeus Stevens [a leading Radical Republican] was right. I had always been taught to regard him as a man of vicious bias. But when I see this sort of thing [violent resistance to integration], I begin to wonder how else you can treat them."[12] The events at Ole Miss and at Birmingham, along with these lessons in revisionist history, led Robert Kennedy to conclude that the President "would never believe a book on Reconstruction again," especially those consisting of "terrible tales of the northern scalawag troops."[13]

The Second Civil War

Kennedy's inauguration in 1961 coincided with the centennial celebration of the American Civil War, a factor that contributed to his initial, halting approach to civil rights. While that war was a century removed, it remained an open sore to those Americans who abided by the precept "hell no, we won't forget," a slogan that appeared on bumper stickers and billboards throughout the South. As William Faulkner noted in his novel *Intruder in the Dust* (1948), "For every Southern boy fourteen years old, not once but whenever he wants it, there is the instant when it's still not yet two o'clock on that July afternoon in 1863, the brigades are in position behind the rail fence . . . looking up the hill waiting for Longstreet to give the word and it's all in the balance."[14] For many Southerners, fourteen years old and beyond, the cause that was lost at Gettysburg was a noble one, one that defended a chivalrous society fighting to keep the cancer of modernity at bay. Defenders of the "Lost Cause" considered the wealthy Yankee in the White House to be a suspect "Democrat" who surrounded himself with Ivy League "do-gooders"— the personification of all that was wrong with modern America.

White America had put a premium on healing the divisions from the nation's bloodiest war, and the Civil War Centennial Commission was determined to continue this theme of reconciliation, which required blotting out any mention of the conflict as a war over slavery. The Commission's executive director observed that "the story of the devotion and loyalty of Southern Negroes is one of the outstanding things of the Civil War. A lot of fine Negro people loved life as it was in the old South."[15] Civic leaders in Montgomery, Alabama, ground zero for the modern civil rights movement, celebrated the anniversary of the inauguration of Confederate president Jefferson Davis in February 1961, with one of the leaders noting that the anniversary instilled among whites "a deeper appreciation of the things the Confederacy fought for, and helped them to realize that unrestrained federal power is destroying this nation."[16]

The Civil War Centennial Commission got off to a horrible start just weeks into Kennedy's presidency, as a Black member of that organization, Madaline A. Williams of New Jersey, was denied a hotel room in segregated Charleston, South Carolina. It is somewhat ironic that first civil rights issue to confront the incoming Kennedy administration occurred in Charleston, the home of Fort Sumter, the site of the attack that began the "War of Northern Aggression." The Charleston incident quickly became a national issue when the commission's chairman, Ulysses S. Grant III, decided he was powerless to do anything regarding the refusal to accommodate Ms. Williams.[17]

President Kennedy was asked about the matter at a press conference on March 23, 1961. Kennedy noted the commission was "an official body of the United States government . . . and it is my strong belief that any program of this kind in which the United States is engaged should provide facilities and meeting places which do not discriminate on the grounds of race or color." He added that he would be in touch with General Grant "because we cannot leave the situation as it is today."[18] Ultimately, after a bruising series of negotiations between Charleston segregationists and cowardly commission members, the White House engineered a compromise, moving the meeting to a US naval base in Charleston, where the delegates would be housed and could conduct their business in an integrated setting.[19] But feelings remained polarized, with civil rights organizations disappointed that segregationist practices were allowed to stand in Charleston, while many Southern and Northern whites saw the compromise as a sellout to "communists." This sentiment was succinctly summarized by commission member Wint Smith, a congressman from Kansas, who "felt from the start that the 'funks' and the liberal 'nit wits' would be using the 'nigger' question to parade their new social theories to the forefront."[20] Kennedy's approach to the Charleston incident typified his administration's response to racial conflict in the early stages of his presidency. The administration sought to accommodate both the "negro" and white Southern perspectives in handling incidents of this type. These incidents, which Kennedy found deeply embarrassing in terms of the nation's standing in the eyes of the world, flared up with distressing regularity in the United States. Damage control was the priority, not the pursuit of equal justice under the law.

Yet despite what some civil rights leaders viewed as a timid approach to racial discrimination, Kennedy held, as Steven Levingston has observed, "a subtle yet steadfast disgust with segregation." His initial actions "pointed to a President who wished to live in an integrated world." He was dismayed at his inaugural parade to see the nearly all-white composition of the Coast Guard contingent and ordered its commandant to diversify its ranks. He was the first American president to dance with a Black woman at an inaugural ball, and he went on to appoint close to fifty Black Americans to senior positions in his administration. He withdrew his request for membership in the Cosmos Club in Washington, DC, after it refused to admit one of these appointees because of his race.[21]

While these actions are often dismissed today as mere symbolic gestures, they were pathbreaking "gestures" signaling that change was coming. It was incremental change, no doubt, and these critics are correct to note that the administration's approach was one of quiet diplomacy, of crisis management if needed, of defusing issues and appealing for moderation. As one historian of the era observed, Kennedy in 1961 "saw the struggle against racism as a conundrum to be managed, not a cause to be championed."[22]

From an electoral perspective, Kennedy's "timidity" made sense. Kennedy's party in the early 1960s continued to rely on the "Solid South" to win presidential elections, and no one knew this better than the man who narrowly won the presidency with the support of white Southern voters. Kennedy carried 52 percent of the white vote in the South, a 3 percent improvement over Democrat Adlai Stevenson's performance in 1956. And the senator from Massachusetts carried seven of the eleven former Confederate states, giving him 63 percent of the South's electoral votes, compared to President Eisenhower's take of 52 percent in 1956. In Georgia, Kennedy carried slightly over 62 percent of the popular vote, a margin exceeding that of the Commonwealth of Massachusetts from which he hailed. It is important to note, however, that Kennedy's impressive performance in the South hinged on the high turnout of Black voters who were in the process of shifting their allegiance from the party of Lincoln to the party that was haltingly picking up Lincoln's mantle.[23]

This high turnout was partly the result of Kennedy's highly publicized intervention on behalf of Martin Luther King Jr., who was arrested for violating his terms of probation (for a traffic violation) by participating in a sit-in at an Atlanta department store. Reluctantly accepting the advice of campaign aides Harris Wofford and Sargent Shriver, Kennedy placed a phone call to Coretta Scott King while his campaign manager Robert Kennedy used his party contacts in Georgia to help release King from a potentially dangerous situation in jail. While King himself would later downplay the importance of this call and of Bobby Kennedy's intervention, as have some historians of the era, Kennedy's call to King was fraught with risk in a party, and a nation for that matter, where race remained the third rail of American politics. The call, and other interventions, led to King's release, and prompted the latter's father to publicly proclaim that he was switching his vote from Richard Nixon to JFK. The elder King famously proclaimed, "I'll take a Catholic or the Devil himself if he'll wipe the tears from my daughter-in-law's eyes. I've got a suitcase full of votes" for Kennedy.[24]

During his first year in office, Kennedy remained hesitant on civil rights, not submitting any legislative agenda on the issue during 1961.[25] Whatever steps he took were in the form of executive orders, including one establishing the Committee on Equal Employment Opportunity, the forerunner to the current EEOC (Equal Employment Opportunity Commission). Martin Luther King initially embraced the idea that Kennedy should make robust use of executive orders, noting in a private letter to Frank D. Reeves, a special assistant to the president responsible for minority issues, that he was "amazed to find the powerful things that the president can do in the civil rights area through executive orders."[26] But that enthusiasm waned over time as King promoted a sweeping legislative agenda that would elevate civil rights into the central moral issue of the day.

President Kennedy was not interested in elevating this issue, in part because moral issues were simply not part of his political DNA, being something of a devotee of pragmatism and unalloyed reason. Arthur Schlesinger

Jr. would later claim that Kennedy was an idealist without illusions, but the idealist elements of the man remained concealed during his first year in office. Kennedy was fixated on one foreign policy crisis after another, and he, along with key members of his administration, viewed civil rights agitation as a nuisance, and worse, a rebuke to a nation seeking to win the hearts and minds of millions of non-whites living around the globe. When an African diplomat from Sierra Leone was refused service at a Howard Johnson's in Maryland in April 1961, this highly publicized incident put the American system of apartheid in the spotlight. The incident became a major propaganda coup for the Soviet Union in its campaign to win worldwide adherents. There were reports that some members of Kennedy's inner circle initially reacted to the diplomat's plight by suggesting he use alternative routes and modes of transport so as not to cause embarrassment.

Kennedy's piecemeal approach and reluctance to challenge the Southern congressional barons began to grate on Martin Luther King and other civil-rights leaders who were tired of being told to wait until the time was "right." For this reason and others, the relationship between President Kennedy and Dr. King was often strained. The latter often seemed ambivalent at best toward Kennedy, even after the famous phone call to Coretta Scott King in 1960. King would later note that while the "Kennedy family did have some part . . . in the release . . . I must make it clear that many other forces worked to bring it about also."[27] There was also a massive cultural void between the Kennedys and King, cogently summed up in a vignette recorded by Kennedy aide Harris Wofford. During one of his visits to the White House, Martin Luther King encountered Jacqueline Kennedy in an elevator, prompting the First Lady to exclaim, "Oh, Dr. King, you would be thrilled if you could just have been with me in the basement this morning. I found a chair right out of the Andrew Jackson period—a beautiful chair. . . . I've just got to tell Jack about this chair."[28]

The relationship between the president, Attorney General Robert Kennedy, and Martin Luther King was further strained by the calculated interventions of FBI director J. Edgar Hoover, who viewed King as a communist and a sexual deviant. Hoover's war against King represents one of the ugliest episodes in American history, an abuse of power that would lead many on the American Left and the Right to claim that a lawless "Deep State" capable of horrific misdeeds existed within the American government. Hoover's war on King would also fuel later allegations that the FBI murdered King. While there is little evidence to support that allegation, it is understandable why many Americans came to that conclusion.

Hoover was convinced, with some reason, that two members of King's movement, Stanley Levison and Jack O'Dell, were communists. While Levison had severed his ties to the Communist Party in 1955, O'Dell's membership status was less certain. Media exposure of even a former communist so close to King would have seriously damaged the civil rights movement, particularly in parts of the country where King's motives were already suspect. Deputy Attorney General Nicholas Katzenbach would later describe the information about King's relationship with Levison as "politically explosive" coming at a time when the Kennedy administration was embracing the goals of King's movement.[29] Hoover used this information to convince Attorney General Robert Kennedy to approve the bureau's request for electronic surveillance of King, which Robert Kennedy did on October 10, 1963.[30] The FBI's electronic surveillance of King began two weeks later and continued until June 21, 1966.[31]

While Hoover's FBI worked to destroy King, right-wing organizations like the John Birch Society and white supremacist entities like the White Citizens Council engaged in a massive public relations campaign to destroy King's image in the American mind. Both groups posted well over two hundred billboards in 1965 with a photograph of King in the front row of a meeting with the headline "Martin Luther King at Communist Training School." A Senate investigative committee determined in 1976 that that neither Levison or O'Dell "attempted to exploit the civil rights movement to carry out the plans of the Communist Party."[32] The committee concluded that the FBI's war on King "continued as long as it did and as intensely as it did only because of Hoover's deep personal dislike for Dr. King. Evidence obtained by the committee indicated that the allegation that Dr. King posed a threat to national security was merely a convenient rationalization used by the Director to justify his personal vendetta against the civil rights leader."[33]

While the surveillance did not uncover evidence that King was a puppet of the Soviet Union, it did uncover the fact that King was a serial philanderer. For Hoover, this behavior was equivalent to working as an agent for the Soviet Union. The electronic evidence of King's robust sexual appetite was surreptitiously sent to King's home, accompanied by a letter suggesting that King kill himself.[34]

The FBI had used embarrassing personal information to sow dissension in the past to disrupt the ranks of the American Communist Party, to great effect. For Hoover, King's connection to Levison and O'Dell justified the use of the same tactics. On June 22, 1963, President Kennedy, building on prior conversations that Assistant Attorney General Burke Marshall and Harris Wofford had had with King, tried to convince King to distance himself from both men during a walk on the White House grounds. The conversation produced mixed results. King agonized for months over what to do about Levison, but the latter took the initiative and scaled back his direct involvement with King, while O'Dell was removed from King's circle within two weeks of the meeting with President Kennedy.[35]

The president's willingness to confide directly in King reveals the extent to which he was trying to establish a trusting relationship with J. Edgar Hoover's "public enemy number one." Kennedy was undoubtedly hoping to protect himself and his legislative agenda, but there was more at work here, in that Kennedy was moving toward an alliance with the leader of the American civil rights movement. Kennedy had come a long way from his youthful disdain for civil rights advocates who had tried to deliver on the promise of the Declaration of Independence and of the Civil War itself, a war that was still underway a century later, and continues to this day.

"We Were . . . Prodding Him, Pushing Him, Sticking Pins and Needles in Him"

No one personified the face of white supremacy more than Theophilus Eugene "Bull" Connor, the commissioner of public safety for Birmingham, Alabama, and a longtime Democratic Party activist on the Alabama political scene. Before making his name as the man who turned fire hoses and police dogs on children and adults protesting for civil rights, Connor had cut his teeth in Alabama politics, serving in the state legislature and twice running unsuccessfully for governor. He served as a delegate from Alabama to the Democratic Party conventions of 1948, 1956, 1964, and 1968, and had made something of a name for himself in leading the walkout of the Dixiecrats who abandoned the Democratic party in 1948 due to the party's adoption of a progressive stance on civil rights.[36]

Kennedy's campaign coterie was familiar with Connor long before the confrontation in Birmingham in 1963. Connor's suspicions about Kennedy's presidential candidacy began when it first appeared that the Massachusetts senator would enter the race. When Alabama's governor, John Patterson, endorsed Kennedy for president in June 1959, Connor was on the alert for any indication that Kennedy opposed racial segregation. Governor Patterson was Connor's rival for statewide leadership, and if Connor detected appeasement on the question of racial supremacy, he could use it not only against Kennedy but against his in-state rival. Connor wrote the Kennedy campaign twice that month demanding clarification on Kennedy's stance on civil rights. "As a citizen of Alabama, I would appreciate it very much if you would inform me what your stand is on integration . . . As far as I'm concerned, this is the number one problem, not only in the South, but all over the nation today."

Kennedy's brother-in-law, Stephen Smith, responded tersely, "In the absence of Senator Kennedy from Washington, I am replying to your letter . . . I am sure you are familiar with the Senator's views, which have been stated many times." Connor, equally abrupt, replied, "I am sorry but I am not familiar with the Senator's views on integration of our schools. I have not seen anything in our Southern papers where he has made a statement in regards to integrating the schools. Therefore, as a prospective candidate to the National Democratic Convention next year, I would appreciate it very much if he would inform me on his views on this matter." The Kennedy campaign opted not to respond to Connor's request.[37]

Connor was likely as irritated about Kennedy's Catholicism as he was about the candidate's murky position on integration. As Governor Patterson, an ironclad segregationist himself, noted, "I didn't realize that people here in Alabama would be as strongly against a man running for President because of his religion. . . . The Baptist and Methodist churches . . . had an organized thing going against him. . . . It was a vicious thing." At one Sunday service, Patterson sat through a lengthy sermon against Kennedy, and "I had words with my own minister about that."[38]

While Kennedy managed to prevail with a narrow win in 1960, his showing in Alabama, with its Byzantine process of presidential selection, was hardly overwhelming. Alabamians cast their votes for individual electors, up to eleven a piece, and Kennedy's slate came in second behind a slate of "unpledged electors" who were in the pocket of the segregationist Senator Harry Byrd of Virginia.[39] Kennedy's Catholicism hurt him in Alabama, as did fears that this Massachusetts Yankee with an odd accent could not be trusted regarding Bull Connor's deepest concern, integrated schools.

Many of the fears held by white Southerners were justified. Encouraged by Kennedy's soaring inaugural address, a group of students decided to challenge one element of the Jim Crow infrastructure, presenting Kennedy with a test of his ability to keep what was left of the fragile New Deal coalition of Southern whites and Black Americans from permanently splintering. The "Freedom Rides" consisted of students mobilized by the Congress of Racial Equality (CORE) who were determined to test various court decisions desegregating public facilities involved in interstate commerce. The rides, which took place from May 4 to December 16, 1961, irritated President Kennedy, who considered them an embarrassment to the United States in the international arena.[40]

The organizer of the rides, James Farmer, noted that Kennedy's election convinced him that the time had come to launch the Freedom Rides. With Kennedy's elevation to the presidency, "there was a spirit of hope which I shared, that the apathy . . . and inactivity of the Eisenhower administration would be at an end. Kennedy was young. His rhetoric was good and seemed to hold some hope."[41] Farmer's hopes were soon dashed as the administration remained silent when he notified the president and the attorney general of his precise plans for the coming months.[42] In his letter to the president informing him of the forthcoming rides, Farmer noted that "Freedom Ride is an appeal to the best in all Americans. We travel peaceably to persuade them that Jim Crow betrays democracy. It degrades democracy at home. It debases democracy abroad."[43] The latter point was clearly designed to appeal to Kennedy's overriding concern regarding civil rights: the damage the issue was doing in the struggle between the free world and the communist world.[44]

Martin Luther King did not participate in the rides and was fearful of what awaited the riders in the Deep South. King told one reporter covering the trip, "You will never make it through Alabama."[45] King's fears were justified, for throughout 1961 there were repeated acts of violence directed at the Freedom Riders. One of the worst incidents occurred in Birmingham, where Bull Connor made sure that his police department avoided a bus terminal long enough for the Ku Klux Klan to savagely attack the Freedom Riders. Connor had promised the Klan "he would see to it that 15 or 20 minutes would elapse before the police would arrive." He added, "by God . . . if you're going to do this thing, do it right."[46] Connor was "just a stone's throw away" from the bus terminal where the Klan and neo-Nazi "storm troopers" beat both Freedom Riders and journalists who attempted to document the rampage.

At the appointed time, a Birmingham police detective told the attackers that they needed to leave the scene to allow for the choreographed arrival of the police. "Get the boys out of here," the detective exclaimed at one point, "I'm ready to give the signal for the police to move in."[47]

In Washington, both the president and the attorney general were caught off guard by the events involving the Freedom Riders in Alabama and elsewhere. It took a piece in the *New York Times* focused on the violence in Birmingham and the firebombing of a Freedom Rider bus in Anniston, Alabama, to bring the story to the attention of the White House. The president angrily directed his civil rights point man, Harris Wofford, to get his "goddamned friends off those buses." At the same time, the attorney general was growing frustrated with the damage done to the nation's reputation due to the chaos surrounding the rides, and asked for a "cooling off period" to stop the violence.

James Farmer's response to the suggestion was to note acidly, and accurately, "We've been cooling off for 100 years."[48] When it was announced that more rides were being planned, the president's old ally John Patterson ignored Kennedy's phone calls and proclaimed in a press conference that "Alabama isn't the Congo."[49] Robert Kennedy dispatched one of his deputies, John Seigenthaler, to negotiate a peaceful transit for the riders. Seigenthaler ended up being beaten in the streets of Montgomery in May 1961 while attempting to protect a female Freedom Rider. These events led Robert Kennedy to order the US Marshals Service to provide protection for the Freedom Riders. It would not take long for white supremacists to turn their attacks against the marshals.[50]

Both Kennedys were criticized then and now for their hesitant approach to providing protection for the Freedom Riders and for not vigorously endorsing the goal of breaking down race-based barriers that impeded the rights of those traveling throughout the United States. But these accounts ignore a significant development that occurred during the rides. Attorney General Robert Kennedy delivered an important address, his first outside of Washington, DC, at the University of Georgia in May 1961, challenging the South as well as the North, and himself, to do better:

The spirit of our democracy, the letter of our constitution and our laws require that there be no further delay in the achievement of full freedom to vote to all. Our system depends upon the fullest participation of all its citizens. . . .

The problem between the white and the colored people is a problem for all sections of the United States. And as I have said before I believe there has been a great deal of hypocrisy in dealing with it. In fact I found, when I came to the Department of Justice, that I need look no further to find evidence of this. I found that very few Negroes were employed above a custodial level. There were nine hundred and fifty lawyers working in the Department of Justice in Washington, and only ten of them were Negroes. At the same moment the lawyers at the Department of Justice were bringing legal action to end discrimination, that same discrimination was being practiced in the department itself. . . .

Financial leaders from the East who deplore discrimination in the South belong to institutions where no Negroes or Jews are allowed. And their children attend private schools where no Negro students are enrolled . . . government officials belong to private clubs in Washington where Negroes including ambassadors are not welcome even at mealtime. . . .

My firm belief is that if we are to make progress in this area, if we are to be truly great as a nation, then we must make sure that nobody is denied an opportunity because of race, creed, or color.

For on this generation of Americans falls the full burden of proving to the world that we—we really mean when we say—we really mean it when we say that all men are created free and equal before the law.[51]

Words do matter, ideas do have consequences, and these words coming from the brother of the president, and one of the most prominent members of a party noted for discriminating against Black Americans for almost 150 years, were truly revolutionary. And to speak these words in the heart of the old Confederacy meant more than was generally acknowledged by the administration's critics. The attorney general's remarks were followed two weeks later by a cautious statement from the president calling for an end to the violence. "The situation which has developed in Alabama is a source of the deepest concern to me . . . I have instructed the Justice Department to take all necessary steps based on their investigations and information." He then called on elected officials in Alabama, specifically the governor and the mayors of Birmingham and Montgomery, to uphold the law, and urged that private citizens avoid "any action" that might "provoke" violence. He added that the United States government "intended to meet its responsibilities."[52] Perhaps this was an occasion where President Kennedy felt his words would only further inflame the situation, and that it would be best to have a subordinate, the attorney general, enlist America's founding principles in the effort to tear down its system of apartheid. Presidents since George Washington had been using subordinates to do the heavy lifting for them on controversial issues, as Alexander Hamilton discovered on multiple occasions.

One critic of President Kennedy's hesitant response to the Freedom Rides was James Farmer, who was uniquely qualified, and justified, to criticize Kennedy. Farmer would later soften that criticism by noting that "while we were criticizing the President from '60 to '63 and were in a way prodding him, pushing him, sticking pins and needles in him, I failed to really understand—we were too much involved in the battle for me to understand—how important the President had been to us. That hit me all of a sudden at the time of his death, of his assassination. And it seemed then, incongruously, as though everything had dropped out of the bottom of the civil rights movement."

Farmer went on to add, "I can look back on it with a little more perspective now and see the forest instead of the trees which were in our eyes at the time. But there is no question but that the President's attitude and the positions he took on issues, as well as his speeches, helped us a great deal in building up the head of steam in the civil rights movement." Farmer recalled that he and other civil rights leaders received a telegram in 1963 from Mao Tse-tung pledging support for the "black man's fight in this country" and accusing Kennedy of being a member of the Ku Klux Klan. "I hit the ceiling—really, this is pure nonsense—and sent a very strong telegram back saying precisely that. I pointed out that it appeared that things had gotten worse because more people were involved in a fight to make them better and the issues were drawn more tightly, and that Kennedy had helped to draw that issue, to draw the lines and bring the controversy out into the open."[53]

Kennedy was not the first American president to wait for public opinion to come around on a vital but divisive issue; Abraham Lincoln had done the same in the early years of his presidency, as had Franklin Roosevelt when he waited for his countrymen to awaken to the dangers posed by Hitler's Germany. Even Barack Obama waited until well into his presidency to endorse same-sex marriage. There are times when presidential silence and caution are warranted. Even when it is unwarranted, and the events of 1961 and 1962 would indicate that it was unwarranted, the fact remains that the United States is a majoritarian regime where public opinion is the ultimate source of power, and for most Americans, white Americans, ignorance was bliss.

It was the Cold War competition with the Soviet Union that dominated the thinking of both elites and rank-and-file Americans at this time. In the 1960 presidential race, John F. Kennedy had outflanked Richard Nixon as a national security hawk, one of a select few Democrats who successfully managed that during the Cold War. Beating the Russians in space and here on earth was *the* issue. To say to Black Americans, then and now, that caution and prudential calculation necessitated presidential restraint until the time was right is asking a lot. But when one looks at Kennedy's record in its entirety, one detects a method to his recalcitrance.

Kennedy's cautious approach to civil rights persisted throughout 1962, but behind the scenes, his Justice Department helped coordinate the Voter Education Project (VEP), an initiative of the Southern Regional Council (SRC), a nonprofit that distributed funds to organizations like King's Southern Christian Leadership Conference. The Project began after conversations between Robert Kennedy; Burke Marshall, the assistant attorney general for civil rights; Martin Luther King; Roy Wilkins; and the leadership of the SRC. Robert Kennedy felt that "a great deal could be accomplished internally within a state if the Negroes participated in elections and voted." While some activists were critical of this nonconfrontational approach, especially members of the Student Non-violent Coordinating Committee (SNCC), the VEP contributed slowly but steadily to the increase in Black voting power in the South, although the VEP encountered such violent resistance in Mississippi that the effort in that state ended prematurely.[54] The VEP was the kind of initiative the Kennedy administration preferred, as they hoped to contain high-profile and frequently confrontational protests like the Freedom Rides. Unlike the Freedom Rides, the VEP did not generate embarrassing headlines, except in white supremacist publications. Nevertheless, while it is sometimes cited as an example of administration timidity, the VEP greatly enhanced Black political power.

The coordination of the Voter Education Project between the SRC and Assistant Attorney General Burke Marshall was extensive. Roy Wilkins of the NAACP (National Association for the Advancement of Colored People) sent copies of the voter registration materials directly to Marshall and to Robert Kennedy; this coordination and other examples prompted the SRC's executive director to observe that Burke Marshall had "done as much as anyone to bring this [VEP] about." When reports of this covert coordination were exposed, it generated considerable ire among Southern members of Congress.

Senator Herman Talmadge (D-GA) pressed the Internal Revenue Service to revoke the tax-exempt status of the foundations who funded the SRC as well as the SRC itself.[55]

But while President Kennedy sought to foster nonviolent change through expanded voting rights, some white Southerners decided to violently resist this "Second Reconstruction." The unrest in the autumn of 1962 shifted to Mississippi, where protestors tried to block a Black Air Force veteran and the grandson of a slave, James Meredith, from registering as a student at the University of Mississippi. Meredith was inspired by John F. Kennedy's election to apply for admission to Ole Miss. The situation came to a head after Mississippi governor Ross Barnett (D-MS) engaged in stalling tactics and repeatedly broke his word to both the president and the attorney general regarding Meredith's registration.[56] At one point in a conversation with President Kennedy, Barnett suggested a decoy plan where the governor would "courageously" stand in the doorway at the university in Oxford while the feds covertly registered Meredith at Jackson, Mississippi. Barnett would then denounce the administration's duplicity, but Meredith could arrive at school after a few days, and all would be well. But the governor abandoned this plan and opted for confrontation.[57]

On the night of September 30, 1962, white supremacist groups mobilized to stop James Meredith from registering, contributing their forces to a nine-hour "Ku Klux Klan Rebellion," as one historian labeled it. Mississippi police officers welcomed cars and buses filled with Klansman and sundry neo-Nazis from Alabama, Arkansas, Florida, Georgia, Louisiana, and Texas. As these same state and local police retreated to the sidelines, snipers wounded thirty US marshals, while an additional 136 marshals were treated for injuries from bricks, bottles, and glass thrown at them. A French journalist was murdered, shot point blank in the back, a case which remains unsolved, while a bystander was killed by a stray bullet fired by the rioters.[58]

President Kennedy delivered a nationally televised address that evening appealing to the patriotism and pride of Mississippians to stop the violence. Kennedy's remarks were an indirect response to Governor Barnett, who had spoken at the Ole Miss football game the night before. With a clenched fist raised high, the governor told a roaring crowd, "My fellow Mississippians, I love Mississippi! I love her people! Our customs. I love and I respect our heritage."[59] There was no mistaking Barnett's intent, for he had observed after his election as Governor that "I'm a Mississippi segregationist and I am proud of it."[60]

President Kennedy was in contact with Justice Department officials in Mississippi throughout that night of violence, and at one point he denied a request from the besieged marshals to allow them to draw their weapons. But the situation fostered by state and local officials spun out of control, forcing Kennedy to nationalize the Mississippi National Guard and order regular United States Army forces to station themselves in Memphis in preparation for possible deployment to Oxford. Deputy Attorney General Nicholas Katzenbach, who was on the scene, spoke with the president in the early morning hours of October 1 "when joyous shouts went up that regular troops had been sighted outside the Lyceum [administration building]" at Ole Miss. It was only then that the Klan members and their fellow travelers began to flee the scene. Meredith registered the day after the riot but had to attend the campus accompanied by a squad of military police.[61]

Remarkably, the actions of the Kennedys in forcing the University of Mississippi to integrate its student body cost the president little support among white southerners, while nationwide, the administration's actions were backed by a majority of Americans.[62] Some elements of American society were simply not open to the idea that admitting Meredith to Ole Miss was a case of equal treatment under the law. For instance, Senator Strom Thurmond of South Carolina, who would soon abandon the Democratic Party, telegrammed the president imploring him not to use force to register Meredith, saying such an action was "unconstitutional, abominable, and dangerous," and accusing Kennedy of advocating self-determination around the world but not for the American South.

The Mississippi State Senate condemned the administration and expressed its "complete, entire and utter contempt for the Kennedy administration and its puppet courts," while the Mississippi House proclaimed that "this man Meredith" was unqualified to be a student and was "in truth and in fact a ward of the President of the United States and his brother" and was therefore "their direct responsibility."[63] White Citizens Councils throughout the south were appalled at the administration's "tyrannical" use of force to admit Meredith to Ole Miss. These Citizens Councils were nothing more than, as one white southern minister put it, the Ku Klux Klan in "grey flannel suits."[64]

On February 12, 1963, Abraham Lincoln's birthday, the Kennedy White House decided to host an event commemorating the one-hundredth anniversary of Lincoln's issuance of the Emancipation Proclamation, which took effect on January 1, 1863. The president had ignored a previous invitation to speak at the Lincoln Memorial on September 22, 1962, to mark the centennial of Lincoln's actual drafting of the proclamation, and he also ignored the anniversary of its issuance on New Year's Day. But the administration did organize the largest gathering of Black Americans in the history of the White House for the February 1963 celebration. Some eight hundred guests met with the president and the First Lady, along with Vice President Johnson, but conspicuously absent was Martin Luther King Jr., who was frustrated with the president's reluctance to take a strong stand on civil rights. King and his lawyers had submitted a draft "Second Emancipation Proclamation" that was sixty-five pages long that they hoped Kennedy would issue on the September anniversary, but the president declined to endorse it.

The February commemoration should have been a bigger media event than it was, but, as Alan Brinkley has observed, "unknown to the visitors, the event was carefully organized to give the reception as little public attention as possible. Guests were greeted at an entrance that would keep them away from photographers."[65] This was done so that the performer Sammy Davis Jr. would not be photographed with his Caucasian wife, in order to keep the event off the front pages of most newspapers. At this time interracial marriage was still prohibited in many US states.[66]

Here was the president of the United States, commemorating a seminal event in American history, trying to protect the sentiments and sensibilities of those white Americans wedded to the principles of the Lost Cause. It was a reminder, if it were ever needed, that "the past," as William Faulkner observed, "is never dead. It's not even past."[67]

Kennedy's hesitancy on civil rights prior to the fall of 1962, while understandable in light of the challenge he confronted in moving his legislative agenda through Congress, is nonetheless disappointing. Kennedy could have advanced the cause of civil rights from the very start of his presidency by capitalizing on his rhetorical skills and his mastery of television. He championed political courage and had the option to exercise that virtue and deliver, sooner rather than later, on this fundamental issue. He had promised in the 1960 election to ban discrimination in federally assisted housing with the "stroke of the pen" applied to an executive order. Candidate Kennedy claimed this order would "assure all citizens that every door will be open . . . to federally financed homes." He belatedly used that pen on November 20, 1962, over two years after he last made that promise, and one year and ten months into his presidency.[68]

But John F. Kennedy did something unusual for a president—he changed, he learned—throughout his presidency. Kennedy was a man of probing intellect who was unwilling to be bound by the deadweight of the past. He did something alien to most adults and most presidents: he continually challenged himself to think and act anew.[69]

3

Finding His Voice
"We Face . . . a Moral Crisis as a Country"

From the perspective of Martin Luther King Jr., John Lewis, Andrew Young, and countless foot soldiers fighting to deliver on the promise of the Declaration of Independence in the early 1960s, John F. Kennedy's evolution was slow in coming. Those who risked their lives, their fortunes, and their sacred honor, to borrow a phrase, have every reason to question Kennedy's belated commitment to equal justice under the law.

For those of us who were not involved, or not alive at the time, it is perhaps prudent to avoid conclusive, sweeping judgments about Kennedy and civil rights. In my view, works that promote such judgments should be read with caution. My assessment of Kennedy and civil rights is rooted in the perspectives of his time and in ours, and in that sense, my judgment is mixed, perhaps excessively nuanced, and not as conclusive as readers might wish. Without question, John F. Kennedy could have thrown the weight of his office behind the civil rights movement sooner than he did. But in looking at the broad sweep of American history as the nation approaches its 250th birthday, Kennedy's belated efforts on behalf of civil rights puts him in the forefront of those white political figures who pressed the nation to fulfill its founding creed.

John F. Kennedy was no Abraham Lincoln. But when it came to racial matters, both presidents were accused of being "cold, dull, and indifferent," as Frederick Douglass said of Lincoln. And they were faulted, with justification, of being "preeminently the white man's president," since they governed within a system where the majority ruled. But looking back on the Kennedy presidency, as

Douglass did with Lincoln, there is a case to be made that "measuring him by the sentiment of his country, a sentiment he was bound as a statesman to consult, he was swift, zealous, radical, and determined."[1]

Abraham Lincoln stands in a league of his own, and drawing comparisons between him and other American political figures is fraught with peril. Those internet memes that allege remarkable similarities between Kennedy and Lincoln ("Kennedy's secretary was Lincoln, Lincoln's secretary was Kennedy," etc.) trace their lineage to a series of urban myths that began in 1964 with the goal of placing Kennedy on the same pedestal as Lincoln.[2] No other president comes near to Lincoln's mastery of democratic statesmanship, including John F. Kennedy. But the fact is that no president after Abraham Lincoln presented the cause of equal rights for Black Americans in such stark moral terms as Kennedy. Kennedy deserves the plaudits of the nation for trying to fulfill its founding creed—a nation that remains divided along racial lines as it approaches the bicentennial of the abolition of slavery.

But while Kennedy was not in the same league as Abraham Lincoln, the claim that John F. Kennedy may not have controlled events but was controlled by them, to borrow from Lincoln, is valid. Both presidents had a finely tuned ear for politics, and they knew that their white brethren had to be coaxed into the kind of change that many whites continue to resist. In this sense, both were content to let events, as abusive and costly as they were to those on the receiving end of racism, run their course, and allow a consensus for change to build within the white majority.

Kennedy's death in November 1963, almost one hundred years to the day after Lincoln delivered his Gettysburg Address, cut short an effort that began the previous June that elevated civil rights to the top of Kennedy's domestic agenda. Had he lived longer, his status as a great president in dealing with the most pressing domestic issue in American history would likely have been secured. If Abraham Lincoln had been murdered in November 1863, instead of after Appomattox, his work would be seen as unfinished. Kennedy's work was unfinished in November 1963, but nevertheless, by embracing the cause of civil rights so starkly, and by proposing far-reaching legislation, he put himself at great political risk. He was, in fact, no "bystander." One speech, his televised civil rights address of June 11, 1963, should be considered a seminal document in American history.

Some observers of the Kennedy presidency argued that Robert Kennedy was *the* Kennedy who cared about civil rights and pushed the issue independently of, or perhaps at odds with, the president. This is a myth, for Robert Kennedy was doing the president's bidding. Paradoxically, members of President Kennedy's own team began to circulate this myth as they transferred their allegiance from President Kennedy to Robert Kennedy. These alterations of the truth to suit the immediate political needs of the family became a recurring practice in the decades following JFK's murder.

Throughout American history, cabinet officers have served as lightning rods to draw political fire and protect the sitting president. Wise presidents will always use subordinates to carry out and shoulder the blame for unpopular policies. Robert Kennedy did precisely that. The notion of a rogue cabinet officer is almost always fiction, a type of myth that is as old as the American republic, when some came to believe that Alexander Hamilton was acting independently of President George Washington. Robert Kennedy was devoted to his brother, and the idea that he was running amuck strains credulity. The relationship between President Kennedy and his attorney general was the closest alliance between a president and a cabinet officer in American history.

Many scholars of this era have been critical of President Kennedy's record on civil rights. As I mentioned at the close of the previous chapter, these critics have a valid point. But while the president did not move as quickly and aggressively on civil rights as the NAACP (National Association for the Advancement of Colored People), SCLC (Southern Christian Leadership Conference), and ADA (Americans for Democratic Action) wished, or as I may have wished, he was well ahead of his fellow white citizens on this issue. The Kennedys were so prominently linked to civil rights that the largely forgotten "Reverse Freedom Rides" of 1962 targeted the president's summer home at Hyannisport, Massachusetts. White supremacists sponsored trips for unknowing Black Americans and deposited them near the president's home for purposes of embarrassing him and revealing the "hypocrisy" behind his policies.[3] Later that year, after the showdown at the University of Mississippi, bumper stickers began to appear throughout the south proclaiming that "The Castro Brothers Have Moved into the White House," or "From Occupied Mississippi," or "We're Backing [Governor] Ross [Barnett]: Beat 'Lil Brother, the South Will Rise Again," the latter adorned with the Confederate battle flag.[4]

"Bull Connor Just Eats This Up"

In 1963, events in Birmingham, Alabama, or "Bombingham" as it would soon become known, prompted John F. Kennedy to find his voice and embrace, first rhetorically, then legislatively, the cause of James Meredith, Martin Luther King, and hundreds of thousands of Black Americans insisting that the United States fulfill its founding creed. No city personified the ideology of white supremacy more than Birmingham, and no state officials, perhaps other than those in Mississippi, were as determined as those in Alabama to use whatever means necessary to keep Jim Crow in place.

Birmingham was an industrial center of the South with a notorious reputation for racially inspired violence. Civil rights activist Fred Shuttlesworth, the leader of a local organization known as the Alabama Christian Movement for Human Rights (ACMHR), joined forces with King's Southern Christian Leadership Conference to organize a boycott of white-owned businesses during the approaching Easter season. Shuttlesworth viewed the boycott as an "attempt to give our community a chance to survive."[5] The Birmingham boycott came on the heels of Governor George Wallace's infamous inaugural address where he pledged "segregation now, segregation tomorrow, segregation forever." On April 12, 1963, a court injunction was issued banning any protests on Good Friday, but Martin Luther King opted to violate the order and was promptly arrested, thus inspiring his famous "Letter from a Birmingham Jail."

King's letter was addressed to "My Dear Fellow Clergymen," and served as a rejoinder to those clerics who had criticized King for his "unwise and untimely" actions in Birmingham.[6] But the letter was also addressed to the entire nation if not the entire world, and King was especially interested in drawing the attention of President Kennedy. King later noted, "When things started happening down here, Mr. Kennedy got disturbed . . . He is battling for the minds and the hearts of men in Asia and Africa . . . And they're not gonna respect the United States of America if she deprives men and women of the basic rights of life because of the color of their skin. Mr. Kennedy knows this." Later, after a famous photograph of one of Bull Connor's police dogs attacking a young Black boy appeared around the globe, King recalled, "When that picture went all over Asia and Africa and England and France, Mr. Kennedy said, 'Bobby, you better get your assistant down there and look into this matter. It's a dangerous situation for our image abroad.'"[7]

But as Jonathan Rieder has observed, President Kennedy was disturbed not only that the images coming out of Birmingham damaged America's international standing, but also because the photos of Bull Connor's police dogs in action "made him sick." Kennedy specifically mentioned Connor throughout his conversation on May 4, 1963, with members of the Americans for Democratic Action. "As it is today Bull Connor's in charge, this is just what Bull Connor wants. . . . Bull Connor just eats this up." And he repeated for emphasis, "The fact of the matter is that's just what Connor wants." The president claimed that "Birmingham is the worst city in the south. They have done nothing for the Negroes in that community, so it is an intolerable situation, that there is no argument about."

The president then recounted a discussion he had with a journalist who said, "'Isn't it outrageous in Birmingham' and I said, 'Why are you over there eating at the Metropolitan Club every day? You talk about Birmingham and you're up there at the Metropolitan Club . . . they wouldn't even let Negro ambassadors in.' So now he (the reporter) said, 'Well we want to work from the inside,' and I said, 'Well your one contribution is that now they won't let white ambassadors in.' So I think that we have worked hard on civil rights. I think it is a national crisis." But he also noted, "We have not done enough . . . the situation is so desperate. But we have shoved and pushed and the Department of Justice has—there is nothing that my brother's given more time to. And I quite agree, if I were a Negro I would be awfully sore." And he added, "I'm not saying anybody ought to be patient."[8]

While King drafted his famous jailhouse letter over Easter Weekend, 1963, his wife, Coretta Scott King, was at home in Atlanta deeply concerned about her husband's treatment in jail and the inability of SCLC lawyers to meet with him. She reached out to the White House to speak with Kennedy, who was visiting his disabled father in Palm Beach, Florida. She was unable to reach the president, but she did receive a call from Robert Kennedy who reassured her and promised to monitor her husband's situation. Within forty-eight hours, the president called Mrs. King directly and reassured her that FBI agents had visited Birmingham and "checked on your husband, and he's all right. . . . I want you to know we are doing everything we can. . . . Your husband will be calling you shortly." (King called 30 minutes later, and Coretta told him the president had tipped her off that he'd be calling; "So that's why everybody is being so polite," King replied.) As the president said goodbye, he told her, "You know how to get me now." Coretta King would later recall, "Even though I understood that there were political overtones, I believed President Kennedy sincerely cared about what happened to us. . . . There was an amazing warmth about him." When Martin Luther King was released, he sent a telegram to the president noting that "your encouraging words and thoughtful concern gave her [Coretta] renewed strength."[9]

"I Don't Want the Enemy to Step on It"

Shortly after the Easter weekend incidents, Governor Wallace met with Attorney General Robert Kennedy on April 25, 1963, at the Statehouse in Montgomery. Normally the Alabama state flag flew over the capitol, but on this day a sole Confederate flag adorned the building. Picketers greeted Kennedy as he entered the building, and a woman who escorted him into the building noted afterwards that she took Kennedy away from the spot where Jefferson Davis had been sworn in as president of the Confederacy. "I don't want the enemy to step on it," she observed. Kennedy and Governor Wallace spoke with one another for an hour and a half, with the two men talking in circles around one another, with Kennedy asking Wallace at one point, "Do you think it is so horrifying to have a Negro attend the University of Alabama?" Wallace responded, "I think it is horrifying for the federal courts and the central government to rewrite all the law and force upon people that which they don't want." He added, "I will never submit myself voluntarily to any integration in a school system in Alabama." After the meeting Robert Kennedy held a press conference where he was asked if he was a communist.[10]

Ironically, President Kennedy and Governor Wallace spent a far more cordial day with one another a short time later, on May 18, 1963. This meeting came after the events in Birmingham and slightly over three weeks before the standoff at the schoolhouse door. Images of Bull Connor's police dogs and high-powered fire hoses breaking limbs were fresh in Kennedy's mind when he visited a Tennessee Valley Authority facility at Muscle Shoals, Alabama. Governor Wallace would later recall that some Alabamans questioned whether he should greet the president, but he responded, "Certainly I'm going to meet the President, unless the President doesn't want me to meet him, because he is the President of the United States and we are happy to have him in the state. It's a great honor."

Wallace noted that during their time together Kennedy was "overly concerned" about the events in Birmingham and that the president wanted "everybody" satisfied. Kennedy urged Wallace to get behind efforts to increase the employment of Black Americans in Birmingham, but the governor questioned Kennedy's understanding of the situation, claiming that there was "no negro, non-white unemployment to speak of in Alabama" at that time. Kennedy's press secretary, Pierre Salinger, was on the helicopter flight from Muscle Shoals to Huntsville and prepared a memorandum after that conversation that quoted Wallace saying that Martin Luther King was a "faker." According to Salinger, the governor then added that King "vied" with Fred Shuttlesworth "to see who could go to bed with the most nigger women, and white and red women too. They ride around town in big Cadillacs smoking expensive cigars."[11]

Wallace later observed that the Kennedy administration was "over-solicitous in their contact with the so-called civil rights leaders" and did not take "into account the attitude of people who were trying to see it more objectively." But Wallace insisted that he liked President Kennedy and that the President had been misled by activists and the media, and that Kennedy's mistakes were of "the head, not the heart." Wallace was effusive in his praise for Kennedy in 1967, noting that "it was good to be around him personally. He was the kind of man that you only wished agreed with you or that you could agree with him a little more. . . . I enjoyed being with him. And I think he was an attractive, intelligent, brilliant man." After the assassination he noted that "it's sort of sad to talk about, to think about what happened. It's hard to believe it. . . . We differed honestly, but he was honest in his attitude."[12]

Their "honest differences" came to a head on June 11, 1963, when Governor Wallace stood in the schoolhouse door to prevent the integration of the University of Alabama. Having learned important lessons from the confrontation at Ole Miss, the Kennedy brothers deftly managed the showdown at Tuscaloosa. Wallace promoted this confrontation widely, seeing it as a fulfillment of his inaugural promise of "segregation now . . . segregation forever." Two Black students, Vivian Malone and James Hood, sought to enroll in summer classes at the university. In the midst of a massive media presence, the governor, equipped with a microphone and a sound system, solemnly condemned "the unwelcomed, unwanted, unwarranted and force-induced intrusion upon the campus of the University of Alabama today," claiming that the attempt by the Justice Department offered a "frightful example of the oppression of the rights, privileges and sovereignty" of the state of Alabama. Wallace portrayed himself as an heir to the American founders, claiming that he was "practicing the free heritage bequeathed to us by the Founding Fathers."[13] These remarks were written by a Wallace speechwriter who was the founder of the "Original Ku Klux Klan of the Confederacy," a group responsible for frequent acts of racial violence in the 1950s, and who had also served as the publisher of a white-supremacist journal called "The Southerner."[14]

Deputy Attorney General Nicholas Katzenbach was the administration's point man during the showdown, and as the media spectacle unfolded, his contempt for Wallace grew. Robert Kennedy had told Katzenbach that "the president wants you to make him look foolish," which is precisely what Katzenbach went on to do.[15] "I'm not interested in this show. . . . From the outset Governor, all of us have known, that the final chapter of this history will be the admission of these students." Which is precisely what happened, as Katzenbach and his deputies returned to their vehicles and drove the students to their dorms. President Kennedy federalized the Alabama National Guard, at which point the choreographed standoff came to an end, but in Wallace's eyes the event simply confirmed that "the trend toward military dictatorship continues."[16]

"That White Man Not Only Stepped Up to the Plate, He Hit It over the Fence"

It was at this moment that President Kennedy decided to give the most important speech of his presidency, and one of the most important speeches ever delivered by an American president. After news came of Wallace's retreat, Kennedy turned to his speechwriter Ted Sorensen and said, "I guess we better make that speech on TV tonight."

"I felt like saying, 'what speech?'" Sorensen later recalled. Sorensen went on to note that "for a long time, there had been internal debate as to whether the President should make a speech [about civil rights]. . . . The politicians inside the White House—Mr. [Kenneth] O'Donnell, Mr. [Lawrence] O'Brien, others—said, 'No, whatever you do, don't make a speech on this. That just makes it a bigger issue.'"[17]

As was somewhat typical of the Kennedy White House, there was an improvised quality to the crafting of the civil rights speech. Sorensen had just six hours to spare before the president would go on the air, and he had little to work with since civil rights was not a centerpiece of either Kennedy's campaign or his presidency. Yet Sorensen managed to cobble together a moving series of remarks partly based on a high school oration he had delivered in the 1950s. A nervous president checked in to Sorensen's office to see how the speech was progressing, which was the only time Kennedy did that during his entire presidency. Reassured by Sorensen that the speech would be ready on time, Kennedy joked that "I thought I was going to have to go off the cuff on national television." One of Sorensen's deputies recalled that despite the jocularity, Kennedy was "extremely nervous. Normally he's not nervous, but he was awfully damned nervous about this one."

Robert Kennedy, Burke Marshall, and the president toned down some of Sorensen's remarks, for instance changing the line "the cesspools of segregation and discrimination exist in every state" to "difficulties over segregation and discrimination exist in every city." The phrase "a social revolution is at hand" was changed to "a great change is at hand."[18] But in the end, despite its somewhat spur-of-the-moment drafting, the speech was a masterpiece.

The president proclaimed that "we are confronted primarily with a moral issue. It is as old as the scriptures and is as clear as the American Constitution," and went on to note:

The heart of the question is whether all Americans are to be afforded equal rights and equal opportunities, whether we are going to treat our fellow Americans as we want to be treated. If an American, because his skin is dark, cannot eat lunch in a restaurant open to the public, if he cannot send his children to the best public school available, if he cannot vote for the public officials who will represent him, if, in short, he cannot enjoy the full and free life which all of us want, then who among us would be content to have the color of his skin changed and stand in his place? Who among us would then be content with the counsels of patience and delay?

One hundred years of delay have passed since President Lincoln freed the slaves, yet their heirs, their grandsons, are not fully free. They are not yet freed from the bonds of injustice. They are not yet freed from social and economic oppression. And this Nation, for all its hopes and all its boasts, will not be fully free until all its citizens are free.

We preach freedom around the world, and we mean it, and we cherish our

freedom here at home, but are we to say to the world, and much more importantly, to each other that this is the land of the free except for the Negroes; that
we have no second-class citizens except Negroes; that we have no class or caste
system, no ghettoes, no master race except with respect Negroes? . . .

We face, therefore, a moral crisis as a country and as a people. It cannot be
met by repressive police action. It cannot be left to increased demonstrations in
the streets. It cannot be quieted by token moves or talk. It is time to act in the
Congress, in your State and local legislative body and, above all, in all of our
daily lives.

It is not enough to pin the blame on others, to say this is a problem of one
section of the country or another, or deplore the fact that we face. A great change
is at hand, and our task, our obligation, is to make that revolution, that change,
peaceful and constructive for all.

Those who do nothing are inviting shame as well as violence. Those who act
boldly are recognizing right as well as reality.[19]

Kennedy did go "off the cuff" at certain points in the speech, having had
some thoughts in the back of his mind if Sorensen or his typewriter failed.
In fact, Robert Kennedy later claimed that the speech would have been more
effective if the president had improvised all of it. One such improvised passage was Kennedy's remark that "this is one country . . . It has become one
country because all of us and all the people who came here had an equal
chance to develop their talents. We cannot say to 10 percent of the population that you can't have the right; that your children can't have the chance
to develop whatever talents they have."[20] The first Catholic president of the
United States may well have had his ancestors in mind when he made this
comment and may have recalled the extent to which his faith cost him in the
1960 election.

The reaction to Kennedy's speech was generally positive. Roy Wilkins
called it "the message I had been waiting to hear" and noted that he "fell
asleep that night feeling new confidence," while Martin Luther King described it as "eloquent" and "profound." Reverend Walter Fauntroy, a King
advisor, recalled years later that he and King watched the speech and when
Kennedy concluded his remarks King jumped up and said, "Can you believe
that white man not only stepped up to the plate, he hit it over the fence."[21]

The American president is in a sense a keeper of the nation's tablets,
the temporary possessor of an office that can ennoble, or demean, the first

modern republic. Franklin Roosevelt's first inaugural address, where he proclaimed that we have "nothing to fear but fear itself," Ronald Reagan's tribute to the astronauts who perished in the Challenger disaster, even George W. Bush's off-the-cuff comments in the rubble at Ground Zero all served to point the nation to something higher, and to remind Americans of their shared heritage.[22] Presidents can seek to divide, as Andrew Jackson, Andrew Johnson, Richard Nixon, and Donald Trump did, or they can appeal to "the better angels of our nature," as John F. Kennedy did on June 11, 1963. Kennedy's invocation of Scripture and the American Constitution in arguing for equal justice for all was precisely such an appeal. This day was the high-water mark of the Kennedy presidency.

Kennedy followed up this address with a sweeping series of legislative proposals in a Special Message to Congress on June 19, 1963. In this message, Kennedy asked Congress to stay in session until it passed some version of what he called the "Civil Rights Act of 1963." He concluded his message by invoking Lincoln's legacy and appealing to the fairmindedness of the American people. He urged the nation to abandon the parochialism that provides the nursery for racism to flourish. "To paraphrase the words of Lincoln, 'In giving freedom to the Negro, we assure freedom to the free—honorable alike in what we give and what we preserve.'" He added:

I therefore ask every Member of Congress to set aside sectional and political ties, and to look at this issue from the viewpoint of the Nation. I ask you to look into your hearts—not in search of charity, for the Negro neither wants nor needs condescension–but for the one plain, proud and priceless quality that unites us all as Americans: a sense of justice. In this year of the Emancipation Centennial, justice requires us to ensure the blessings of liberty for all Americans and their posterity—not merely for reasons of economic efficiency, world diplomacy and domestic tranquility—but, above all, because it is right."[23]

Kennedy had submitted to Congress the most comprehensive civil rights legislation ever proposed by an American president. This legislation included provisions to protect the voting rights of Black Americans, ensure equal access to public accommodations, further the desegregation of public schools, and provide for workplace training and an end to discriminatory hiring practices. For the remainder of his presidency, he met with business leaders, clergymen, union representatives, educators, and state and local officials, urging them to back his legislative package and exhorting them to act in their communities. Kennedy lobbied his Republican opponents in Congress and enlisted the support of former President Dwight Eisenhower. Kennedy's efforts were described by Ted Sorensen as "the most intensive use of the educational powers of the presidency that I have ever seen." And while Sorensen was prone to hagiographical overstatement when it came to his beloved boss, in this instance he was correct.[24] Unfortunately, a large segment of the American public rejected the "educational" message conveyed by the President.

In the aftermath of Kennedy's nationally broadcast speech, his poll numbers began to drop, as many white Americans began to believe that Kennedy was being overly aggressive on civil rights. Thirty-six percent of Americans believed this in June, 41 percent by July, and 50 percent by August. Kennedy held a remarkably high approval rating in February 1963 of 70 percent, but by October of that year it had fallen to 59 percent. This decline began after his June 11 civil rights speech, and the decline was most pronounced in the South, where his approval fell from 60 to 40 percent.[25] 70 percent of Southern whites believed that Kennedy was pushing too aggressively on integration, while his support among Black Americans remained at an impressive 89 percent.

One consequence of Kennedy's decision to embrace the civil rights movement, which led to his drop in the polls, was that congressional Democrats from the South and the border states were more reluctant than ever to support his legislative agenda.[26] Asked to comment on this troubling polling data, Kennedy observed:

The fact of the matter is this is not a matter on which you can take the temperature every week or two weeks or three weeks, depending on what the newspaper headlines must be. I think you must make a judgment about the movement of a great historical event which is taking place in this country, after a period of time. You judged 1863 after a good many years, its full effect. . . . The fact is that same poll showed 40 percent or so thought it was more or less right. I thought that was rather impressive, because it is change; change always disturbs.[27]

Kennedy's precarious standing in the South was part of the reason for his trip to Texas a year before the 1964 presidential election. A myth would emerge that Kennedy was murdered in a "city of hate" due to his civil rights stance. He was not killed because of this but rather he was murdered, as Jacqueline Kennedy put it, by a "silly little communist."[28] But one should not dismiss the political risk Kennedy took for himself and his party in embracing equal rights for all.

"And You Had a Dream"

So much violence lay ahead despite Kennedy's appeal in his June 11 speech for the public to embrace the noblest aspirations of the American political tradition. Just hours after Kennedy went off the air, Medgar Evers, a World War II veteran and state field secretary for the Mississippi chapter of the NAACP, was assassinated in his driveway as he returned home from work. The assassin was a member of the White Citizens' Council and the Ku Klux Klan; two separate all-white juries in Mississippi failed to reach a verdict in the 1960s. He was not convicted until 1994, a miscarriage of justice lasting thirty-one years.[29] Attorney General Robert Kennedy attended Evers's funeral at Arlington National Cemetery, where the veteran of the Normandy invasion was given full military honors. This enraged white supremacists, one of whom wrote to President Kennedy arguing that this "neurotic" "rabble rouser" should not be buried at Arlington. The honors accorded Evers were a "national disgrace," another letter writer informed the president.[30]

On September 15, 1963, four Black girls attending Sunday school were killed when members of the Ku Klux Klan detonated explosives at the 16th Street Baptist Church in Birmingham. The bombing occurred shortly after Governor Wallace told the *New York Times,* "What this country needs is a few first-class funerals, and some political funerals too," a statement the governor later claimed was intended as a warning of a forthcoming voter uprising, but was open to a more sinister interpretation by white supremacist organizations.[31]

After hearing the news of the Birmingham church bombing, Martin Luther King sent a telegram to Kennedy with a warning, "I WILL SINCERELY PLEAD WITH MY PEOPLE TO REMAIN NON VIOLENT IN THE FACE OF THIS TERRIBLE PROVOCATION HOWEVER I AM CONVINCED THAT UNLESS SOME STEPS ARE TAKEN BY THE FEDERAL GOVERNMENT . . . MY PLEAS SHALL FALL ON DEAF EARS AND WE SHALL SEE THE WORST RACIAL HOLOCAUST THIS NATION HAS EVER SEEN."[32]

The following day Kennedy expressed his "outrage and grief over the killing of the children" and took a swipe at Governor Wallace for encouraging an atmosphere of "violence which has fallen on the innocent." He added, "If these cruel and tragic events can only awaken that city and state—if they can only awaken this entire nation to a realization of the folly of racial injustice and hatred and violence, then it is not too late for all concerned to unite in steps toward peaceful progress before more lives are lost." The four criminals responsible for the bombings also walked free for years; two of the terrorists were not convicted until the twenty-first century.[33]

While President Kennedy was losing support in what was left of the Democratic Party's "Solid South," he was also denounced by the more radical leaders of the civil rights movement. The leading proponent of Black separatism, Malcolm X of the Nation of Islam, condemned Kennedy's endorsement of integration and disputed the idea that anything positive came out of the administration's effort to enroll James Meredith at the University of Mississippi. The entire effort was a waste of time and money, for "what was accomplished?" According to Malcolm, "It took 15,000 troops to put Meredith in the University . . . those troops and $3,000,000 . . . to get one Negro in." That money "could have been used much more wisely by the Federal Government to elevate the living standards of all the Negroes in Mississippi." Offering a unique understanding of executive power, Malcolm claimed that a President "doesn't have to fight" to achieve his goals but could do whatever he wished. But "when it comes to the rights of the Negro, who helped to put him [Kennedy] in office, then he's afraid of little pockets of white resistance."

Malcolm X would go on to celebrate the assassination of President Kennedy as a vindication of his view of the violent nature of the United States and especially the wicked ways of whites. Malcolm noted that Kennedy's death was a case of "chickens coming home to roost" and added that "chickens coming home to roost never did make me sad; they've always made me glad."[34]

John Lewis of the Student Nonviolent Coordinating Committee, who was one of the speakers at the famous March on Washington on August 28, 1963, included a passage in his original text that Kennedy's civil rights proposals were "too little and it was too late," although other civil rights leaders convinced him to remove that passage, along with the line calling for a march "through the heart of Dixie, the way [General William T.] Sherman did." President Kennedy originally opposed the March on Washington, thinking it would only bolster congressional opposition to his civil right proposals, but in the end he was impressed by what he saw. As Lewis recalled, "President Kennedy was so proud at the end of the march. He was beaming like a proud father. He was almost giddy. He went around, he shook every single hand. He said: 'You did a good job. You did a good job,' and when he got to Dr. King, he said 'And you had a dream.'"[35]

John Lewis would eventually conclude that President Kennedy "was a man that I admired. . . . His whole demeanor and personality sort of gave you a sense of hope and optimism, the sense that you could do almost anything, you could go almost anyplace you wanted to go." Lewis came to believe there was "something magic about the man."[36] Reflecting on Kennedy on the fiftieth anniversary of the President's assassination, Lewis observed, "when President Kennedy was assassinated, something died in those of us who knew him, and something died in America. He was the first American President to say that the issue of civil rights . . . was a moral issue."[37]

As the Kennedy presidency neared its end, 52 percent of Americans viewed race relations as the most important issue confronting the nation, displacing the Cold War as the top concern of citizens. This was due primarily to the exertions of Martin Luther King, John Lewis, James Farmer, and all the Freedom Riders, black and white, male and female, who were genuine "profiles in courage." They put their lives on the line for a noble cause. Their courage, coupled with the draconian response of Ross Barnett, Bull Connor, and George Wallace, shifted public opinion and helped the Kennedy administration build a consensus that something needed to be done. But President Kennedy also displayed a different kind of courage, the kind he had celebrated in *Profiles in Courage* just a few years earlier. In the end, Kennedy threw the entire weight of his office behind civil rights for Black Americans. He was no longer a bystander but was now a "co-conspirator" with Martin Luther King and all that King's movement represented. Kennedy moved far beyond the legalistic, managerial approach of the first months of his presidency, and well beyond that of President Eisenhower, and by so doing put himself at great political risk.

There are noteworthy similarities between John F. Kennedy's handling of the civil rights issue and Abraham Lincoln's approach to emancipation and abolition. Both men recognized the injustice of situation, both men seemed to temporize at times, both were accused by opponents of either moving too fast or too slow, both men took advantage of events and shifts in opinion in terms of timing their respective declarations of Black equality. And both men tried to lead their fellow countrymen, or more accurately their white countrymen, to fully embrace the nation's founding creed. Without downplaying the frustrations and hardships experienced by the victims of slavery or of Jim Crow, it is nonetheless true that in a majoritarian regime a sense of timing, of prudence, an awareness of how much change a society can bear, must enter into a statesman's calculation.

While that fact offers little solace to the victims of injustice, nevertheless the injustice of it all does not negate the fact that any political order rooted in the consent of the majority requires even the noblest statesman, a Lincoln for instance, to trim at times. As historian James Giglio has observed, both Lincoln's and Kennedy's restraint made the change that ultimately did occur more acceptable to the majority.[38] As mentioned, Kennedy was no Lincoln, and he did not live long enough to earn the sobriquet of "statesman," but he was on his way toward achieving that status as he entered the final months of his life. And while he had trimmed, he ultimately pointed the way for his fellow countrymen to live up to the ideal that "all men are created equal."

The Dream Deferred

Shortly after President Kennedy's assassination, George Wallace took his "states' rights" campaign on the road, challenging President Lyndon Johnson's support for desegregation and other civil rights initiatives. Wallace's racist message began to resonate in the North in reaction to Kennedy's and Johnson's civil rights agenda. Wallace did remarkably well in the Democratic primaries in 1964, running against a series of favorite-son candidates pledged to President Johnson. Wallace garnered 34 percent of the vote in Wisconsin, a state where he was projected to get approximately 10 percent of the vote; 30 percent in Indiana, where his campaign was coordinated by two members of the Ku Klux Klan; and 43 percent of the vote in Maryland.[39]

In the general election that fall, Republican Barry Goldwater, an opponent of civil rights legislation and a champion of states' rights, carried Mississippi, Alabama, Georgia, South Carolina, and Louisiana. Kennedy had carried Georgia, South Carolina, and Louisiana, and a portion of Alabama's electoral votes in 1960. By 1964, those states were solidly in Goldwater's camp. Eight years later, at the time of his attempted assassination on May 15, 1972,

George Wallace had won the most votes of any Democrat in the party's presidential primaries that year.

In no location was the flight of white voters away from the Democratic Party more glaring than in President Kennedy's hometown of Boston, which became a focal point of racial discord just a few years after his murder. The president's brother, Edward Kennedy, who held the Senate seat John Kennedy once held, was chased off Boston's City Hall Plaza in 1974 when he tried to calm a crowd of white protesters upset over court-ordered school desegregation. As Ted Kennedy worked his way through the mob, they shouted, "Why don't you put your one-legged son on a bus for Roxbury," "Let your daughter get bused there so she can get raped," and "Why don't you let them shoot you like they shot your two brothers," all the while chanting "pig" as they pursued him into the John F. Kennedy Federal Building. There, the mob shattered panes of glass as they pressed against the entryways. One anti-busing advocate observed of that day, "It was great. It's about time the politicians felt the anger of the people." Another activist, Flossie O'Keefe of South Boston, observed in 1976 that "I cried for his brothers" but "today I'd dance on his [Edward Kennedy's] grave."[40]

John F. Kennedy and Lyndon Johnson are the two twentieth-century Democratic presidents most responsible for breaking the historic hold of segregationists on their party. What began as a trickle of defections starting under President Truman became a tsunami in response to Richard Nixon's "Southern Strategy" in 1968. In the twenty-first century, the "party of Lincoln" attracted white voters in droves and established a near lock on the electoral votes of the "Solid South," abandoning its founders' commitment to equal justice under the law. Closer to our time, the same party that led the drive for emancipation and full citizenship for freedmen is now in the forefront of efforts to tighten election laws with the intention of making it more difficult to vote. The resurgence of white supremacist movements during the Trump presidency and recurring cases of excessive police force, most notably the case of George Floyd in Minneapolis in 2020, was yet one of many indicators of the long road ahead in completing John F. Kennedy's Second Reconstruction.

Cuba

The Sins of William McKinley

My earliest memory as a child is of President Kennedy on my family's grainy black-and-white television announcing the blockade of Cuba in October 1962. I had no idea what he was discussing, but I could tell from the concerned look on my parents' faces that something was amiss. The next day at the dinner table, my older brother said that his school classmates were all talking about war with Russia. Shortly thereafter my father came home with blueprints for a bomb shelter. These are my first memories, and they were all rooted in fear.

No other events of Kennedy's presidency generated as much criticism as his campaign to remove Fidel Castro from power and his alleged culpability in bringing the world "to the brink of destruction" in October 1962. Liberal and conservative commentators, along with Kennedy's courtiers, promoted misleading accounts of his administration's policies toward Cuba, with the Left seeing him as a warmonger and the Right viewing him as a feckless commander in chief. And while I agree with the courtiers' fulsome praise of President Kennedy's handling of the missile crisis, these mythmakers were right for all the wrong reasons.[1] Granted, John F. Kennedy went eyeball to eyeball with Khrushchev, but both fellows blinked, and at just the right time.

While President Kennedy's support for regime change in Cuba remains controversial, for better or worse it was consistent with American's founding principles, which were rooted in the idea of the universality of liberty. While there was pressure to "liberate" Cuba to restore American corporate holdings on the island (and return the casinos and prostitution dens to their organized crime owners), this was not the primary motive for regime change. Kennedy's policies were consistent with seminal American documents such as the Monroe Doctrine, in which the nation drew a line in the sand regarding any European attempts to "extend their system" into the Americas. This mix of ideals and interests has always animated American foreign policy and was no different here. Kennedy, and his predecessor Dwight Eisenhower, believed Cuba was being transformed into a Soviet base that would be used against the United States.

The Cuban missile crisis also remains shrouded in myth, a myth carefully propagated by Robert Kennedy, Arthur Schlesinger Jr., and Ted Sorensen. Most of what the American public thought at time, and in the decades since, is inaccurate, a result of a spin placed on the event to keep Robert Kennedy's presidential ambitions afloat, and since that time, keep the entire Kennedy brand in good stead. The mythologized version of the missile crisis is still accepted by far too many scholars, rendering it a suspect teaching tool.

This mythologized interpretation holds that the young president, aided by his brother Robert, rebuffed the "hawks" in his administration who wanted to attack Cuba, but the secret tape recordings of the ExComm (Executive Committee of the National Security Council) meetings show a different Robert Kennedy, one who was repeatedly hawkish in his advice to his brother about the Soviet missiles in Cuba.[2] It was President Kennedy, defying the wishes of most of his key advisers, including his brother, who opted for a way out of the missile crisis and prevented the crisis from escalating into a nuclear war.

It is important to note that Cuba had long held a place in the hearts and minds of Americans as something equivalent to an American state, and in fact, throughout the nation's history, numerous proposals to acquire Cuba were proposed by American political figures. Thomas Jefferson wrote in 1803 that the acquisition of Cuba would give the United States "control . . . over the Gulf of Mexico . . . [filling] up the measure of our political well being." Twenty years later, he wrote President James Monroe warning that if Cuba was taken by the British, it would be a "great calamity to us."[3] Absent the divisive issue of the expansion of slavery, it is quite likely Cuba would have been annexed at some point in the early nineteenth century. As it was, the United States would later declare Cuba a protectorate in 1898 under President William McKinley after the American victory in the Spanish-American War. After Cuba won its independence in 1902, the island remained dominated by American economic interests and by threats of, and occasional use of, American military power. During the period from 1902, after Cuban independence, until the rise of Fidel Castro in 1959, Cuba was a wholly owned subsidiary of the United States. This explains the shock most Americans felt when Castro successfully toppled the corrupt regime of President Fulgencio Batista and began to steer his nation toward becoming a full-fledged ally of the Soviet Union.

Fulgencio Batista fled Havana on New Year's Day in 1959, and exactly four months later, on May Day, 1959, Castro nationalized American property on the island. He went on to sign the Cuban-Soviet Trade Agreement in February 1960, raising further concerns in Washington, and by July of that year the first Soviet weapons began to arrive. The United States implemented a partial trade embargo on Cuba in October, just prior to the American presidential election. One of President Eisenhower's last acts in office was to break diplomatic relations with Cuba on January 3, 1961, seventeen days before Kennedy's inauguration.

"Moscow Is Our Brain and Our Great Leader"

Cuba was central to John F. Kennedy's campaign for president in 1960. He defeated Richard Nixon in 1960 partly because he outflanked Nixon on the Cuba issue, essentially turning the Republican talking point of "who lost China," which had worked effectively against Democrats during the Truman years, to "who lost Cuba," against Eisenhower and Nixon and the Republican Party. As Kennedy told Arthur Schlesinger Jr., in deciding to attack the Republicans on Cuba, "What the hell, they never told us how they would have saved China."[4] Kennedy was one of the few Cold War–era Democratic candidates for president to successfully portray his Republican opponent as weak on national security, a charge usually directed at Democrats with devastating effect.

President Eisenhower's failure to block Fidel Castro's rise to power was a major foreign policy setback, Kennedy argued, and he pledged to reverse the "loss" of Cuba as part of his vow to get the United States "moving again." Kennedy claimed in his final televised debate with Richard Nixon that "the Communists have been moving with vigor—Laos, Africa, Cuba—all around the world today they're on the move. I think we have to revitalize our society.

I think we have to demonstrate to the people of the world that we're determined in this free country of ours to be first—not first if, and not first but, and not first when—but first." On the campaign trail, Kennedy asserted that the nation's "enemies" had "rolled the Iron Curtain to 90 miles from our shores onto the once friendly island of Cuba."[5] He accused the Eisenhower administration of passively standing by as a dangerous "missile gap" emerged with the Soviet Union, but more importantly, he viewed the rise of a communist Cuba as the Republican administration's "most glaring failure"—a failure that threatened the "whole Western Hemisphere."[6]

The Eisenhower-Nixon record on Cuba was one of "blunder, inaction, retreat, and failure," and candidate Kennedy promised to assist Cuban "fighters for freedom" who had received "virtually no support from our government."[7] Richard Nixon would later contend that Kennedy knew the latter statement was false, claiming that CIA Director Allen Dulles had briefed Kennedy on the training of a Cuban invasion force in July 1960. Dulles denied this in an interview conducted in late 1964, and historian Tim Naftali and author Peter Kornbluth find this denial to be credible.[8] However, it is known that Alabama governor John Patterson briefed Kennedy about four weeks prior to the election regarding the recruitment of Alabama National Guard pilots for the CIA's planned operation in Cuba.[9]

The question of whether Castro was pushed into the arms of the Soviet Union by the United States or had planned to embrace the Kremlin from the start has been debated by students of American foreign policy for decades. Castro's own words seemed to indicate that his alliance with Moscow came naturally to him. "I have been a Marxist from my student days and have pulled together all of the fundamental works of Marxism," he announced in November 1960. He began to read Marxist tracts in high school and noted that he "introduced" Marxism to his brother Raul, whom he described as "the original revolutionary Marxist." He argued that there was "no other path for Cuba but the construction of socialism" and proclaimed that only Communists could hold "all of the key positions . . . in the government, the cultural apparatus, the army and the state economy" in the new Cuba.[10]

Scholars Alexander Fursenko and Timothy Naftali concluded that Raul Castro became a communist by the early 1950s, Che Guevara by 1957, and Fidel by late 1959 or early 1960.[11] However, Raul Castro's wife later observed that Fidel had approved of his brother joining the Cuban Communist Party in 1953, and while Fidel was already a Marxist, he felt that he could not join because "his fledging political career would be doomed if he were a party member."[12] While there remains some dispute over Castro's claim that he was a Marxist since he was a teenager, it does appear that the Castro brothers kept their conversions to communism under wraps until their power was fully secured, misleading supporters both at home and abroad.

Whatever doubts there were about Fidel's stance regarding the Cold War competition between the United States and the Soviet Union ended on November 8, 1960. After attending an event at the Soviet Embassy commemorating the forty-third anniversary of the Bolshevik Revolution, Castro pronounced that "Moscow is our brain and our great leader, and we must pay attention to its voice."[13] On the same day that Castro was proclaiming his allegiance to Moscow, Americans were participating in the election of a new president, selecting John F. Kennedy by a razor-thin margin.

Phase one of the Cuban Revolution involved toppling Batista, while phase two involved eliminating those "counterrevolutionaries" who were opposed to installing a one-party Marxist state allied with the Soviet Union. Grizzled veterans from the Spanish Civil War living in Moscow were dispatched to Cuba to serve as trainers to form a cadre of shock troops loyal to the new Marxist regime. So, while Fidel was trying to assure Western audiences that he was not a communist, his brother Raul was securing internal security support from the Kremlin.[14] It was this "phase two" that produced the deep and abiding hostility that fueled the ranks of opponents to Castro's regime that exists to this day. This method of co-opting well-intentioned democratic revolutionaries and then excommunicating them upon the successful completion of a revolution was an oft-used template for Marxist-Leninist movements.

Both the Soviet Union and the United States fought for the allegiance of other nations, and there was always a temptation to adopt the edict that you were either with us or against us. However, Kennedy rejected this Manichean view of the world. One sees this reflected in American policy toward Tito's Yugoslavia, which was conducted with a degree of nuance that offended those on the Far Right.[15] Cuba, however, due to its proximity to the United States and to its explosive resonance on the domestic American political scene, was a different story.

Castro's decision to ally himself with the Kremlin led to American efforts under Eisenhower and Kennedy to overthrow his regime. Yet America's economic domination of the island and its imperialist past made any hostile actions toward Castro's Cuba suspect in the eyes of the rest of the world, and to many Americans as well. Those who saw American policy toward Cuba in the Cold War as a continuation of its imperialist past had the weight of history behind them, but at the same time, proponents of this position tended to ignore Castro's pro-Soviet inclinations and his behavior during the Cuban missile crisis. If Fidel Castro rather than Nikita Khrushchev had directed the response to the American blockade, some type of nuclear exchange would likely have occurred.

"I Can Assure You . . . This Flag Will Be Returned to This Brigade in a Free Havana"

In the aftermath of what turned out to be the "fiasco" at the Bay of Pigs, critics often asked how someone as smart as John F. Kennedy could have approved what some have described as the "perfect failure."[16] But there was a certain inevitability about the entire Bay of Pigs operation. John F. Kennedy tried to deliver on one of the key promises from his presidential campaign— to remove the cancerous communist growth ninety miles from Key West. Kennedy was determined to reverse Dwight Eisenhower's "lethargic" foreign policy and saw a chance to do so within three months of his inauguration. A successful overthrow of Castro would have been a signal that American complacency had been replaced with a renewed "vigor," a favorite term from the New Frontier. Toppling Castro would fulfill Kennedy's inaugural pledge to "pay any price, bear any burden . . . support any friend, oppose any foe to assure the survival and the success of liberty." More directly, it would fulfill his promise to "let every other power know that this hemisphere intends to remain the master of its own house."[17]

President Kennedy's approval of the Bay of Pigs operation, codenamed "Operation Zapata," is rightly considered the low point of his presidency. Critics on the Left viewed it as an example of superpower bullying, an immoral act that violated international law. Howard Zinn, whose *People's History of the United States* is widely used in the nation's classrooms, saw the Bay of Pigs as an extension of America's "imperialistic, militaristic, and expansionist" history, part of the perennial quest to make Cuba an "economic vassal" of the United States.[18] Kennedy's conservative critics saw it as an example of a feckless president approving an invasion and then withholding American air support at the moment victory hung in the balance. Richard Nixon had urged Kennedy to "find a proper legal cover . . . and go in," while former president Eisenhower privately criticized Kennedy as a "profile in timidity and indecision."[19]

Kennedy's defenders engaged in an effective campaign both at the time and after the president's death to pin the blame on the Central Intelligence Agency (CIA) for misleading the young president about the chances for success. They also argued that Kennedy "inherited" the operation, or some version of it, from President Eisenhower, and while that is true, Kennedy was under no obligation to approve the invasion. The disaster at the Bay of Pigs on April 17, 1961, was of his own making, as Kennedy candidly admitted.

A CIA-trained force of fourteen hundred exiles were all captured or killed within seventy-two hours of the landing. Kennedy refused to commit American air power to provide cover for the invasion force, "Brigade 2506," while they were pinned down on the beach, despite pleas from some of his advisors. (2506 was the number given an exile who had been killed in a training accident prior to the invasion. The CIA decided to name the brigade after him).[20] Approximately twelve hundred men were taken prisoner, and the president and Attorney General Robert Kennedy devoted considerable energy in the following months to secure their release. Castro's victory was due in part to the lack of the element of surprise which was lost when a bombing campaign directed against the Cuban Air Force began on April 15, two days prior to the landing. Realizing that something was afoot, Castro's security forces rounded up any suspected "counterrevolutionaries," dashing the CIA's hopes for an indigenous uprising in support of the landing force.

Geography also played a role in the fiasco, as the exile force was surrounded not only by Cuban forces but by swamps that made escape from the beach improbable. The landing at this swampy location was the result of President Kennedy ordering the CIA to find an obscure location in order to preserve plausible deniability for the United States. Additionally, President Kennedy canceled a second airstrike on the morning of the invasion that might have eliminated the remainder of Castro's airpower and provided some relief to the embattled force trapped on the beach, and he denied the use of American fighters to cover the invasion force as it disembarked. The *USS Essex* with its fighter aircraft, visible on the horizon, was told to pull back and not launch its aircraft.[21] In its post-mortem, the CIA concluded that the Soviet Union had learned around April 9 that the attack was planned for the 17th. Despite this serious breach of operational security, which the CIA discovered almost immediately, no one at the agency warned President Kennedy that the Soviets had obtained this information.[22]

Castro and the Soviets had also learned valuable lessons from successful American covert operations in the 1950s. Castro's military was loyal to him, which had not been the case with CIA-backed operations in Iran and Guatemala, where the agency had been able to enlist, or in some cases buy, the support of disgruntled members of the officer corps. The Bay of Pigs, as historian Timothy Naftali has argued, was "round two of the Guatemala operation." Castro's military, Naftali added, had been equipped with an impressive array of firepower by April 1961. This weaponry was provided by the Soviet Union and its Warsaw Pact allies and consisted of some "167,000 rifles . . . 125 tanks. There were 41 MiG jets that were on their way . . . and 400 artillery pieces."[23]

There were several consequences stemming from Kennedy's failure at the Bay of Pigs. Some were significant, others less so. Allen Dulles was removed as CIA director seven months after the failure of Operation Zapata. Kennedy told Dulles, "Under a parliamentary system of government it is I who would be leaving office . . . but under our system it is you who must go."[24] While it has become one of the main talking points of the post-Bay of Pigs, pro-Kennedy narrative, it is nonetheless true that he became more suspect of expert advice, including from the military and the intelligence community. Ted Sorensen recalled Kennedy saying to him on April 17, "I got where I am by not trusting experts. But this time I put all my faith in the experts and look what happened."[25]

Another repercussion from the Bay of Pigs turned out to be a boon for future historians, as President Kennedy secretly installed a tape-recording system in the White House to make sure that he, and he alone, would have important discussions "on the record." Some advisors who favored the invasion claimed in off-the-record discussions with reporters that they had opposed it, and this duplicity irked Kennedy.[26] He may have intended to use these recordings to write a memoir someday.

But the most important consequence of the failure at the Bay of Pigs was the president's decision to intensify covert efforts to topple the Castro regime. The president placed his brother, Attorney General Robert Kennedy, in charge of the effort, codenamed "Operation Mongoose." Mongoose was designed, according to Robert Kennedy, to "stir things up" with "espionage, sabotage, general disorder." But it also involved eliminating Castro by any means necessary, a point Robert Kennedy left out of his oral history. At least eight attempts were made on Castro's life, with the CIA enlisting the help of American organized crime to do their bidding.[27]

Robert Kennedy was informed by J. Edgar Hoover on May 22, 1961, of the mafia's involvement in assassination attempts to kill Castro, this collaboration having been initiated at the end of Eisenhower's presidency. The attorney general was briefed again in May 1962 about the CIA's connections with organized crime, and while Robert Kennedy expressed some discomfort with this, the collaboration continued. Richard Helms, who served as the CIA's deputy director for plans, later testified that "it was made abundantly clear to everyone involved in the operation that the desire was to get rid of the Castro regime and to get rid of Castro. No limitations were put on this injunction." Helms stated that Robert Kennedy "would not have been unhappy if [Castro] had disappeared off the scene by whatever means," and added that the pressure from RFK to remove Castro was akin to "white heat." Bobby Kennedy viewed the Bay of Pigs as an "insult that had to be redressed," and he pressured a sclerotic bureaucracy to ensure that Mongoose received all of the funding it needed to carry out its campaign to topple the Castro government. The assassination element of the campaign saw the CIA develop a variety of means to eliminate Castro, including various poisons and exploding seashells designed to lure the curious scuba-diving dictator to his death.[28]

Operation Mongoose was formally shut down at the end of 1962. But during its brief existence, Mongoose became one of the largest covert operations in the CIA's history, involving some four hundred agents and an annual budget of over fifty million dollars. But while Operation Mongoose was terminated, covert efforts to overthrow the Castro regime continued through the end of Kennedy's presidency. Lyndon Johnson ordered the end of these operations in April 1964 and would later observe that the United States had operated a "Murder, Inc." in the Caribbean.[29]

President Kennedy was dead serious when he pledged at a rally at the Orange Bowl in Miami to the recently released veterans from Brigade 2506 on December 29, 1962, that "I can assure you . . . that this [brigade] flag will be returned to this brigade in a free Havana." This promise was not to be, as the flag was unceremoniously returned to the brigade during an exchange between the Kennedy Library's Museum Curator, Dave Powers, and the brigade's lawyer at Boston's Logan Airport on April 15, 1976, two days before the fifteenth anniversary of the invasion. The brigade had demanded that the flag be returned after Senator Edward Kennedy came out in favor of lifting the embargo against Castro's Cuba.[30]

Operation Mongoose was publicly revealed in 1975 by a Senate committee chaired by Senator Frank Church (D-ID) that examined abuses of power by the CIA and the FBI. Only a handful of high-ranking US government officials, out of the 189 million Americans alive in November 1963, were aware that assassination had been adopted as a tool of American foreign policy by Eisenhower and Kennedy.[31] These 1975 revelations would fuel the already flourishing Kennedy assassination conspiracy complex, providing endless and fruitless leads for those intent on proving that Lee Harvey Oswald did not act alone.

"The Back Alleys of the World"

Americans were shocked to learn in the mid-1970s that two beloved leaders, Eisenhower and Kennedy, one a victim of assassination, had authorized similar attempts against foreign leaders. No "smoking gun" existed to prove either man signed off on these actions, as the concept of plausible deniability in these cases proved somewhat effective at masking their involvement. A myth would soon arise that the CIA was "acting like a rogue elephant on a rampage" by committing these deeds without presidential approval.[32] This was fiction, but it had the bipartisan benefit of protecting the reputation of two giants of mid-century American life.

The doctrine of plausible deniability was not something imposed on the nation by the so-called "imperial presidency," in fact it was a concept widely accepted at this time by members of Congress. Congress cut itself out of the loop in terms of oversight of these types of sensitive operations, much to the relief of many of its members. John F. Kennedy's fellow senator from Massachusetts, Leverett Saltonstall, observed in 1956 that "it is not a question of reluctance on the part of CIA officials to speak to us. Instead, it is a question of our reluctance, if you will, to seek information and knowledge on subjects which I personally, as a member of Congress and a citizen, would rather not have."[33] That attitude prevailed in Congress as late as 1973, when Senator John Stennis (D-MS) once stopped a CIA director from briefing him on an impending clandestine operation by observing, "No, no my boy, don't tell me. Just go ahead and do it, but I don't want to know."[34]

There was also a somewhat callous attitude adopted by the World War II generation regarding these kinds of "special operations." After all, the Western allies were aware of the conspirators within the German military who plotted to kill Adolf Hitler, an assassination that would have been warmly welcomed throughout the world. The United States military had killed the commander of the Imperial Japanese Navy, Admiral Isoroku Yamamoto, when decoded intercepts revealed his flight plans, while the British had trained the assassins of the "Butcher of Prague," SS-Gruppenführer Reinhard Heydrich.

While American history is littered with examples of American presidents ordering all types of clandestine operations, from kidnapping to bribery to support for insurgent movements and employing journalists and clergymen for secret operations, it does appear that Eisenhower's and Kennedy's approval of assassination represented a significant break with the past. Thomas Jefferson once observed that "assassination," while considered a "legitimate" weapon during the "dark ages," was "held in just horror in the 18th century."[35]

But the twentieth century offered a type of threat Jefferson could not have envisioned. The prospect, regardless of whether it was real or imagined, of impending nuclear annihilation tended to focus the mind and led to a robust embrace of the old nostrum that the ends justify the means. This made the transition from contemplating killing Hitler to killing Castro seem perfectly rational. The United States had emerged from World War II as one of two superpowers and was opposed by a regime that had murdered more people than Hitler's Germany. It was not a great leap for members of this generation to conclude that Castro was a puppet of that regime; he was to Khrushchev as Mussolini was to Hitler. One simply could not afford to be morally fastidious when faced with such a deadly foe. As Kennedy's secretary of state, Dean Rusk, once observed, the CIA was locked in a struggle in "the back alleys of the world," where standards of decency and restraint were in short supply.[36] Nevertheless, the guardians of President Kennedy's reputation decided early on that defending the president's policies toward Castro was not a hill they were willing to die on. As the Vietnam War dragged on and Americans began to question their nation's role in the world, Cuba became the totem for those convinced that American bullying and imperialism caused the Cold War and threatened to destroy the planet.

John F. Kennedy's reputation has always been held hostage to the

Kennedy family's political ambitions, and when Robert Kennedy began to shift his views leftward after his brother's death, sympathetic accounts from chroniclers such as Schlesinger and Sorensen shifted along with it. Airbrushing Operation Mongoose out of the historical record was a prerequisite to launching Bobby Kennedy's presidential race in 1968 and Ted Kennedy's bid in 1980. Keeping JFK's presidency in tune with the prevailing ideological sentiments of the Democratic Party is an ongoing process.

At a certain point it was determined to place the blame for Mongoose on the agency that did the president's bidding, the CIA. Arthur Schlesinger Jr. argued that a rogue CIA, acting beyond the control of two American presidents, had attempted to kill Castro. This notion was rebuffed by David Eisenhower, the grandson of Dwight D. Eisenhower, in a discussion with Schlesinger over President Eisenhower's legacy. Schlesinger was mortified when David Eisenhower bluntly, and rightly, rejected Schlesinger's "rogue CIA" theory by indicating that the World War II generation had a different take on the propriety of assassination.[37]

As recently as 2008, Ted Sorensen was adhering to the mythology that the CIA misunderstood JFK's interest in "deposing" Castro, for "that did not mean he wanted him [Castro] murdered."[38] Yet all of those who were directly involved with Operation Mongoose, including Richard Helms, the CIA's deputy director for plans; Ray Cline, the agency's deputy director for intelligence; and U. Alexis Johnson, the State Department's Mongoose liaison, insisted that the agency was doing the president's bidding. As Ray Cline put it, "The assassination of Castro by a Cuban . . . might have been viewed as not very different in the benefits that would have accrued from the assassination of Hitler in 1944." Alexis Johnson added, "There was never, to my knowledge, any foundation for charges of freewheeling by the CIA."[39] Testifying years later, Secretary of Defense Robert McNamara noted that "the C.I.A. was a highly disciplined organization, fully under the control of senior officials of the Government."[40]

The Fictional "Thirteen Days"

It was the "white heat" of Operation Mongoose that led Nikita Khrushchev to gamble on what became known as the Cuban missile crisis of October

1962. Khrushchev's audacious move had the potential to solve a myriad of problems for the Kremlin. If the Soviets could install ballistic missiles in Cuba prior to their discovery by the Americans, this would enhance Russian bargaining power regarding the status of western forces in Berlin and would alleviate a gnawing sense of insecurity regarding the lopsided American lead in intercontinental ballistic missiles. A successful deployment of these missiles might also lead the United States to reconsider its own missile bases in Italy and Turkey and ensure the survival of Castro's regime. Additionally, Khrushchev was determined to convince anti-colonial movements around the globe that the Kremlin was as committed to revolutionary struggle as Mao Zedong's China.[41]

The "Missiles of October" have been dissected far beyond the point of diminishing returns, providing endless fodder for doctoral dissertations and case studies in crisis management. The lessons from this crisis may not be as applicable as is generally assumed, for this was a unique situation involving the potential loss of millions of lives. President Kennedy's micromanagement of the crisis, while admirable, is not necessarily a suitable model for managing lesser crises. This is not to suggest that the Cuban missile crisis is undeserving of study; it was, by far, the closest the world came to a nuclear exchange between two great powers. Kennedy and Khrushchev brought the world to this dangerous tipping point, but they also deserve credit for stepping back from the brink.

The Camelot version of the missile crisis has been exhaustively deconstructed by Sheldon Stern, a former historian at the Kennedy Library, who was the first outsider to listen to the secret tape recordings of the meetings of the ExComm. In his seminal work *The Cuban Missile Crisis in American Memory: Myth versus Reality* (2012), Stern traces the evolution of the "heroic" interpretation of Kennedy's actions in the missile crisis. This "'heroic' but historically one-dimensional rendering" was "created and promulgated by JFK, RFK, and key members of the administration, eagerly swallowed by gullible journalists . . . and popularized by the selective and manipulative writings of administration insiders like Arthur Schlesinger Jr. and Theodore Sorensen."

And, it should be noted, the manipulation of the historical record involved members of the Kennedy circle publishing unflattering accounts of the role of Dean Rusk, Lyndon Johnson, and Adlai Stevenson, all of whom were disliked by Robert Kennedy. Stevenson was accused by the Kennedy circle of advocating a "Munich" [appeasement] even though President Kennedy secretly adopted Stevenson's proposal to diffuse the crisis.[42] Shortly after the missile crisis ended, Robert Kennedy falsified documents to ensure that no paper trail existed regarding President Kennedy's secret commitment to remove the missiles from Turkey.[43] Thus began, as Stern notes, the "deliberate falsification of the historical record" which was "the first step in writing [Robert Kennedy's] *Thirteen Days*." This book, which was finished by Ted Sorensen after Robert Kennedy's murder in 1968, became the "template" of the "heroic" interpretation of the missile crisis. Despite being a deeply flawed account of the missile crisis, the book, and later movie, "continues to frame the discussion" of the events of that October.[44]

The "heroic" interpretation, according to Stern, focuses on a "courageous and determined young American President" who maintained his cool throughout the missile crisis and through a blend of toughness and restraint successfully forced an aggressive Soviet Union and its puppet dictator in Cuba to blink, winning a decisive Cold War victory and learning lessons that led him to reach out and press for better relations with the Kremlin, and seek to limit the spread of nuclear weapons. A typical example of this narrative can be seen in the work of Arthur Schlesinger Jr., who rhapsodized that President Kennedy's handling of the missile crisis revealed a "combination of toughness and restraint, of will, nerve, and wisdom, so brilliantly controlled, so matchlessly calibrated, that [it] dazzled the world."[45]

As Sheldon Stern puts it, "President Kennedy often stood virtually alone against warlike counsel . . . during those historic thirteen days."[46] Kennedy agreed secretly to the removal of American missiles in Turkey and gave a no-invasion pledge (to take effect after verification of the removal of the Soviet missiles) that Premier Khrushchev was seeking. And, showing the same type of courage he would later demonstrate in dealing with the civil rights crisis, he approved a plan to make these secret deals public if that was needed to strike a deal with the Soviets and avert the "final failure" of nuclear war. It never came to that, but as Stern notes, such a revelation was fraught with "domestic political risks," to say the least.[47]

Prior to the missile crisis, Kennedy was already the target of conservative criticism for being "soft" on communism, for being an "appeaser like his father." Concessions of the type he made to Khrushchev, had they been revealed at the time, would have become a major issue in his reelection campaign in 1964. That Kennedy even considered making those concessions public is somewhat remarkable; he would have been excoriated by his opponents had that happened.

The "Reckless" President

It was often asserted that John F. Kennedy drove the world to "the brink," and that his effort to topple Castro was "reckless." Canadian prime minister John Diefenbaker believed this, noting in his memoir that Kennedy was "perfectly capable of taking the world to the brink of thermal-nuclear destruction to prove himself . . . a courageous champion of Western democracy."[48] As we shall see in chapter 8, this indictment of Kennedy became the conventional narrative in the ensuing decades, shared by a number of prominent American scholars. But it was Castro who exhibited, according to Nikita Khrushchev, irrational and suicidal inclinations in the midst of the Cuban missile crisis. Castro seemed to relish an impending confrontation with the United States, a confrontation he viewed in apocalyptic terms. "The result of aggression against Cuba will be the start of a conflagration of incalculable consequences, and they will be affected too," Fidel noted, and "it will no longer be a matter of them feasting on us. They will get as good as they give." Castro's forces and their Russian advisors would resist the Americans "to the last day and the last man, woman or child capable of holding a weapon."[49]

Castro pleaded with the Soviet ambassador to Cuba to shoot down American U-2 spy planes flying over Cuba photographing the progress of the missile sites. His wish was granted when Major Rudolf Anderson's spy plane was shot down on the orders of a Soviet general during the crisis, moving the world closer to "the brink." Khrushchev's son Sergei later recalled that a message was sent to Cuba from the Soviet leadership after the downing of the U-2 reading, "We consider that you were in a hurry to shoot down a U-2 spy plane." Sergei Khrushchev added that from that point on, no antiaircraft activity was to take place without permission from Moscow, but "at almost the same time Father sent orders not to shoot down American planes, Fidel Castro issued a command to open fire on them. Castro's injured pride demanded revenge."[50]

Fortunately, cooler heads than Castro's prevailed in Moscow and

Washington after Rudolf Anderson's death. On October 27, day twelve of the thirteen days, Castro wrote to Khrushchev urging him to use his nuclear arsenal to destroy the United States in the event of an attack. "If they attack Cuba, we should wipe them off the face of the earth!" In pleading for a first strike in the event of an American invasion, Castro told Khrushchev that this was an opportunity to eliminate the chance for the Americans to strike first against the Soviet Union. "An American invasion would be the moment to eliminate such danger," Castro told the Kremlin. This "harsh and terrible . . . solution" was the only solution, "for there is no other." In Moscow, Khrushchev, the man who once promised to bury the capitalist West and who had flaunted the possibility of nuclear war during his summit with Kennedy in Vienna on June 3, 1961, was astounded by Castro's proposed final solution. "This is insane; Fidel wants to drag us into the grave with him!"[51]

Sergei Khrushchev recalled his father's shock at Castro's remarkable proposal. "Is he proposing that we start a nuclear war? That we launch missiles from Cuba? . . . That is insane. We deployed missiles there to prevent an attack on the island . . . But now not only is he ready to die himself," he wanted the Soviet Union to go down in flames as well. "Remove them," Khrushchev's son recalled his father saying, "and as soon as possible. Before it's too late. Before something terrible happens."[52]

Toward the end of the crisis, Khrushchev dispatched his deputy prime minister Anastas Mikoyan to make sure that the mercurial Castro did not undermine the Soviet deal with the Americans. Castro was looking for an assurance that the Russians would leave nearly one hundred "tactical" nuclear weapons (equivalent to those dropped on Hiroshima and Nagasaki) in Cuban hands. But after dealing with the unstable dictator, Mikoyan rejected this idea by claiming that Soviet law prohibited the transfer of these tactical nuclear weapons. Mikoyan came to believe that Castro could not be trusted, and that the "Cuban tail was quite capable of wagging the Soviet dog." Castro had planned to make a dramatic announcement through his United Nations ambassador telling the international community that Cuba was now a member of the elite club of nuclear powers. The Soviets, seeing up close and personal Castro's recklessness, prevented this from happening. Mikoyan's son, who journeyed with his father to Havana for part of this mission, would later note that the Kremlin came to believe that Cuba was led by "hotheads who were preparing their country to die in the fire of a nuclear confrontation with the United States in the name of world socialism."[53]

Kennedy and Cuba in Retrospect

There is an element of presentism at work in modern-day criticism of Kennedy's policies toward Cuba. In the fourteen years prior to Kennedy's election, there was good reason to believe the worst about the Soviet Union and its proxies. The targeting of Cuba was done during a Cold War that threatened to turn hot at any moment and had already done so in places like Greece, Korea (where Josef Stalin had given the approval for the invasion of South Korea), and Vietnam, and came close to doing so during the Berlin blockade of 1948. The Soviet Union had repressed democratic uprisings in Poland, East Germany, and Hungary, and sponsored a coup in Czechoslovakia that ensured one-party communist rule.

Exactly two weeks prior to John F. Kennedy's inauguration, Nikita Khrushchev pledged his nation's support for "wars of national liberation" around the globe. In Kennedy's view, Castro's government was central to this effort, supplying men and material in the service of Soviet foreign policy. Former president Eisenhower believed that Kennedy overreacted to Khrushchev's speech, and many scholars have since echoed this theme, noting that Khrushchev's remarks were largely directed at his own party apparatchiks and designed to counter the Chinese claim that the Kremlin was going soft on its commitment to revolution.[54] While that speech may have been misinterpreted by the Kennedy administration, there was nonetheless a bipartisan consensus that Castro's embrace of America's adversary made him our adversary.

Which brings this account to an important point—that Kennedy's support for the Bay of Pigs and of Operation Mongoose was primarily the result of domestic American politics. At the strategic level, Kennedy's policy toward Cuba was remarkably counterproductive—Senator J. William Fulbright (D-AR) told Kennedy in March 1961, that Castro was a "thorn in the flesh, not a dagger in the heart." Fulbright and others warned that an American-sponsored invasion would play right into Castro's hands and damage Kennedy's efforts to improve his country's relations with governments throughout the Americas.[55] Additionally, the decision to pursue regime change in Cuba solidified Castro's power not only at home but made him a hero to revolutionary movements around the globe.

But while Kennedy's clandestine efforts to topple Castro continue to be subject to intense criticism, there is evidence, often overlooked, that Kennedy was moving toward a two-track approach to Cuba, employing both carrots and sticks. While he never halted the effort to eliminate Castro, during the final year of his life Kennedy approved an initiative to gauge Castro's willingness to improve relations with the United States. On November 18, 1963, speaking to an audience composed partly of anti-Castro Cubans in Miami Beach, Kennedy noted that Castro had betrayed his nation's sovereignty to "forces beyond the hemisphere" who were intent on subverting the nations of Latin America. "As long as this is true, nothing is possible. Without it, everything is possible." Kennedy had asked his speechwriter Ted Sorensen to include this remark as a signal to Castro that there was a possibility for improving relations, and it was also a signal to help an American envoy at the United Nations, William Attwood, in his secret dealings with Castro's representatives.[56]

Attwood was told by Cuba's UN ambassador in September 1963 that Castro wanted to open back-channel communications with the United States. Attwood was in the process of arranging to meet with Castro to discuss improving relations and was set to meet President Kennedy and receive his instructions upon the latter's return from his trip to Dallas. As Attwood later recalled, "As a result of the ensuing informal talks I had with the Cuban Ambassador, the President decided that it might be useful for me to go down to Cuba and see Castro."[57] These steps were very much in their preliminary phase, and the prospects for success were slim. But these initial movements toward some rapprochement fit with Kennedy's overall approach to the Cold War: secure his domestic political front against allegations of being soft on communism, use rhetorical and covert means as a stick against opponents, but leave yourself room to maneuver and never back yourself or your adversary into a corner.

Kennedy, in keeping with his foreign policy views about the developing world, had observed to a French emissary in October 1963 that American policy during the Batista years had contributed to "economic colonization, humiliation and exploitation" of Cuba, a message this emissary likely relayed on his forthcoming trip to Cuba. Attwood's nascent effort to reach out to Castro ended when Lyndon Johnson became president, as there was little appetite to pursue such an initiative in an election year. In January 1964, President Johnson nominated Attwood to be the United States ambassador to Kenya, and as Attwood noted regarding the fate of his secret Cuban diplomacy, "That was it."[58] It is my belief that some effort at rapprochement would have been made secretly in the remaining months of Kennedy's first term, followed by more serious public efforts during his second term. But as with so many issues related to this presidency, that prospect remains eternally confined to the realm of speculation.

5

Khrushchev, Kennedy, and the "Nuclear Sword of Damocles"

As I mentioned in the previous chapter, I vividly recall the fear I felt about impending war with Russia in October 1962. Yet if the conflict were to occur, in my mind, and in the minds of my gaggle of baby-boomer friends, we were the good guys, and the Russians, especially some guy named Khrushchev, were the bad guys. We used to sing a song that was a variant of "Whistle While You Work," which was a standard from the Disney film *Snow White and the Seven Dwarfs*. The only line I remember sixty years later is "Whistle while you work, Khrushchev is a jerk."

In the later years of my life, I taught at the Naval War College, and one of my faculty colleagues was Nikita Khrushchev's son, Sergei, who was a professor at Brown University and taught an elective at the War College. I would see him infrequently, but in one instance I debated whether to tell him my story from the 1960s. I opted not to, but I never adjusted to the surreal vision of this son of the evil empire teaching at an American military institution, standing in front of me paying for his coffee. Thanks, arguably, to his "jerk" of a father, and to John F. Kennedy, I managed to survive to adulthood.

Of course, it was the policies of those two men that brought the world to the most dangerous point in the Cold War. Yet both had the courage to compromise to avert a catastrophe, and both spent their last months in power seeking to move beyond a world where an unstable peace was preserved by the prospect of "mutual assured destruction."

The Missile Gap and "Doubting Thomases"

John F. Kennedy successfully outflanked Richard Nixon on the national security issue in 1960, claiming that Eisenhower and Nixon slept while Cuba went communist and Sputnik was launched. With Sputnik, the Russians demonstrated that they were winning the space race, and according to Kennedy, this gave them superiority over the United States in terms of launching a nuclear attack. "We are losing the satellite missile race with the Soviet Union," he argued, repeating this allegation throughout the campaign. Nevertheless, Kennedy's promotion of a nonexistent "missile gap" and his hostility to Castro should not distract from the fact that he despised nuclear weapons and avoided war with the Soviet Union using politically risky back-channel diplomacy.

In February 1960, shortly after announcing his presidential candidacy, Kennedy noted:

Whether the missile gap (that everyone agrees now exists) will become critical in 1961–62 or 63—whether during the critical years of the gap the Russian lead will be 2–1, 3–1 or 5–1—whether the gap can be brought to a close (by the availability in quantity of Polaris and Minuteman missiles) in 1964 or in 1965 or ever—on all these questions experts may sincerely differ . . . the point is that we are facing a gap on which we are gambling with our survival.

"Time is short," Kennedy added, and "this situation should never have been permitted to arise." But if the nation moved quickly, "if we are willing to gamble with our money instead of our survival," the nation would prevail.[1]

None of this was true, and sometime later it was determined that the Soviets had only three intercontinental ballistic missiles (ICBMs) capable of hitting the United States.[2] But Kennedy's "missile gap" allegation fit with his broader theme of getting America moving again, of making sure that the United States was first in any area of competition with the Soviet Union.

In fairness to Kennedy, the "missile gap" allegation grew out of a CIA National Intelligence Estimate from 1957 that claimed the United States had fallen behind the Soviet Union in long-range missiles. Kennedy's allegation was bolstered by the Gaither Report, a study commissioned by President Eisenhower in 1957 that claimed Russian ICBM technology had eclipsed that of the United States. General Curtis Lemay of the Strategic Air Command and the chairman of the joint chiefs of staff, Admiral Arthur Radford, both believed there was a missile gap, and a "bomber gap" as well. Future president Gerald Ford would later recall the briefings he received from Eisenhower's CIA director, Allen Dulles, when he was a member of the Defense Appropriations Subcommittee. "Dulles and others from the CIA would come in and paint the most scary picture possible about what the Soviet Union would do to us. We were going to be second rate; the Soviets were going to be Number One. I didn't believe all that propaganda."[3]

The origin of, and support for, Kennedy's argument came from within the Eisenhower administration. Stuart Symington (D-MO), the nation's first secretary of the air force and one of the most respected members of the Senate when it came to defense matters, was another leading proponent of the existence of a missile gap. Senator Symington lambasted Eisenhower's secretary of defense, who announced that the administration would not try to "match the Soviets missile for missile." Symington curtly responded, "Then as I understand it your position is that we are voluntarily passing over to the Russians production superiority in the ICBM missile field . . . despite the great damage that we know we would suffer if they instigated an attack?"[4] Symington, like Kennedy, was a potential presidential candidate in 1960, and he believed he had latched on to a winning campaign issue as well.

Both the Eisenhower and Kennedy administrations misinterpreted Soviet capabilities and believed that Russia was stronger than it was. This was partly due to a Soviet disinformation campaign celebrating nonexistent advances in the field of ICBM technology. Premier Khrushchev knew his nation was behind the United States but did not want to tempt the Americans to take advantage of the situation. Ironically, around the very time that Kennedy began a remarkable buildup of America's nuclear might, Khrushchev had already decided to shift resources from his military to the civilian sector.[5]

Kennedy is frequently portrayed as having lied about the "missile gap," for he continued to decry the existence of the gap after General Earle Wheeler briefed him in September 1960 and dismissed the idea. But Kennedy had legitimate grounds to distrust the word of an emissary from Eisenhower's Pentagon. Kennedy listened to Wheeler's briefing, and asked, "General, don't you have any doubting Thomases in the Pentagon?" Wheeler reassured him that there were plenty of doubting Thomases in both the Pentagon and the CIA.[6]

There were good reasons for Kennedy to continue asserting there was a missile gap beyond a cynical desire to exploit an effective campaign message. It was not the case, as many scholars have suggested, that Kennedy decided to simply keep lying. Many of the nation's best national security experts believed the missile gap was a legitimate issue. While the missile gap turned out to be a myth, the difficulties of penetrating a closed society, coupled with an effective disinformation campaign approved by Nikita Khrushchev, made it all seem plausible. It was not until well after America's Corona surveillance satellites began to operate in August 1960 that the US government began to see a more complete picture of Soviet capabilities.[7] As the United States has painfully learned time and again, intelligence estimates are frequently wrong. They were wrong in 1957, and closer to the truth in 1960, but again, no one was certain at the time.

Harold Brown, a future secretary of defense who held his first Pentagon position under Kennedy, recalled his own surprise at realizing the advantageous position held by the United States. Brown "gradually came to believe that our position vis-à-vis the Soviets in strategic matters was very much more powerful than we had thought." But President Kennedy "was perhaps even more" surprised.

Brown noted in 1964, "After all, it was his missile gap." As Brown observed, Kennedy, as well as many others, were operating on the basis of limited information enhanced by Soviet bluffing. "I had had rather little exposure to intelligence information, but probably more than he [Kennedy] as a comparatively junior member of the Senate had had, and this is an inference on my part—he must have been even more surprised." The intelligence bonanza that Corona produced "became available during 1961 [and] I think made this clearer and clearer. Although I think it was fairly clear to the Eisenhower administration in 1960, but they didn't quite know how to handle it in 1960, I don't think. They had evidence, but it wasn't conclusive, that the Soviets didn't have any ballistic missiles. This evidence I think became clearer in 1961," after Kennedy became president.[8] To its credit, Kennedy's Pentagon went on to dismiss the missile gap, a little over two weeks into the administration.

Brown was impressed that Kennedy remained interested in the question of how so many policymakers, Republican and Democrat, were wrong about the missile gap. According to Brown, "This was a subject that . . . intrigued President Kennedy, the history of the missile gap." As late as January 1963, when the issue was long removed from the front pages, Kennedy "got to talking about the missile gap and said that it was very important to have a history of the missile [gap]."[9] Some of this might have been to prepare for the 1964 presidential campaign, when Kennedy's erroneous allegations might be used against him, but some of it was good policy, a practice that other administrations presiding over failed intelligence estimates could use to their benefit.

The day before his inauguration, when John F. Kennedy met with outgoing president Dwight Eisenhower, Ike assured Kennedy that his allegations of a missile gap were unfounded. The United States had nothing to fear from advances in Soviet nuclear weapons technology, due to the presence of American submarines armed with nuclear weapons lurking off the Russian coast. "You have an invulnerable asset in Polaris [nuclear-firing submarines]. It is invulnerable."[10] Eisenhower's celebrated farewell address warning of the dangers of a military-industrial complex was prompted in part by the constant drumbeat directed against his administration to increase defense spending across the board.

Secretary of Defense McNamara dismissed Kennedy's missile gap allegation with a "not for attribution" briefing at the Pentagon on February 5, 1961. The secretary noted that it was the Soviet Union that lagged behind the United States. McNamara told reporters that there are "no signs of a Soviet crash effort to build ICBMs" and concluded that "there is no missile gap today."[11] The next day Kennedy was not pleased to read a story in the *New York Times* headlined, "Kennedy Defense Study Finds No Evidence of a 'Missile Gap.'" Kennedy ordered his press secretary to flatly deny the story, and on February 8, the president himself claimed at a press conference that it was "premature" to conclude whether there was a gap or not.[12]

By the fall of 1961, the administration had abandoned any discussion of a missile gap. Deputy Defense Secretary Roswell Gilpatric delivered a speech in October making it clear that the United States held a commanding lead over the Soviet Union in terms of its ability to strike the enemy with nuclear weapons. Gilpatric's message was unequivocal regarding American superiority in the arms race. "The fact is that this nation has a nuclear retaliatory force of such lethal power" that any enemy that attacked the United States first would be engaging in "an act of self-destruction." He added that the United States had "hundreds of manned intercontinental bombers capable of reaching the Soviet Union" as well as "six Polaris submarines . . . carrying dozens of intercontinental ballistic missiles. The total number of our nuclear delivery vehicles, tactical as well as strategic, is in the tens of thousands." No Soviet "sneak attack" could disarm the United States, for if such an attack were to occur, the United States could respond with a force "as great as—perhaps greater than" that which the Soviets could launch in their first strike.[13]

Within a matter of days, both Secretary of State Rusk and Secretary Mc-Namara added to the chorus of administration voices crowing over America's nuclear superiority. Even the president himself, when asked about American military might in comparison to the Soviet Union, noted that he "would not trade places with anyone in the world." And he added, "I have stated that I thought the United States was in a position that was powerful. Mr. Gilpatric said second to none. I said it was our obligation to remain so."[14] These coordinated statements were designed to pressure the Kremlin, which not only faced a militarily superior opponent in the United States but was now openly challenged by the People's Republic of China for leadership of the communist world. Mao Tse-Tung remained committed to Stalinism and considered Khrushchev to be soft on capitalism and hostile to Stalinist regimes such as Albania. Chinese Premier Zhou Enlai stormed out of a Moscow summit around the time of Gilpatric's speech, leaving Khrushchev anxious to find some opening where he could emerge victorious in the Cold War.[15]

"You Can Give Gifts Even before a War"

Perhaps no Cold War presidency got off to a worse start than John F. Kennedy's. The humiliation at the Bay of Pigs in April was followed less than two months later by a Vienna summit meeting where a sickly Kennedy was manhandled by a bullying Nikita Khrushchev, or so the story went, who leavened his insults with stale Marxist talking points. The Soviet premier was festooned with two medals that struck Kennedy's curiosity; when the president was told they were Lenin Peace Prize medals, Kennedy quipped, "I hope you get to keep them," prompting one of the few laughs from Khrushchev during their time together that weekend.[16] Kennedy's commitment to arms control and nuclear disarmament was deep and abiding, as we shall see, but for Khrushchev this commitment was a sign of weakness that he hoped to exploit.

One member of the presidential delegation to Vienna was Dr. Max

Jacobson, a physician from New York City known as "Dr. Feelgood," who administered amphetamines (legal at the time) to Kennedy to counteract the effect of Addison's disease and multiple other ailments afflicting the president. Kennedy was repeatedly tormented by constant back pain that had been aggravated by a tree-planting ceremony in Ottawa with Canadian prime minister John Diefenbaker, whom Kennedy strongly disliked.[17] In addition to his degenerative back issues, Kennedy suffered from high cholesterol, gastrointestinal issues, urinary tract issues, allergies, and sleeplessness.

Much has been made of Kennedy's physical state at the time of the June 1961 summit in support of the narrative that an unprepared and sick president was flummoxed by a cunning Khrushchev in Austria. That Kennedy was not in top condition is undoubtedly true; what is less clear is whether Dr. Jacobson's concoction of amphetamines, human placenta, and vitamins ("I don't care if it's horse piss. It works," was Kennedy's response to those expressing concern over this quack "medication") affected his performance at the summit.[18] Historian Robert Dallek contends that as an afternoon session with Khrushchev dragged on and the effect of an injection wore off, Kennedy may have lost his edge. But this is all speculation that emerged years later after Jacobson's death in 1979; at the time of the summit, Khrushchev's bullying and Kennedy's ineffectual appeals to reason dominated the coverage; no report mentioned that Kennedy appeared to be under the influence of drugs or "out of it."

In fact, throughout his entire presidency, despite the suspicions of some close observers, Kennedy seemed to live up to the image of a young president filled with vigor. He was, in fact, sickly, and concealed it, but as Robert Dallek has argued, Kennedy surmounted his significant medical challenges.[19] The secret recordings of Kennedy's conversations, even during incredibly stressful times such as the Cuban missile crisis, reveal Kennedy's quick mind, insightful questioning, innate curiosity, and an uncanny sense of how an adversary may look at a problem. This does not appear to be a sick man unable to fulfill his duties as president. Frederick Kempe, a diplomat turned author who is critical of Kennedy's Cold War policies, has noted that "history would never record how this medication influenced President Kennedy's performance in Vienna."[20] This may be because no one noticed anything out of the ordinary to record.

Kennedy's negotiating stance in Vienna undermines the argument that he pushed the world toward a nuclear confrontation. Kennedy generally did not parry Khrushchev at the summit with the usual American talking points about Soviet repression in Eastern Europe and the constant flow of refugees from East Germany seeking freedom in the West (although Kennedy would later refer to West Berlin as "an escape hatch for refugees"). He attempted to engage Khrushchev in a discussion over the dangers that both sides might miscalculate and lead the world into nuclear war. Khrushchev bridled at these attempts to tilt the conversation in this direction, instead demanding that the West surrender West Berlin to the Soviets and their East German protégés. Khrushchev engaged in saber rattling throughout the weekend and seemed comfortable with the prospect of a conflict between NATO and the Warsaw Pact.

Kennedy's critics, then and now, ignore the reckless image that Khrushchev deliberately promoted both in Vienna and beyond, a remarkably risky strategy that set the stage for the confrontations to follow. "Berlin is the testicles of the West," Khrushchev was fond of saying. "Every time I want to make the West scream, I squeeze on Berlin."[21] The Berlin crisis of 1961 was entirely of Khrushchev's making. It was yet another example of his seemingly blasé attitude toward war, which pushed the world to the brink on more than one occasion. As Robert Dallek has observed, Khrushchev had "not come to Vienna to negotiate. He had come to compete." Prior to traveling to Vienna, he approved a list of gifts for President and Mrs. Kennedy and observed, "Well, you can give gifts even before a war."[22]

Kennedy believed, as an amateur student of history, that miscalculation had contributed to the start of both world wars of the twentieth century. "If our two countries should miscalculate they would lose for a long time to come," Kennedy told Khrushchev, while the latter responded that the use of the term "miscalculation" was a veiled attempt to force the Soviet Union to "sit like a school boy with his hands on the table." Kennedy persisted, noting that "the purpose of this meeting is to introduce precision" into the judgments of the two nations. The two men went back and forth on the merits of their respective political and economic systems and on the status of "national wars of liberation" in the developing world including Cuba, Laos, and Vietnam; the legitimacy of the governments of Poland, Turkey, Iran, and Spain; and the foreign military presence in these nations. The leaders presented differing theories as to the role of ideas versus the role of force in shaping these regimes, or as Khrushchev noted, "The two sides differed as to their understanding of what popular or anti-popular movements were." For

Khrushchev, the United States was acting as a modern day "Spanish inquisition" in its attempt to "dam" the flow of revolutionary ideas sweeping the Third World.[23]

Khrushchev allegedly left Vienna thinking Kennedy was "young enough to be my son" and "not strong enough" and "too intelligent and too weak."[24] The notes taken at the meeting reveal that Kennedy tended to give as good as he got, but that was not the way the event was spun, not just by the Kremlin, but by the president and some members of his team. Perhaps this was designed to convince Americans and their NATO allies to brace themselves for conflict, likely in Berlin, where the premier had threatened to cut off Allied access to the city and callously observed, "Force would be met by force. If the US wants war, that's its problem." Khrushchev added, "It is up to the US to decide whether there will be war or peace. . . . The decision to sign a peace treaty [with East Germany] is firm and irrevocable, and the Soviet Union will sign it in December, if the US refuses an interim agreement." Kennedy responded, "Then, Mr. Chairman, there will be a war. It will be a cold winter."[25]

The administration may have been spinning the Vienna summit as negatively as possible to convey that fact that Khrushchev was not someone you could do business with, in fact he was slightly unhinged, and no amount of discussion could avert the coming conflict. Kennedy told *New York Times* columnist James Reston that Khrushchev "beat the hell out of me," adding that his experience in Vienna was "the worst thing in my life. He savaged me." Kennedy told Hugh Sidey of *Time* "I never met a man like this . . . [I] talked about how a nuclear exchange would kill 70 million people in 10 minutes, and he just looked at me as if to say, 'So what?'"[26]

Nevertheless, a witness to the Kennedy and Khrushchev exchanges in Vienna differed with the media narrative of a young president bullied by a Stalinist apparatchik. Charles E. "Chip" Bohlen noted after Kennedy's death that the president performed "excellently—I mean, he was a very good listener. . . . He had an intensity of attention which was quite remarkable. You really felt as though he was drawing out from you every aspect of a subject and he was certainly able to keep from talking himself until the other fellow had completely exhausted his views, so while he was quiet in his dealings with Khrushchev, he was perfectly firm, in my opinion."[27] Yet it is also true that Kennedy was flustered by his inability to charm Premier Khrushchev.

In late July 1961, Kennedy belatedly reported to the nation on his meeting with Khrushchev and on further developments in the Cold War. Khrushchev, who had fought with the Red Army at Stalingrad, no doubt took notice of this passage in Kennedy's speech: "I hear it said that West Berlin is militarily untenable. And so was Bastogne. And so, in fact, was Stalingrad. Any dangerous spot is tenable if men—brave men—will make it so." And he reminded Khrushchev that "we are there [in West Berlin] as a result of a victory over Nazi Germany—and our basic rights to be there, deriv[e] from that victory. . . . Berlin is not part of East Germany, but a separate territory under control of the allied powers." Kennedy requested additional defense appropriations from Congress and an increase in manpower for all the services, as well as a "doubl[ing] and tripl[ing]" of draft calls "in the coming months," while asking Congress for the authority to order reservists into active duty.

Yet in the same speech, Kennedy acknowledged the sacrifices made by the Soviet Union in World War II, praising the Russian people "who bravely suffered enormous losses" and warning that the next struggle would be worse. It was not the United States that sought to upend the postwar status quo, Kennedy observed. "There is peace in Berlin today. The source of world trouble and tension is Moscow, not Berlin. And if war begins, it will have begun in Moscow and not Berlin." And to add to the point, "It is the Soviets who have stirred up this crisis. It is they who are trying to force a change."[28]

In this gloomy speech, the president also called for a crash program in civil defense, a call that has generated criticism from many scholars examining the events of 1961. From the vantage point of hindsight, Kennedy's request may appear to be a case of scaremongering. But considering that Kennedy had just witnessed Khrushchev's bullying tactics and blasé attitude toward war over Berlin, the appeal was entirely appropriate. Kennedy would have been derelict if he had not called for bolstering the nation's civil defense infrastructure in the face of a Soviet leader whose nation had lost millions of citizens and emerged stronger, and who appeared to cavalierly accept the prospect of a superpower confrontation.

Khrushchev's saber rattling was a bluff, but it was a lot to ask that Kennedy read Khrushchev's mind and conclude that his warlike bluster was simply for show. Predictably, the call for bolstering the nation's civil defense infrastructure led to sporadic outbreaks of hysteria, from profiteering on the part of bomb shelter manufacturers to armchair ethicists arguing that shooting your unprepared neighbors who attempted to enter your shelter was entirely appropriate.[29]

There were credible reasons for President Kennedy to believe that Khrushchev was not an idle boaster but someone intent on, as the premier once put it, "burying" the West. The shoe-banging (or perhaps it was fist-banging) Khrushchev was not seen at the time as a moderate reformer but as a somewhat unhinged leader of a regime incapable of feeding its own people but presiding over an impressive array of military might. Khrushchev's own granddaughter once described him as a person "known for strong language, interrupting speakers, banging his fists on the table in protest, pounding his feet, even whistling." During his shoe- or fist-banging episode at the United Nations, the leader of the one of the world's great powers interrupted a speech by the head of the Filipino delegation to the United Nations, taking the podium, brushing the speaker aside, and referring to him as "a jerk, a stooge, and a lackey of imperialism," among other epithets.[30] It is not surprising that in the aftermath of the Vienna summit, Kennedy told British prime minister Harold Macmillan that Khrushchev was "much more of a barbarian" than he expected him to be, a conclusion that some advisors felt he should have known going in to Vienna.[31]

While he is seen somewhat positively in the West today, Khrushchev was viewed at the time as a mercurial leader inclined to bravado and caustic comments about the coming collapse of capitalism. Khrushchev may have given a "secret speech" condemning Stalin's excesses, permitted a degree of artistic and cultural liberalization, and set some limits on the secret police, but he was no social democrat. A CIA report on Khrushchev prepared for President-elect Kennedy had warned that his buffoonish nature concealed a man of shrewd "ambition and ruthlessness."[32] Khrushchev had cut his teeth as one of Stalin's apparatchiks and was comfortable with the idea that mass sacrifice in the service of Marxism-Leninism was entirely appropriate. Despite some initial hesitation, Khrushchev ultimately approved the ruthless suppression of the Hungarian Revolution of 1956, which led to thousands of casualties and effectively snuffed out "Khrushchev's Thaw" or what some have called the first "Russian Spring." He had little toleration for speech that challenged the legitimacy of the Soviet Union or criticism of its occupied territories in Eastern Europe.

Whatever inclinations Khrushchev might have had for liberalization in

Eastern Europe were held in check by the fear that a permissive attitude toward dissent provided an opening for Beijing to emerge as a replacement for Moscow. The Kremlin feared the loss of prestige due to the rise of the People's Republic of China as a beacon of ideological orthodoxy in the eyes of true believers. This was the context in which the Kremlin confronted the flood of East Germans fleeing to the West in droves, "voting with their feet," as Dean Rusk put it.[33] Consequently, Berlin became something of a test case for Khrushchev and for the legitimacy and survival of communism itself.

Up against the Wall

In the summer of 1961, the United States and the Soviet Union appeared headed toward a conflict over Berlin. Remarkably, tensions began to ease on August 13, 1961, with the erection of the Berlin Wall, or as many in the West came to describe it, that "wall of shame." The wall was installed with extraordinary efficiency under a veil of secrecy that caught Allied forces off guard. The barrier was initially composed of barbed wire and later transformed into a more permanent concrete behemoth that stretched for ninety-six miles around West Berlin.

The East German leader, Walter Ulbricht, issued a number of Orwellian statements in defense of the wall. The barrier was erected due to the "filthy head-hunting" of the Western intelligence services who lured East German refugees, including many talented engineers and scientists, into West Berlin. Ulbricht went on to add that "no one should think we are in love with the Wall; that is by no means the case . . . The anti-fascist protective rampart was necessary to stand up to the military adventurers."[34] Ulbricht had been criticizing Nikita Khrushchev for some time over his failure to adequately stand up to Western depredations against East Germany and viewed Khrushchev's communist bona fides as suspect.

President Kennedy was also the subject of suspicion, but from markedly different quarters. Before the wall was erected, Kennedy was accused of ignoring Allied rights in East Berlin that grew out of postwar agreements between the great powers. He was also criticized for "abandoning" the captive residents in the Soviet-controlled sector of the city. Right-wing activists at home and abroad accused him of appeasement and noted that his father had displayed a similar propensity regarding German aggression in the late 1930s and early 1940s. Some Americans began to send black umbrellas, an accoutrement associated with that personification of appeasement, Prime Minister Neville Chamberlain, as a sign of protest to the White House (one of those umbrellas would appear in Dealey Plaza on November 22, 1963). Former vice president Richard Nixon accused Kennedy of suffering from a "Hamlet-like psychosis" that led to indecisiveness in the Cold War.[35]

It is safe to assume that Kennedy and Khrushchev viewed Berlin as an irritant for themselves and as a threat to the uneasy peace that existed between East and West. Kennedy's priority was to remove the prospect of a clash between the two superpowers because Berlin had become "a bone in the throat of Soviet-American relations," as Khrushchev called it.[36] The solution, one that Khrushchev knew would represent a propaganda coup for the West, was to deny his people the freedom to move. But for Kennedy, the wall represented an end to the crisis over Berlin. As the president put it to his aide Kenneth O'Donnell, "This is his [Khrushchev's] way out of his predicament. It's not a very nice solution, but a wall is a hell of a lot better than a war." The idea that the wall was Khrushchev's way of avoiding a war was shared by the Soviet expert George Kennan, the famous "Mr. X" who wrote the "Long Telegram," and by Charles "Chip" Bohlen, who had served as President Eisenhower's ambassador to the USSR from 1953 to 1957.[37]

While Kennedy may have been relieved that the wall had reduced the chances for war, events in Berlin still threatened the peace. The wall symbolized the failure of communism, but the initial reaction in much of the West was that Kennedy "stood by" while the wall was erected. West Berlin mayor Willy Brandt was furious at this "passive" response to the wall, and so were many of his constituents. The message got through to Kennedy, who asked the hero of the 1948 Berlin Airlift, retired General Lucius Clay, a revered figure in West Berlin, to serve as his special representative to the city.

The arrival of the hero of the airlift revived the sagging spirits of the people and signaled a renewed American commitment to the besieged city. Vice President Johnson was dispatched as well, even though he feared he might be killed. But the most serious move was Kennedy's decision to send a convoy of fifteen hundred American soldiers through East Germany to West Berlin, where they were greeted by General Clay and the vice president on August 20, 1961. Khrushchev was pressured by his defense minister and by

Walter Ulbricht to stop the American convoy. Unknown to American officials, Khrushchev gave orders to the contrary, and the convoy's safe arrival had a remarkable impact on public opinion inside West Berlin.

Lucius Clay may have, at times, exceeded his instructions with an aggressive approach to handling the Berlin crisis, an approach undermined by Dean Rusk's State Department and at times by the military chain of command. Rusk was dismissive of Clay's mission, as were many civilian and military leaders within the Department of Defense. Clay deployed American tanks at Checkpoint Charlie in late October 1961, in response to East German harassment of Allied officials crossing into East Berlin. Dean Rusk later described Clay's gambit as that "silly tank confrontation . . . brought on by the macho inclinations of General Clay."[38] The idea that the West responded fecklessly in Berlin is often attributed to Kennedy's alleged weakness, but as Clay himself would later note, "The President was all right. Every time I went to the President, I got support." Clay believed that Kennedy was determined to stay the course in Berlin, more so than any of his advisors. "Above all, I was sure that he was not going to let the situation deteriorate. I had complete confidence that in a real emergency we would get approval from the President to act."[39]

However, Clay's understanding of the situation was limited, for he, and most of those outside a narrow circle of senior officials in Moscow and Washington, were unaware of Kennedy's back-channel dealings with the Kremlin. As with the Cuban missile crisis a year later, Kennedy mixed firmness with secret diplomacy to bring an end to the Berlin crisis. The president asked his brother to discretely contact a KGB operative attached to the Russian embassy in Washington named Georgi Bolshakov. The hope was that Bolshakov could circumvent the usual bureaucratic impediments and communicate directly with the Politburo. Bobby Kennedy met with Bolshakov on October 27, 1961, and the two men exchanged messages committing both sides to withdrawing their tanks from Checkpoint Charlie. A choreographed withdrawal soon ended the sixteen-hour standoff at the checkpoint.[40]

Kennedy's mix of firmness and covert diplomacy with the Kremlin averted a potential disaster. Despite repeated portrayals of an "unprepared," "naïve," and "weak" president attending a "disastrous" summit, the fact is that Kennedy and Khrushchev developed something of a personal relationship in Vienna which averted disaster at Berlin in October 1961 and Cuba in October 1962. The two men were aware that they were both trapped in a perpetual cycle of having to prove their toughness.[41]

Critics of Kennedy's handling of the Berlin standoff sometimes argue that he "caved" on Berlin. These critics ignore the fact that America's allies, the British and the French, were more passive both in their response to the building of wall and to Ulbricht's attempt to keep Westerners from approaching the wall on the allied side of the barrier, which led to Clay's stationing of American armor right up to the wall. French president Charles de Gaulle seemed more interested in sowing discord between the allies than in checking Soviet behavior in Berlin.[42] American efforts in Berlin were consistently undermined by French and British dithering, so much so that, in contrast to President de Gaulle, Kennedy conducted himself like Leonidas at Thermopylae.

Both Kennedy and Khrushchev displayed remarkable restraint at critical moments in 1961: Kennedy in the face of Khrushchev's warlike chest thumping in Vienna and his approval of the Berlin Wall, Khrushchev in the face of warlike advice from those who urged him to halt, by whatever means necessary, the American convoy dispatched that August. Armchair warriors suggested that Kennedy should have ordered American forces in Berlin to "knock the wall down," since it violated a postwar agreement between the victorious powers. This idea still has currency, but it requires its advocates to dismiss the fact that this might have ignited World War III.

In the end, the Berlin Wall became a symbol of the failure of communism. It was a semi-permanent monument to a bankrupt ideology at odds with human nature. President Kennedy highlighted this fact during his visit to Berlin on June 26, 1963, where he delivered one of the most impressive speeches of his presidency. Kennedy had visited the wall earlier in the day and was moved by what he saw. He was not satisfied with the bureaucratically sterilized speech he was set to deliver that afternoon, so he took a quick break in Mayor Willy Brandt's office and made some alterations. When he stepped to the podium at Berlin City Hall, some claimed he was still angry from his visit to the wall. The speech built to a crescendo:

There are many people in the world who really don't understand, or say they don't, what is the great issue between the free world and the communist world. Let them come to Berlin . . . There are some who say that communism is the wave of the future. Let them come to Berlin . . . And there are even a few who say that it's true that communism is an evil system, but it permits us to make economic progress. *Lasst sie nach Berlin kommen*—let them come to Berlin!

He noted that "freedom has many difficulties, and democracy is not perfect but we have never had to put a wall up to keep our people in." Kennedy concluded by observing, "All free men, wherever they may live, are citizens of Berlin, and therefore, as a free man, I take pride in the words *Ich bin ein Berliner*." Years later an urban myth began to circulate claiming that Kennedy had declared himself a jelly donut when he uttered that line. The story first appeared in the *Baltimore Sun* in 1972, followed by the *Keene Sentinel* (NH) in 1979, and was then circulated internationally in Len Dighton's spy thriller *Berlin Game* (1983). The claim, like Dighton's novel, is complete fiction.[43] Kennedy's audience of possibly four hundred thousand Germans knew exactly what he meant, and were deeply moved, chanting "Kennedy" as the speech progressed.[44] It was a remarkable moment in the history of the Cold War and would be matched only by President Reagan's plea to a new leader in the Kremlin twenty-four years later to "tear down this wall." Kennedy grasped the import of what had happened that day, remarking to Ted Sorensen on Air Force One as it left Berlin, "We'll never have another day like this as long as we live."[45]

"You Mean It's in the Rain Out There?"

While the possibility of a conflict in Berlin abated, the fallout from the standoff persisted for months. In the midst of all the machinations in Berlin, the Soviets resumed nuclear testing on September 1, 1961; "Fucked again" was Kennedy's private reaction to the news.[46] The Soviets proceeded to test at a remarkable brisk pace into 1962, conducting fifty-nine tests in 1961, followed by seventy-nine in 1962.[47] Three weeks after the Soviets resumed testing, the president spoke before the United Nation's General Assembly and argued that nuclear weapons were a "source of horror, and discord and distrust." The existence of these weapons, and their proliferation, brought the world closer to "the day when this planet may no longer be habitable." He added, "Every man, woman and child lives under a nuclear sword of Damocles, hanging by the slenderest of threads, capable of being cut at any moment by accident or miscalculation or by madness. The weapons of war must be abolished before they abolish us." And he challenged Premier Khrushchev "not to an arms race, but to a peace race." "Let us call a truce to terror," he urged, but for the time being his plea was ignored.[48]

The Soviets continued to test, with the worst yet to come. On October 30, 1961, just three days after the tank showdown at Checkpoint Charlie, the world's most powerful nuclear weapon, "Tsar Bomba" (King of Bombs), also known as "Big Ivan," was detonated. With its fifty-seven-megaton yield, "Big Ivan" was the largest nuclear weapon ever detonated; the detonation was the largest man-made explosion ever recorded. It was more than fifteen hundred times as powerful as both the Hiroshima and Nagasaki bombs combined, and ten times more powerful than all the bombs dropped during World War II. Sensors detected the bomb's shock waves orbiting the earth three separate times. One Russian town, thirty-four miles from ground zero, was destroyed. Soviet towns hundreds of miles from ground zero saw buildings collapse, windows shatter, and roofs cave in. If the Politburo hoped to send a message to the world about its ability to destroy much of the planet, they succeeded, although "Big Ivan" turned out to be too unwieldy to deploy.[49]

In response to the Soviet tests, President Kennedy ordered a resumption of American nuclear tests on March 2, 1962, with the first test scheduled for late April. In his televised address to the nation announcing the resumption of testing, Kennedy included a plea for a mutual ban on testing enforced by inspections. He emphasized that the United States would do everything in its power to limit the fallout from its tests, contrary to Soviet practice, adding that "I find it deeply regrettable that any radioactive material must be added to the atmosphere." He noted that if the Soviet tests were merely for "intimidation and bluff," that would be one thing, but their tests were designed to develop highly sophisticated technology, leading him to conclude that these tests were aimed at unleashing increasingly destructive power. Kennedy mentioned the detonation of "Big Ivan" the previous October and emphasized that the Soviet tests which began the previous fall did not give the Russians superiority over the United States but did give them important data and experience on which they could base further tests.

The president noted that these Russian tests could well provide the Soviet

Union with a nuclear attack and defense capability so powerful that if the West were to stand still, the free world's ability to deter and, if necessary, survive a nuclear strike "would be seriously weakened." Continued Soviet testing in the absence of further Western tests ran the risk of undermining the core concepts of deterrence. Kennedy concluded by noting that he had a "solemn obligation" to defend American freedom, but he hoped and prayed "that these grim, unwelcome tests will never have to be made" and that "these deadly weapons will never have to be fired."[50] Kennedy's thirty-two-minute speech was remarkable for its somewhat sophisticated discussion of nuclear strategy and the scientific and technological issues surrounding it. Such a speech today would flummox many Americans.

Harold Brown, Kennedy's director of defense research and engineering, was struck by the president's concern over fallout from nuclear testing. "He was obviously reluctant to resume atmospheric testing. . . . This is something which I think President Kennedy had quite a different view of from the beginning. He placed considerable stress on the fallout issue, and not just for political reasons. I think he really believed that it was a menace, although I don't think he got any responsible scientific advice that said it was a real problem."[51] Kennedy's science advisor, Jerome Wiesner, shared the president's concern over fallout, and movingly described a scene in the Oval Office where Kennedy was quietly staring out the window as it rained. "I remember one day when he asked me what happens to the radioactive fallout, and I told him it was washed out of the clouds by the rain and would be brought back to earth by the rain." "You mean it's in the rain out there?" the President asked. "Yes," Wiesner responded. Kennedy "looked out the window, very sad, and didn't say a word for several minutes."[52]

Kennedy's commitment to countering the spread of nuclear weapons can be seen in his request to Congress to create the Arms Control and Disarmament Agency (ACDA), which was approved on September 26, 1961, the day after the president delivered his moving plea at the United Nations for an end to the arms race. Kennedy's position on arms control and disarmament had been relatively consistent since 1956, when he had first proposed a ban on nuclear weapons testing. While he had outflanked Vice President Nixon on the hawkishness quotient in the 1960 campaign, his saber-rattling bona fides were always questioned by conservative Americans, and his decision to create ACDA was considered further evidence of his "soft" approach.

A July 1961 Gallup poll showed that the American public approved by a margin of two-to-one the resumption of nuclear testing, but Kennedy resisted testing until the spring of 1962, all the while seeking an agreement with the Russians for a permanent end to the tests. The risks he took on this issue are an underappreciated aspect of his presidency. In both stalling on resuming the tests and by spending significant political capital to secure a Nuclear Test Ban Treaty, he demonstrated true political courage.[53]

When ACDA was created, the president had been in office for eight months, during which time he relied on one of the pillars of the foreign policy establishment, John McCloy, to serve as his de facto arms control advisor. In September, Kennedy appointed William C. Foster, a Republican, to be the first director of ACDA, a smart political move on Kennedy's part in light of Republican suspicions that he was too eager to strike a deal with Khrushchev.[54] Foster noted that with the erection of the Berlin Wall and the Soviet resumption of testing on September 1, it was somewhat counterintuitive for President Kennedy to push at that time for an arms control entity within the executive branch. "It is true that this was a dark period and one would have thought that this might kill the chances for our type of establishment being set up. Actually, the darkness of the period formed a backdrop against which our activities seemed clearly more essential than it might otherwise have been and the bill of goods was sold with the strong personal support of the President." Foster added that Kennedy had "a deep and abiding sense of the importance of moving in the direction of arms control and disarmament." Kennedy considered himself an expert on this subject, and William Foster believed that he was. "Therefore, he did not participate just as an observer. He participated, shifted, added, moved things, sometimes by a quantum leap beyond what had been developed."[55]

Kennedy was always offering "bold additional suggestions. He didn't want just short briefs. He wanted to have details when we presented a paper. . . . He required detailed presentation and would ask about technical details. This is one of the fields on which he spent much personal time." Foster added, in an assessment frequently heard from Kennedy's colleagues and subordinates, that the president was "always the quickest man in the room to grasp the implication of a basic proposal."[56] Foster was by no means part of the "Irish Mafia" that surrounded Kennedy but was a Republican who had little reason to bolster the mythological account of Kennedy's talents. Critics of Kennedy who suggest he was nothing but an empty suit who mastered the public relations game must contend with the testimony of scores of eyewitnesses such as Foster who attest to Kennedy's incisive intellect.

"I Want to Leave It Far behind Me When I Go"

There was something else at work in Kennedy's commitment to arms control and disarmament. This was Kennedy's belief, carefully concealed during an era where political viability depended on tough talk and saber rattling, that war was an abomination. For all his wartime heroism (he remains the only American president awarded the Purple Heart, as well as the Navy and Marine Corps medal) in rescuing his PT boat crew in the South Pacific, Kennedy despised war. Historian Sheldon Stern has done impressive work in undermining the conventional narrative that claims Kennedy had a cavalier attitude toward armed conflict. As Stern observes, "All his life JFK had a high regard for personal courage and toughness, but at the same time, he loathed the brutality and carnage of war.[57]

As a twenty-two-year-old writing after the Nazi invasion of Poland in 1939, Kennedy warned that World War II would be "beyond comprehension in its savage intensity, and which could well presage a return to barbarism." In the spring of 1943, Lieutenant (JG) John F. Kennedy wrote to one of his paramours, "I understand we are winning it [the war], which is cheering, albeit somewhat hard to see, but I guess the view improves with distance. . . . I wouldn't mind being back in the States picking up the daily paper, saying 'Why don't those bastards out there do something?' It's one of those interesting things about the war that everyone in the States . . . want[s] to be out here killing Japs, while everyone out here wants to be back [home]." He added in another letter that the "boys at the front" hardly ever talked about the war but instead talk almost exclusively about "when they are going to get home." His letters to his parents were equally jaded about the war in the Pacific: "When I read that we will fight the Japs for years if necessary and will sacrifice hundreds of thousands if we must—I always like to check from where he is talking—it's seldom out here."[58]

Kennedy noted bitterly that "to see that by dying on Munda [in the Solomon Islands] you are helping to ensure peace in our time takes a larger imagination than most men possess." A place like Munda was a "God damned hot stinking" corner of the world "we all hope never to see again." And he wrote movingly about the death of a member of his crew whom he wished he had assigned to desk duty. "There was a boy on my boat, only twenty-four, had three kids" who hardly ever spoke again after Kennedy's boat was almost hit by two Japanese bombs. After that incident, "he told me one night he thought he was going to be killed. I wanted to put him ashore to work, [but] he wouldn't go. I wish I had." The sailor was in the forward gun turret of PT-109 and was immediately killed when it was hit by a Japanese destroyer. Kennedy was not much more than a boy himself, only twenty-six years old when he wrote this. It is no wonder that he concluded this account by noting that "I want to leave it far behind me when I go."[59] One can safely assume that losing his older brother in the skies over the English Channel only deepened Kennedy's contempt for war.

Kennedy's concern about modern weapons that could destroy entire civilizations became evident in his postwar career. He briefly toyed with the idea of going into journalism and covered the founding of the United Nations for the Hearst Newspapers. He was dismayed by the "inadequate preparation and lack of fundamental agreement" among its founding members. This did not bode well for the future, one that he believed would lead to "the eventual discovery of a weapon so horrible that it will truthfully mean the abolishment of all the nations employing it." After his election to the House of Representatives in 1946, he warned that Russia "will have the atomic bomb" and this could lead them to engage in "aggressive war," a war that would "truly mean the end of the world."[60]

The notion that the United States and the Soviet Union had the capacity to destroy much of the world dominated his thinking throughout his brief presidency. This was a consistent concern during the Cuban missile crisis, where Kennedy displayed a remarkable capacity to place himself in his adversary's shoes. And he had, as his ambassador to France Charles Bohlen noted, "a mentality extraordinarily free from pre-conceived prejudices, inherited or otherwise, and that he approached any problem with a clarity that was certainly a pleasure to hold in operation. You felt that when he came to a subject it was almost as though he had thrown aside the normal prejudices that beset human mentality." Regarding the nuclear standoff with the Russians, Bohlen noted that Kennedy considered the Soviet Union to be "a great and powerful country and we were a great and powerful country and it seemed to him that there must be some basis upon which the two countries could live without blowing each other up."[61] Others heard him remark that "it is insane that two men, sitting on opposite sides of the world, should be able to decide to bring an end to civilization."[62]

There was, he believed, no more important task for a president "than thinking hard about war." He was deeply impressed by B. H. Liddell Hart's book *Deterrent or Defense: A Fresh Look at the West's Military Position* (1960) and highlighted a few lines that could have served as a set of fundamental precepts for the way he managed the conflict with the Soviet Union. "Keep cool. Have unlimited patience. Never corner an opponent, and always assist him to save his face. Put yourself in his shoes—so as to see things through his eyes. Avoid self-righteousness like the devil—nothing is so self-blinding."[63]

Kennedy welcomed debate and abhorred those "yes-men" who gravitate toward the powerful. He was a critical thinker in the truest sense of the term and possessed that rarest of qualities for a politician: an open mind. Kennedy understood this attribute came with a cost, including projecting an image of indecisiveness, for "there's no doubt that any man with complete conviction, particularly who's an expert, is bound to shake anybody who's got an open mind. That's the advantage of having a closed mind."[64] He recognized the complexity of the issues confronting him, noting that "there are few if any issues where all the truth and all the right and all the angels are on one side."[65]

During the Cuban missile crisis, Kennedy often stood alone at meetings of the Executive Committee, as almost everyone around him pressed for a military response. He argued that using military force to destroy the Russian missile sites in Cuba was "one hell of a gamble" and wondered aloud whether this was a "gamble we should take." He told both the Joint Chiefs of Staff and members of Congress that any use of force could quickly spiral out of control and lead to "a nuclear exchange." Such an exchange could lead to "the destruction of a country," the United States, that would sustain "80–100 million casualties." Kennedy was aware that the United States maintained an edge in terms of its nuclear arsenal, but "we can't use them," for "the decision to use any kind of nuclear weapon, even the tactical ones, presents such a risk of it getting out of control so quickly."

In the midst of being berated by Senator Richard Russell (D-GA) and Senator J. William Fulbright (D-AR) for not attacking the Soviet missile sites and invading Cuba, Kennedy raised the prospect that "you'd have those bombs [nuclear warheads] go off and blow up fifteen cities in the United States." At another point when the discussions turned to the question of a Russian move against West Berlin if the United States attacked Cuba, General

Maxwell Taylor noted that if American forces were attacked "they [would] fight," leading Kennedy to suggest they would be overrun. At that point, Taylor argued, you "go to general war." "You mean nuclear exchange?" Kennedy asked, prompting Taylor to observe "guess you have to." The ultimate insult came from Air Force chief of staff General Curtis LeMay, who "did not see any other solution except direct military intervention [in Cuba]." If Kennedy continued to opt for a blockade instead of an invasion, this would be "almost as bad as the appeasement at Munich."[66]

Remarkably, in terms of the depths of his disdain for nuclear weapons, the Cold War president who compares most closely to Kennedy is Ronald Reagan. Both men's contempt for these weapons was sometimes difficult to discern due to their equally vociferous disdain for communism. And the two occasionally concealed their hatred of weapons of mass destruction to remain politically viable within their own political parties. Kennedy may have gone to greater lengths to conceal his dovish streak, except toward the end of his presidency, but he was operating in an era when conciliatory gestures to the Russians were seen as prima facie evidence of treason. Both men favored complete nuclear disarmament, as Kennedy suggested in his commencement address at American University in June 1963, and as Reagan did, albeit briefly, at the Reykjavik Summit with Gorbachev in October 1986, although he never fully abandoned the idea.

Some of President Kennedy's contemporaries detected this dovish streak and did not like what they saw. General Curtis LeMay, who seemed unperturbed at times over the prospect of mass casualties, sensed a whiff of pacifism in Kennedy, and this contributed to the mutual contempt the two men felt for one another. Kennedy's handling of the Cuban missile crisis only deepened LeMay's suspicions, for the resolution of the crisis represented "the greatest defeat in our history."[67] The right-wing fringe that dogged Kennedy until the moment he died (see the Umbrella Man in Dealey Plaza) were in fact on to a kernel of truth.[68] This president was a pacifist when it came to nuclear weapons (interestingly, his alter ego, speechwriter Ted Sorensen, was an avowed pacifist.) Kennedy once wrote to an old PT boat comrade that "war will exist until that distant day when the conscientious objector enjoys the same reputation and prestige that the warrior does today."[69] Kennedy was as far removed as one can get from the Barry Goldwater and Curtis LeMay school of thought that nuclear weapons were "merely another weapon." In Kennedy's mind, nothing, not Berlin or Cuba, was worth a nuclear exchange.

"Our Most Basic Common Link Is That We All Inhabit This Small Planet"

American and Soviet policy during the Cold War had a certain logic to it, in that every action generated an equal and opposite reaction. In response to continued Soviet testing, Kennedy announced on November 2, 1961, that the United States was preparing to resume testing. Kennedy had been under intense pressure from his military advisors and members of Congress to take such a step, and opinion polls revealed that the American public also favored the resumption of testing. This decision was opposed by some members of the administration who believed the American refusal to match Khrushchev's tests represented a public relations coup for the United States. The president himself shared many of these reservations. But when the American ambassador to the United Nations, Adlai Stevenson, argued that "we were ahead in the propaganda battle," Kennedy dismissed this claim by noting the limited condemnation from nonaligned nations regarding the Soviet tests. Kennedy argued that Khrushchev wanted to "give out the feeling that he has us on the run." "Anyway," Kennedy told Stevenson, "the decision has been made. I'm not saying it was the right decision. Who the hell knows?"[70]

Throughout the winter of 1961 into 1962, Kennedy seems to have vacillated on the issue of resuming the tests, in part due to the opposition of British prime minister Harold MacMillan. But after meeting with President Kennedy in Bermuda for two days in December 1961, MacMillan reluctantly agreed with the decision to resume testing.[71] On February 27, 1962, Kennedy decided at a meeting with his national security team to begin the tests. As noted earlier, Kennedy announced the decision on March 2, observing that if the United States did not respond, the American people and the nation's allies would "lose faith in our will and our wisdom, as well as our weaponry."

The United States conducted its first atmospheric test of the year on April 25, 1962, and the next day, Secretary of State Dean Rusk defended the decision by noting repeated Soviet rejections of a verifiable, comprehensive test ban treaty. The United States, Rusk added, would cease testing upon agreement of a verifiable treaty with the Soviet Union.[72]

The United States and Great Britain proposed two draft treaties for consideration in August 1962, in hopes of reaching an agreement on testing. The first called for a comprehensive test ban enforced by internationally supervised on-site inspections, while the second called for a ban on all tests except those conducted underground. The second proposal contained a sweetener for the Soviets, as the Anglo-Americans dropped any demand for on-site inspections. The latter proposal held out the prospect of moving the negotiations forward since the issue of inspections had always been a deal breaker for the Soviets. While this proposal was devoid of any international inspection regime, the belief was that existing American and British technology would be able to detect any Soviet violations.[73] Less than two months later, the Cuban missile crisis brought the world to the brink and prompted many in Washington and in Moscow to heed Kennedy's plea to "call a truce to terror."

Kennedy pressed hard for an agreement with the Soviet Union throughout the spring of 1963 despite constant criticism from Republicans and even some members of his own party. There was significant media skepticism as well; one reporter pressed him in a March 1963 news conference about the "years of failure in attempting to reach a nuclear test ban agreement." Kennedy responded that "I still hope" for an agreement and made it clear that he was not going to abandon his efforts. "The human race's history, unfortunately, has been a good deal more war than peace, [and] with nuclear weapons distributed all through the world, and available, and the strong reluctance of any people to accept defeat, I see the possibility in the 1970s of the president of the United States having to face a world in which 15 or 20 or 25 nations may have these weapons. I regard that as the greatest possible danger and hazard." The continued testing of these weapons, beyond contaminating the atmosphere, allowed nations to develop weapons that lacked the sophistication of American or Soviet weapons, but were nevertheless unimaginably destructive. "The fact of the matter is that somebody may test 10 or 15 times and get a weapon which is not nearly as good as these megaton weapons, but nevertheless, they are two or three times what the weapon was which destroyed Hiroshima, or Nagasaki, and that was dreadful enough."[74]

It was President Kennedy's speech in June 1963 at the American University in Washington that removed the final impediments to a deal on atmospheric testing. The speech was remarkable on so many levels. It was the first time an American president explicitly praised the Soviet Union for its sacrifices in World War II and acknowledged its status as a great power.[75] And in a series of passages that roiled those already convinced that Kennedy was weak, the president committed the United States to "general and complete disarmament—designed to take place by stages." He pledged that the United States sought "not a Pax Americana enforced on the world by American weapons of war. Not the peace of the grave or the security of the slave. I am talking about genuine peace, the kind of peace that makes life on earth worth living, the kind that enables men and nations to grow and to hope and to build a better life for their children—not merely peace for Americans but peace for all men and women—not merely peace in our time but peace for all time." And he added, "we [the United States and the Soviet Union] are both caught up in a vicious and dangerous cycle in which suspicion on one side breeds suspicion on the other, and new weapons beget counter weapons." And this cycle must be broken, Kennedy proclaimed, so that the world "moves not toward a strategy of annihilation but toward a strategy of peace." Near the end of the speech, Kennedy announced that high-level discussions would begin in Moscow between the United States, Great Britain, and the Soviet Union to seek a test ban treaty, and that the US was halting atmospheric testing as long as other states refrained as well.[76]

One unabashed admirer of the American University speech was Nikita Khrushchev. The Soviet leader told Kennedy's arms control negotiator in Moscow, Averell Harriman, that the American University speech paved the way for the Nuclear Test Ban Treaty. Khrushchev permitted the speech to be broadcast to the Russian people via the *Voice of America* and had it published in the state-controlled newspapers.[77]

Glenn Seaborg, a Nobel Prize–winning scientist and Kennedy's appointee to chair the Atomic Energy Commission, served as a member of Kennedy's Moscow negotiating team. Seaborg would later argue that the test ban treaty "owes its existence to John Kennedy's passionate commitment." Kennedy not only set the parameters of the American negotiating position; the negotiators operated "under [his] daily supervision." An agreement was reached in Moscow after only twelve days of negotiation, some six weeks after Kennedy's American University speech.[78]

The treaty was signed in Moscow by Secretary of State Dean Rusk, British foreign secretary Alec Douglas-Home, and Soviet foreign minister Andrei Gromyko on August 5, 1963, the eve of the eighteenth anniversary of the atomic bombing of Hiroshima. But Senate approval was in no way guaranteed, as Seaborg recalled. "Kennedy faced an unenthusiastic Senate" in 1963, "but he took the offensive, marshaling the vocal support needed to gain ratification." Initially, even members of his own party on the Senate Armed Services Committee were lukewarm to the treaty. But due to Kennedy's personal lobbying and his advice to interest groups that he helped create, including the Citizens' Committee for a Nuclear Test Ban, public opinion began to shift in favor of the treaty, and ultimately members of the Senate shifted as well.

Kennedy took every opportunity at his televised press conferences to lobby for Senate ratification, for he wanted as large a margin as possible beyond the two-thirds vote required for approval. Kennedy pulled out all the stops in his vote-gathering effort, including meeting with the Republican leader of the Senate, Everett Dirksen (R-IL), who had earlier condemned talks with the Russians over nuclear testing as "an exercise not in negotiation . . . but in give-away." In the end, Dirksen endorsed the treaty.[79] Kennedy also twisted the arm of Republican senator George Aiken of Vermont, urging him to attend the final meeting of the negotiating session and witness the signing ceremony in Moscow to give it a bipartisan flavor. "I'd rather go to Vermont," Aiken protested; "after all, it t[akes] about the same time to get to Moscow that it takes me to drive to Vermont." The senator bowed to Kennedy's request and went to Moscow.[80]

On September 23, 1963, the Senate approved the Nuclear Test Ban Treaty by a vote of eighty to nineteen, with Kennedy signing the ratified treaty on October 7, 1963. Three days later the treaty went into effect. In the end, Glenn Seaborg believed that had the president not been murdered, Kennedy and Khrushchev, whose time in office was also cut short, would have reached a comprehensive test ban and taken additional measures to reduce superpower tensions.[81]

Kennedy's exertions on behalf of the Nuclear Test Ban Treaty refute the argument that he recoiled from the taxing work of lobbying Congress. In the case of the test ban treaty, this was simply not true. It was the president who oversaw the negotiations within his administration over the correct approach to Moscow, it was the president who brought Prime Minister MacMillan along, it was the president who closely supervised his negotiators in Moscow, and it was the president who directed the campaign for Senate ratification. The idea that Kennedy was a failure in terms of moving legislation through Congress is an entrenched part of the conventional narrative surrounding his presidency. There is much to support this argument, but it is important to recall that Kennedy's "failures" are often contrasted with his successor, who won a landslide in 1964 and carried into Congress many Democrats on his coattails. This landslide was due in part to the impact of Kennedy's assassination, as was Johnson's subsequent legislative successes—not to diminish Johnson's talent for congressional arm twisting. But Kennedy's deft management of the Nuclear Test Ban Treaty from start to finish is a classic case study in effective presidential leadership.

President Kennedy was "elated" with the ratification of the Nuclear Test Ban Treaty. And it was his personal persistence that made it happen. In the face of repeated rebuffs from the Kremlin, and with the intense disagreement of members of his own military, Kennedy kept pushing and prodding. Even close allies such as his ACDA director William Foster were ready to abandon the effort in the face of Russian intransigence. Foster gave all credit to Kennedy for staying the course, for his "last letter or two" to Khrushchev, which Foster and others believed was "perhaps a little undignified," helped to break the logjam. "Kennedy would not give up before one more try because the stakes were so high," Foster noted. "Let us take another crack at this thing," Foster recalled Kennedy saying, "because this is too important to let nature take its course. He, of course, was so right." Charles "Chip" Bohlen attested to Kennedy's "emotional" commitment to the disarmament and noted that it stemmed from "the responsibility of sitting over a button which you could press and blow up the world, this was one very terrible and heavy responsibility." As a result, Kennedy was determined to "push back the frontier of danger."[82]

Countless authors from Thomas G. Paterson to Garry Wills to Christopher Hitchens have argued that Kennedy was a slave to his macho instincts and led the world to the brink of a nuclear holocaust. There are elements of truth in these accounts, in that Kennedy's hard-line campaign rhetoric limited his options upon becoming president, particularly when it came to Cuba.[83] But a truly nuanced account of these events would reject Garry Wills's claim that it was Khrushchev who acted with restraint during the Cuban missile crisis, that Kennedy was concerned about "macho appearance, not true security," that he would "risk nuclear war" in order to save face.[84]

These allegations ignore the culpability of the Kremlin in escalating world tensions during this era, disregard Kennedy's remarkable concessions during the Cuban missile crisis, omit the fact that he refused to retaliate when an

American U-2 aircraft was shot down at the height of the crisis, and most importantly, slight his leadership in securing the Nuclear Test Ban Treaty. More recently, author Robert Dean, in his book, *Imperial Brotherhood: Gender and the Making of Cold War Foreign Policy* (2003), added to the theme of Kennedy as a prisoner of his own machismo, a captive to an "ideology of masculinity." Kennedy, according to Dean, "identified his own body with the state," a deteriorating body that had to be compensated for—thus the pursuit of policies endangering the peace and leading to, among other things, the quagmire in Vietnam.[85]

6

"In the Final Analysis, It Is Their War"

As a young boy interested in politics, I was an avid consumer of print and television news, and I would often watch the National Broadcasting Company's "Huntley-Brinkley Report," where each week the respective body counts from Vietnam would be posted. Inevitably the American forces suffered the fewest losses, while the number of dead or wounded North Vietnamese and Viet Cong was enormous. As a result of these weekly statistics, I was convinced that our side was winning.

The war in Vietnam was brought close to home for me in March 1968 when nineteen-year-old Private First Class Ralph Berg of the United States Marine Corps was killed during the Tet Offensive. Ralph was from my hometown of Paxton, Massachusetts, and although I did not know him, my mother and his mother were acquaintances. Paxton at that time was a small town of approximately 3,500 residents, most of whom knew one another, and Berg's death sent a shock wave through the community. Later that same year, I went to see John Wayne's movie *The Green Berets* (1968) and found myself confused by the pro-war message of the film and the antiwar sentiment I heard at home from my parents and from political figures I admired, including Robert Kennedy. As the war dragged on, I remember my mother's fear that my older brother might end up being drafted, a fear that subsided when the despised Richard Nixon moved to abolish the draft.

For much of my life I had assumed, as have many scholars, that President Kennedy would have followed the same course of action in Vietnam as Lyndon Johnson. After all, it was Kennedy's team, the "best and the brightest," that led the United States into the quagmire, so the conventional wisdom holds. It was this same team, led by Robert Mc-Namara, Dean Rusk, Walt Rostow, and others, that continued to direct the war well into the late 1960s.

Nonetheless, President Kennedy's private doubts were apparent from the beginning to the end of his Vietnam decision-making process. This was a man who outflanked Richard Nixon in the 1960 election by taking a hard-line stance on foreign policy, but by 1963 his critics considered him to be the personification of "weakness." "Wanted" posters adorned the streets of Dallas on November 22, 1963, due to Kennedy's "treason" in dealing with the Soviet Union and its Third World proxies. His electoral calculations as 1964 approached only deepened his instinctive tendency to feint, mislead, and conceal his true intentions beneath a barrage of impassioned rhetoric. All of this makes the task of discerning Kennedy's true intentions in Vietnam quite daunting.

John F. Kennedy kept his own counsel; he was as Machiavellian as any man ambitious for power. Kennedy's public words, even the ones that support the thesis that he would have prevented Vietnam from becoming an American quagmire, which I now believe to be the case, must be read with caution. So, the question of what Kennedy would have done in Vietnam must remain forever in the realm of speculation.

But not all speculation is equal; some conjectures are more rooted in facts and reason than others. As his private letters during World War II revealed, and his policies toward the Soviet Union demonstrated, John F. Kennedy hated war. As he told journalist Hugh Sidey in 1960, "I really did not learn about the [Great] Depression until I read about it at Harvard. My experience was the war. I can tell you about that."[1] Sidey added, "If I had to single out one element in Kennedy's life that more than anything influenced his later leadership, it would be a horror of war, a total revulsion over the terrible toll that modern war had taken on individuals, nations and societies."

The same president who canceled American air strikes at the Bay of Pigs, refused to block the construction of the Berlin Wall, agreed to the neutralization of Laos, and secretly agreed to Khrushchev's demands during the missile crisis, would not have turned Vietnam into America's deadliest war save the Civil War and the two world wars.

"We're Going Nowhere Out Here"

President Kennedy expanded America's involvement in the war in Vietnam and recruited the cadre known as the "best and the brightest" who would go on to preside over an American quagmire. When he took the oath of office on January 20, 1961, there were just under seven hundred American advisors in South Vietnam, and by the time he died, that number had risen to just over 16,700. He gave conflicting statements as president that provided fodder for those on both sides of the hypothetical question, "What would he have done about Vietnam had he lived?" Intellectual honesty requires anyone dealing with this question to begin with an obvious but seldom-utilized disclaimer: this is all conjecture. But as mentioned, conjecture rooted in the precedents Kennedy set during his brief presidency and even as a United States senator provides a greater sense of certainty than some of the theories emerging from the Camelot camp or from the inveterate Kennedy haters.

As a United States senator, Kennedy sympathized at times with the proponents of the domino theory. In 1954, President Eisenhower described the domino theory as a situation where "you have a row of dominoes set up; you knock over the first one, and what will happen to the last one is that it will go over very quickly."[2] One would assume that Kennedy, whose senior college thesis *Why England Slept* examined the failure of the British to stop Hitler before it was too late, would have been one of the more vocal champions of the domino theory. He was not, and in fact he repeatedly warned that the United States should embrace anticolonial independence movements.

Interestingly, Kennedy did not accept the conventional narrative when it came to Neville Chamberlain, Munich, and appeasement. In Kennedy's view, Chamberlain pursued appeasement at least in part to allow time for the British armaments industry to catch up to the Germans. "Munich," according to Kennedy, "was the price she [Britain] had to pay for this year of grace." Kennedy did not exclusively blame Chamberlain or Foreign Secretary Viscount Fairfax for allowing the Nazi menace to metastasize. He contended that the entire British society was averse to another conflict so soon after the disastrous Great War. In Kennedy's view, the British balked at the idea of rearming, seeing those inanimate objects as the cause of war.[3]

Yet the Massachusetts senator was far more sympathetic to the nationalist yearnings of emerging Third World nations than many of his peers. During the 1960 campaign, he criticized the Eisenhower administration for its knee-jerk hostility to nonaligned nations, and was a frequent critic of European, particularly French, attempts to preserve the remnants of their Third World empires. Kennedy endorsed Algerian independence from France in 1957, a controversial move that garnered international publicity. As chairman of the newly created Senate Foreign Relations Subcommittee on Africa (a chairmanship that no one else apparently wanted), he became especially sensitive to the issue of African nationalism. Remarkably, he mentioned Africa 479 times during the 1960 campaign. His high-ranking State Department appointees reflected his sympathy toward Third World nationalists, as did his ambassadorial appointments. The latter nominees were first-rate, and Kennedy required many of them to speak the languages of their host countries. Kennedy went out of his way to accord the leaders of newly independent nations full-blown honors at White House state visits—some eleven in 1961, ten in 1962, and seven in 1963.

The president, along with members of his family, developed close personal relationships with a number of these leaders. The creation of the Peace Corps (a proposal that originated with Senator Hubert Humphrey) and the Food for Peace program, the Alliance for Progress in Latin America, and a doubling of the number of loans issued by the Agency for International Development were all part of Kennedy's larger agenda of outreach to emerging nations. This was all smart international politics, as these new states were joining the United Nations, and their votes had the potential to change the tenor of that body.

It was also smart domestic politics for a president who sought to broaden his support among Black voters. On a deeper level, as historian Anna Kasten Nelson has pointed out, John F. Kennedy believed in American exceptionalism and that the United States had a special obligation to serve the needs of newly independent nations.[4] That desire clashed with the hardcore realities of the Cold War, and he did not always deliver on his promises, but in comparison to his predecessor and his successors, his commitment set him apart. There is a reason why, to this day, Kennedy's image can be found in remote outposts around the globe.

One of Kennedy's most impressive ambassadorial appointments was his selection of Edmund A. Gullion to be his envoy to the Republic of the Congo. Kennedy first met Gullion in the late 1940s when the young congressman was seeking information for a foreign policy speech, and then again in 1951 when Kennedy traveled to Vietnam while Gullion was serving as the political counselor at the American embassy in Saigon. Gullion was impressed by this young man with "an air of physical frailty," who arrived at a "sorely divided" American embassy. The embassy was divided over whether French colonial rule could prevail in Indochina, and over the appropriate role for the United States in the region.

Kennedy's visit was unusual, Gullion noted, because he did not observe the usual protocol regimen. Kennedy was "challenging the establishment... his stance on Indochina certainly went against the prevailing opinion.... His challenge here to what was thought and believed in Indochina was quite important." Kennedy's French military guides felt that the young congressman was "rocking the boat," and Gullion believed that Kennedy learned lessons from this visit that he carried over into his presidency. As Gullion would later observe, the lessons from this trip "cast quite a shadow into the future." The visit reinforced Kennedy's preexisting attitude about assessing reports from abroad, and about the importance of "having direct contact with men behind the reports." In general, Kennedy developed a new way of looking at the dynamics between colonial powers and emerging nations.[5]

Gullion was part of a faction within that divided American embassy that was skeptical about French prospects in their fight against Vietnamese nationalists. At dinner one night, as artillery shells fired by the Viet Minh exploded in the distance, Gullion bluntly responded to Congressman's Kennedy's question, "What have you learned here?" The lesson Gullion learned was that "in twenty years there will be no more colonies. We're going nowhere out here. The French have lost. If we come in here and do the same thing, we will lose, too, for the same reason. There's no will or support for this kind of war back in Paris. The home front is lost. The same thing would happen to us."[6] In his travel diary from that journey to Vietnam, Kennedy asked rhetorically, and prophetically, "Could anyone subdue Ho?" And he added, "We are more and more becoming colonialists in the minds of the people."[7]

Congressman Kennedy bluntly rejected the idea that the United States should attempt to fill the void left by the withering European colonial empires. This put him at odds with both the Truman and Eisenhower administrations, who viewed European security, and thus keeping the Europeans happy, as the linchpin of America's containment policy toward the Soviet Union. Kennedy argued in the House of Representatives in 1951, "We cannot ally ourselves with the dreams of empire. We are allies with our Western

European friends and we will aid and befriend them in the defense of their own countries. But to support and defend their colonial aspirations is another thing. That is their problem, not ours."[8]

Kennedy would later report on his return to the United States that "in Indochina we have allied ourselves to the desperate effort of a French regime to hang on to the remnants of empire. There is no broad, general support of the native Vietnam Government among the people of that area."[9] In March 1952, he spoke to an audience in Everett, Massachusetts, while campaigning against incumbent senator Henry Cabot Lodge Jr. (R-MA), arguing that the United States should not send American forces to assist the French in Vietnam. He then expanded on these comments a month later in Lynn, Massachusetts, arguing that "we should not commit our ground troops to fight in French Indo-China."[10]

Kennedy's victory over Lodge in the 1952 Senate race was one of the few bright notes in an otherwise dismal year for the Democratic Party. Despite rampant illnesses, Kennedy quickly emerged as a bright young star in the Senate and invested considerable time and effort in the Senate burnishing his foreign policy credentials. During the summer of 1953, the junior senator from Massachusetts proposed an amendment to a foreign aid bill to pressure France to give more independence to Vietnam, Laos, and Cambodia. The amendment was opposed by the Eisenhower administration, which viewed such pressure as counterproductive to Franco-American relations, and it went down to defeat.[11]

The Domino Theory

On April 6, 1954, during the climactic battle at Dien Bien Phu, Kennedy spoke on the floor of the Senate about the conflict in Vietnam. Kennedy recounted repeated American and French pronouncements regarding the "light at the end of the tunnel," all of which proved to be false. Kennedy struck a middle course, arguing that the United States assist the French in their fight against communism, but only if the French abandoned their commitment to "ancient colonialism." If the French were to support Vietnamese independence, then there was a chance to salvage the situation in Indochina, in part through the "united action" of the "associated states" [Laos and Cambodia] who were also determined to secure their own independence. But he added,

"To pour money, materiel, and men into the jungles of Indochina without at least a remote prospect of victory would be dangerously futile and self-destructive. I am frankly of the belief that no amount of American military assistance in Indochina can conquer an enemy which is everywhere and at the same time nowhere, 'an enemy of the people' which has the sympathy and covert support of the people."

Kennedy rightly noted that Vietnam's neighbors had "made it clear that they regard this as a war of colonialism" and that the prospects for "united action," which the Eisenhower administration claimed was necessary for victory, required France to abandon its colonial designs. The United States needed to withdraw its support for European colonial holdings in the Third World, and Kennedy hoped that the Eisenhower administration recognized that without a French commitment to Vietnamese independence, the United States would have to unilaterally assist France and alienate all of Vietnam's neighbors. That simply should not happen, Kennedy pleaded, insisting that the administration recognize "the futility of channeling American men and machines into that hopeless internecine struggle."[12] America must throw its weight behind the forces of nationalism if it were to prevail in the long, twilight struggle between the free world and the communist world. It would lose that struggle if it backed colonial puppet regimes simply because they were anticommunist.

Kennedy focused on the situation in Vietnam both in senatorial venues and in speaking engagements around the country. Whether he sought to bolster his foreign policy credentials or simply because he viewed it as an intellectual challenge, Vietnam captured his imagination. As with all political figures, it was likely a mixture of both motives. But what he had to say was eerily prescient. Shortly after his speech on the floor of the Senate, and after the French defeat at Dien Bien Phu, Kennedy spoke to a group of business executives in Chicago. He warned that the United States and its European allies did not always have the same interests when it came to the emerging world. "The political and economic interests of ourselves and our European allies in the area were not on the same level . . . the West is reaping a bitter harvest of decades of mistakes and exploitation in Asia." And, in an analysis that would become hauntingly familiar to Americans over the next twenty years, the senator noted that if the United States were to intervene in Vietnam, "the terrain in Indo-China is more complex than Korea; and we would not have the support of a friendly population. We would be forced to throw our widely dispersed ground troops into the jungle war where conditions favor the Communists."[13]

By 1956, as mentioned, Kennedy began to see Ngo Dinh Diem, a pro-Western Vietnamese Catholic, as the answer to America's policy conundrum in Vietnam. Kennedy had first met Diem at a dinner hosted by Justice William O. Douglas of the Supreme Court on May 7, 1953.[14] Diem was the type of pro-Western nationalist that the United States could support, a champion of Vietnamese independence who was anti-French but also a devoted anti-communist. Kennedy referred to Diem's success after the partition of Vietnam in 1954 as the "Diem Miracle." Kennedy's hope was that Diem would not only resist Communist North Vietnam but also preside over "a political, economic and social revolution far superior to anything the Communists can offer," a revolution that was peaceful, democratic, and controlled by the Vietnamese. The United States should commit itself not to "handouts" for the Vietnamese but help them replenish all they had lost due to the colonial pillaging they were subjected to for centuries.[15]

On June 1, 1956, with an eye toward possibly becoming a running mate for presidential candidate Adlai Stevenson, Senator Kennedy spoke to The American Friends of Vietnam. In this speech, Kennedy proclaimed that South Vietnam represented a test of American resolve. Preventing that nation from falling into the communist camp was a crucial step toward containing another expansionist totalitarian dictatorship. Kennedy's speech reflected a near consensus among American foreign policy makers at the time that Ho Chi Minh was a dupe of Moscow, and to a lesser extent of Mao Tse-Tung's China, the latter still seen as a puppet of the Kremlin. The senator observed that "Vietnam represents the cornerstone of the Free World in Southeast Asia, the keystone to the arch, the finger in the dike." He added that "Vietnam represents a proving ground of democracy in Asia." All of Southeast Asia, along with Japan and the Philippines, were at risk if "the Red Tide of Communism overflowed into Vietnam."[16]

Kennedy adopted a hard-line stance on the proposed referendum question regarding a unified Vietnam that came out of the Geneva Accords of July 21, 1954. The North Vietnamese had committed to the accords due to a pledge from France that elections would be held in 1956 regarding a potential unification of North and South Vietnam. The Eisenhower administration promoted the idea of partitioning Vietnam rather than permitting a vote on unification. The administration adopted this position out of a belief that Ho

Chi Minh's regime would never permit a fair vote on the referendum, and due to the continued attacks of the Viet Minh, supported by the North, in South Vietnam.

Encouraged by the United States, Ngo Dinh Diem, won a rigged election in October 1955, "defeating" former Emperor Bo Dai to become the first president of the Republic of Vietnam [South Vietnam]. Diem owed his victory in good part to the machinations of the Central Intelligence Agency. With the support of the Eisenhower administration, Diem then reaffirmed his commitment to rejecting the proposed unification referendum of 1956. The Eisenhower administration's policies toward South Vietnam led the United States, as historian David L. Anderson has noted, into becoming "the guarantor not only of an independent South Vietnam but of a particular Vietnamese leader."[17]

The events of 1955–56 moved the United States further toward war in Southeast Asia. Yet none of this seemed to disturb Senator Kennedy, who noted in 1956, "Neither the United States nor Free Vietnam was a party to that agreement—and neither the United States nor Free Vietnam is ever going to be a party to an election [the unification referendum] obviously stacked and subverted in advance." It would be unconscionable if the United States permitted "any diplomatic action adverse to this, one of the youngest members of the family of nations." And he added, "this [South Vietnam] is our offspring—we cannot abandon it, we cannot ignore its needs."[18]

As for Ngo Dinh Diem, Kennedy celebrated "the amazing success of President Diem in meeting firmly and with determination the major political and economic crises which had heretofore continually plagued Vietnam," and he hailed Diem's pursuit of social reforms to improve the lives of his people, including "legislation for better labor relations, health protection, working conditions, and wages." All of this "has been completed under the leadership of President Diem." Additionally, the Diem government had constructed "approximately 45,000 houses . . . 2,500 wells . . . 100 schools and dozens of medical centers and maternity homes."[19] The focus on the number of wells dug is yet another small reminder of the pathological American practice of focusing on metrics as way of measuring success, a practice that would become commonplace in Robert McNamara's Defense Department.

The Ugly American

Senator Kennedy cruised to reelection in 1958, the same year that the situation in Laos took a turn for the worse in the struggle between communists and pro-Western forces. Kennedy observed that the Eisenhower administration, with its doctrine of massive retaliation, was in no position to respond to aggression in Laos that was a fight against "guerilla forces." These "peripheral wars" could not be dealt with by a doctrine of massive retaliation. Eisenhower's policies drove "ourselves into a corner where the choice is all or nothing at all."[20]

Kennedy was influenced that same year by the publication of a work of fiction called *The Ugly American* by Eugene Burdick and William Lederer, a tale of diplomatic malpractice by Americans who lacked familiarity with the language, culture, and traditions of a fictional Southeast Asian country that resembled South Vietnam. The book became an instant sensation, remaining on the bestseller list for seventy-eight weeks and ultimately selling over four million copies. Hollywood bought the rights to the book and turned it into a movie starring Marlon Brando. The ugly American of the title, Homer Atkins, was actually the hero of the book, for he was unafraid to dirty himself in helping local villagers build wells and otherwise enjoy the blessings of the twentieth century. The villains were American diplomats and Defense Department bureaucrats unwilling to leave their embassy cocktail parties and mingle with the masses. Kennedy was so impressed with the book that he sent copies to all his fellow senators.[21]

Kennedy sponsored a full-page advertisement in the *New York Times* on January 23, 1959, where, along with other prominent figures of the day, he praised *The Ugly American*. The ad's sponsors argued that the book offered an insightful look at "the Americans who go overseas for the various governmental agencies, their activities abroad, and the policies they are entrusted to carry out." Kennedy sent a private letter to the book's coauthor, Eugene Burdick, noting that it was "a pleasure for me to give a public endorsement of *The Ugly American*, which I also feel has begun to have some visible influence both in Congress and in Foggy Bottom [the State Department]."[22]

Kennedy was something of a rarity in political circles, both then and now, with his interest in books. He also had a ferocious appetite for magazine and journal articles focused on both the higher and the lower aspects of the human experience. *The Ugly American* was precisely the kind of book that appealed to Kennedy, who, as a consequence of his frequent travels abroad, had come to the conclusion that the nation's diplomacy was crippled by the inclination of American envoys to ignore the harsh reality outside the embassy walls. In the years prior to the 1960 election, Kennedy hammered away at the growing "economic gap" between the First and Third World and argued for the creation of "a volunteer corps" that would, as Steven Watts, has noted, "personify the physical and personal virtues of the effective Americans praised in the novel." As the senator put it, "Many have been discouraged at the examples that we read of 'the ugly American.' And I think the United States is going to have to do much better in this area if we are going to defend freedom and peace in the 1960s."[23] *The Ugly American* was tailor-made for a presidential candidate committed to the idea that victory in the Cold War required unconventional thinking, unconventional diplomatic and military measures, and innovative approaches involving both public and private initiatives.

Considering all the attention given to Vietnam in the latter half of the 1950s, one would have expected the issue to feature prominently in the 1960 presidential campaign. It did not. In the second presidential debate, Vice President Nixon referred once to Vietnam, noting that "we've stopped them [the communists] in Indochina." The candidates were specifically asked a question about Vietnam, and other Cold War issues, during the third debate. Vice President Nixon argued that "as far as Indochina was concerned, I stated over and over again that it was essential . . . that the United States make it clear that we would not tolerate Indochina falling under Communist domination. Now, as a result of our taking the strong stand that we did . . . the Communists have moved out and we do have a strong, free bastion there." Kennedy rejected Nixon's claim that the strong stand of the United States prevented Vietnam from falling to the communists. "Mr. Nixon talked . . . before the newspaper editors in the spring of 1954 about putting, and I quote him, 'American boys into Indochina.' The reason Indochina was preserved was the result of the Geneva Conference."[24] Kennedy seemed to suggest that if Nixon had his way, American soldiers would have been, and could be in the future, fighting in Southeast Asia.

"Shit Man, He's the Only Boy We Got Out There"

Vietnam was a third- or fourth-tier issue in the pecking order of Kennedy's foreign policy priorities. When it came to the developing world, Kennedy focused more on Africa and Latin American than on Southeast Asia. But all these issues were eclipsed by the constant crises related to Berlin and Cuba, and other bilateral issues between the United States and the Soviet Union. This explains Kennedy's halting and at times contradictory policy on Vietnam.

Shortly after the disaster at the Bay of Pigs, President Kennedy created a Vietnam task force headed by Deputy Defense Secretary Roswell Gilpatric. The deputy secretary would later note that "none of us . . . who were charged with the responsibility for this area, had any preparation for this problem."[25] Gilpatric would later observe that President Kennedy "seemed to me to be at times rather irked or distracted at having to focus his attention on Vietnam as opposed to the problems of the Atlantic Alliance; the relations with the Soviet Union . . . which fascinated him, and occupied a good deal of his thinking and time."[26]

Gilpatric's team was charged with assessing the Diem government's vulnerabilities and recommending any strategic changes to prevent South Vietnam from falling into communist hands. "South Vietnam is nearing the decisive phase of its battle for survival," the Gilpatric report concluded on May 1, 1961, adding that the United States must show "our friends . . . and our foes, the Viet Cong [South Vietnamese communists], that come what may, the United States intends to win this battle." The task force recommended increasing the size of the Army of the Republic of Vietnam (ARVN) and continuing support for the Diem government while pressuring the same for economic and political reforms. Kennedy accepted some of the task force's recommendations and followed up on May 11, 1961, by dispatching four hundred Army Green Berets trained in counterinsurgency tactics, along with additional advisors, as part of the American effort to bolster the Diem government.[27]

Two days before Kennedy approved some of the task force's recommendations, the president dispatched Vice President Lyndon Johnson on a tour of Asia that included a stop in Vietnam. Johnson did not want to make the trip, and only found out about it from listening to news on the radio. The vice president arrived in Saigon the same day Kennedy approved the request for the Green Berets. Johnson would go on to proclaim Ngo Dinh Diem as the "Winston Churchill of Southeast Asia." The vice president allegedly told a journalist who asked if such praise was warranted, "Shit man, he's the only boy we got out there."[28] Johnson was widely ridiculed for his comment about Diem's Churchillian stature, but he had been instructed by the administration to bolster Diem's esteem and convince him of America's resolve to "join with you in an intensified endeavor to win the struggle against communism."[29] But Diem proved to be a constant problem, at least from the American perspective, because he was fiercely independent and sensitive to the charge that damaged both him and his regime, that the Americans had replaced the French as South Vietnam's colonial masters.

In the late summer and fall of 1961, the Viet Cong intensified their attacks on South Vietnamese forces, essentially taking control of almost all of rural South Vietnam. Serious concerns were raised in Saigon and in Washington about President Diem's ability to defeat the Viet Cong and govern a unified republic. Presidential chronicler Theodore White wrote Kennedy that August after a trip to South Vietnam, "The situation gets steadily worse almost week by week . . . What perplexes the hell out of me is that the Commies, on their side, seem able to find people willing to die for their cause."[30]

Kennedy announced on October 11, 1961, that he was sending General Maxwell Taylor and Walt Rostow to lead a delegation to Vietnam to examine "ways in which we can perhaps better assist the government of Viet Nam in meeting this threat to its independence." When asked if American ground forces might be the answer, Kennedy demurred, noting, "We are going to wait until General Taylor comes back and brings an up-to-date description of the situation . . . in Viet Nam."[31]

Taylor's delegation, top-heavy with military personnel, reported that the situation required an enhanced American military response. The task force saw Vietnam as a test for the United States' ability to respond to Premier Khrushchev's January 6, 1961, address committing the Soviet Union to support "wars of national liberation." This address was viewed as Khrushchev's embrace of a Hitlerian doctrine of world domination by some American scholars and policymakers. Stefan Possony, a Pentagon consultant and a professor at Georgetown University, claimed that Premier Khrushchev's speech revealed that he was the new Hitler. It was "becoming very clear," according to Possony, that Americans should view the "January speech and *Mein Kampf*" in the same light.[32]

In hindsight, Possony's argument was overblown, but a substantial number of Americans, including many high-ranking policy makers, considered the Kremlin of 1961 to be the equivalent of the Reich Chancellery of 1939. Kennedy should have been more attuned to the false equivalencies at work here; his judgment and insight in cases such as these was usually quite acute. In this instance perhaps it eluded him, or as is more likely the case, these were the actions of a skilled politician with a prudential understanding of the pitfalls of getting too far out of step with public opinion. Moving the American body politic, not to mention his own government, required incremental moves.

"Flexible Response"

The perception that the Soviet Union was repeatedly probing and exploiting Western vulnerabilities, and that the Eisenhower administration was hamstrung by its reliance on "massive retaliation," led General Maxwell Taylor and others to embrace the doctrine of "flexible response." Taylor's doctrine was promulgated in his 1959 book *The Uncertain Trumpet*, where he claimed the Eisenhower administration's reliance on nuclear weapons to hold the Kremlin in check had handcuffed the United States from responding to non-nuclear acts of aggression, including what were later termed "wars of national liberation." The United States needed capabilities that allowed it to respond to different levels of aggression by applying methods equal to a specific threat. Having seen successful counterinsurgency tactics applied in places like Malaya (soon to be known as Malaysia) and the Philippines, Taylor believed the same techniques, if adequately bolstered by American weaponry and intelligence capabilities, could lead to victory for the Republic of Vietnam.

America's reinvigorated special forces, particularly the Green Berets, would provide the flexibility needed to counter communist aggression in Vietnam. Taylor saw Vietnam as a test case for the doctrine of flexible response and viewed the ongoing struggle there as a "laboratory" for the development of American strategy and tactics. Walt Rostow was also a believer in deploying American special forces to save South Vietnam: "In Knute Rockne's old phrase, we are not saving them for the junior prom." If America was able to secure South Vietnam's independence, Khrushchev's national liberation strategy would unravel.[33] President Kennedy seemed onboard with this as well, although, as we shall see, he harbored doubts, often in private but occasionally in public, about the prudence of using South Vietnam as the bulwark against Khrushchev's doctrine.

Taylor's report recommended escalating America's presence in Vietnam, including the deployment of anywhere from eight to ten thousand combat troops. "South Vietnam is in serious trouble . . . but if the U.S. promptly and energetically takes up the challenge, a victory can be had without a U.S. takeover of the war," the report argued. But "some combat troops" would be needed to defend areas controlled by the Americans and to allow for the protection of American and ARVN logistical operations. The report added that the same message could be heard all around Southeast Asia, that "vigorous American action is needed to buy time for Vietnam to mobilize."[34]

Several administration officials disagreed with the Taylor Report, including Assistant Secretary of State for East Asian and Pacific Affairs Averell Harriman; Ambassador John Kenneth Galbraith; and Undersecretary of State Chester Bowles, who observed that Taylor's recommendations would send the nation "full blast up a dead-end street." George Ball, who would shortly succeed Bowles as the number two man at the State Department, was even more blunt and remarkably prescient, arguing that "Taylor is wrong . . . Within five years, we'll have three hundred thousand men in the paddies and jungle and never find them again."[35] Senator Mike Mansfield (D-MT), a student of Asia who considered himself a friend of the Republic of Vietnam, told the president in the aftermath of the Taylor Report that "armed power" was no substitute for "political, economic, and social" changes that offered "the best resistance to communism."[36]

The president himself was arguably the greatest skeptic of all when it came to escalating American involvement in Vietnam. Kennedy told *New York Times* columnist Arthur Krock in October 1961 that "United States troops should not be involved on the Asian mainland." His comments to Arthur Schlesinger Jr. were even more acerbic. If the war in Vietnam "were ever converted into a white man's war, we would lose the way the French had lost a decade earlier." The deputy assistant secretary for international security affairs for the Department of Defense, William Bundy, whose brother served as the president's national security advisor, noted at one critical juncture that autumn that "the thrust of the President's thinking was clear—sending organized forces was a step so grave that it should be avoided if this was humanly possible."[37]

Taylor's task force met with the president for over an hour on November 3, 1961, and told Kennedy that if he acted decisively on their recommendations, "a victory could be had without a U.S. takeover of the war." Twelve days later, Kennedy met with his National Security Council and continued to express concerns about deepening American involvement. The prospect of having to fight the Soviets over Berlin and at the same time deal with a conflict thousands of miles away in Asia was deeply unsettling. Kennedy deferred any decision at this meeting, waiting until November 22, 1961, to issue National Security Action Memorandum #111, which codified decisions Kennedy had reached a week earlier. The memorandum committed the United States to providing helicopters, military transports flown by American servicemen, increased surveillance, and increased economic assistance to South Vietnam.[38]

A short time after NSAM #111 became administration policy, Kennedy approved "Operation Ranch Hand," which authorized the widespread use of defoliants and crop-destroying chemicals to assist with "the clearance of key routes" in South Vietnam and "proceeding thereafter to food denial" to the enemy. While Agent Orange would not be introduced until 1965, other chemicals were employed to deprive the enemy of both food and the foliage that concealed their movements.[39]

Nevertheless, Kennedy, to the surprise of some members of his national security team, decided not to commit American combat forces to the conflict. Maxwell Taylor later noted that he could not recall anyone who was strongly against deploying combat troops "except one man and that was the President. The President just didn't want to be convinced that this was the thing to do." Kennedy had recently met with retired General Douglas MacArthur, who warned him, "Above all things, Mr. President, never commit your forces to a ground war in Asia." As Taylor noted, whenever Kennedy was pressed to commit such forces, he would respond, "Well, now, you gentlemen, you go back and convince General MacArthur, then I'll be convinced." As Taylor drolly commented, "none of us undertook the task."[40] Taylor noted that Kennedy peppered him with questions during a meeting held to discuss the report's recommendations. In the aftermath of that meeting, Taylor wrote that the President "is instinctively against introduction of U.S. forces."[41]

In hindsight, knowing how the quagmire played out, many Americans asked how so many administrations, and so many experts, could have gotten it so wrong in Vietnam. But hindsight, as the cliché goes, provides a dramatically clearer picture than the view available at the time. Robert D. Schulzinger summed up the quandary confronting policymakers before, during, and after the Kennedy years: When looking at the cost and balance sheet regarding Vietnam, these policymakers tended to view the short-term cost of exiting Vietnam as too great to bear. "A departure of the United States from Vietnam or even a diminution of the U.S. commitment there would lead to a communist victory. The sight of the unification of Vietnam under Ho Chi Minh would be tangible. The costs of an enhanced U.S. presence in Vietnam could only be imagined."[42]

There were significant domestic American political costs that would arise from an American withdrawal from Vietnam, whether it happened under Eisenhower or Kennedy. "Who lost Vietnam?" would have become a rallying cry for whichever political party stood to benefit. But there was also a cost in American credibility in the international arena. Premier Khrushchev had taken the measure of President Kennedy at the Vienna summit in June 1961 and thought he had found a young, sickly, and somewhat callow president overly eager to avoid conflict. Khrushchev underestimated Kennedy and opted to test him wherever possible. Consequently, Berlin, Cuba, Laos, and yes, Vietnam, became a test of American resolve.

"The Basic Problems Facing the World . . . Are Not Susceptible of a Military Solution"

Nevertheless, by late 1961, John F. Kennedy, as he had earlier and would again, opposed the introduction of American combat troops in Vietnam. He opted for something of a middle course, which American presidents are fond of doing, involving increased covert operations and stepping up the number of advisors working with the South Vietnamese military. Granted, one can get into a debate involving the semantics of the word "advisors." But there appeared to be a line that Kennedy simply would not cross—that American soldiers would not carry the weight of the war in Vietnam. As Senator J. William Fulbright (D-AK) put it, Kennedy's objective was to prevent the United States from becoming "formally involved." Fulbright added that Kennedy was committed to this "informal basis" because "we couldn't withdraw if it gets too formal."[43]

Perhaps Kennedy was fooling himself with his "red line" on "formal involvement," since American soldiers were already in the thick of combat as the slowly growing rate of casualties revealed."[44] Yet even if one accepts that Kennedy contrived some imaginary distinction between "formal" and "informal," it is nevertheless consistent with a president unwilling to take those final steps authorized by Lyndon Johnson in the spring of 1965.

During much of 1961 and 1962, the administration was negotiating a settlement with the Russians to neutralize Laos.[45] An agreement was reached in June 1962, a development which relieved Kennedy from having to make an overt commitment of American forces to that nation. The agreement effectively took the issue off the front pages, but it did not end the struggle. Strategically speaking, the "neutralization" of Laos allowed North Vietnam a sanctuary from which to run men and material into South Vietnam; however, Kennedy authorized a covert war against the communists in the face of their repeated violations of Laotian neutrality. It should be noted that it was the Chinese who were more deeply involved in Laos than the Soviets, and that the violence in that nation was the result of genuine indigenous grievances. Contrary to most of his contemporaries, Kennedy was often acutely aware of these factors, but in the case of Laos that quality seemed to have deserted him.

Kennedy's decision to opt for a political settlement in Laos pitted him against the Joint Chiefs of Staff, who had urged him to intervene in April 1961, just days after the Bay of Pigs. The chiefs recommended air strikes against the communist forces in Laos followed by the deployment of American troops to halt a North Vietnamese–sponsored offensive. According to Robert Kennedy, when asked what the American response should be if these forces were attacked, the chairman of the Joint Chiefs, Lyman Lemnitzer, argued, "You drop a bomb on Hanoi . . . and you start using atomic weapons." In another discussion, Lemnitzer claimed, "If we are given the right to use nuclear weapons, we can guarantee victory."[46] Kennedy's critics would later claim that his failure to act with alacrity and ruthlessness in this early phase of the conflict in Southeast Asia contributed to the ultimate defeat of the United States.

Nevertheless, the Laotian neutrality solution was more to Kennedy's liking than a massive combat role for the United States in Southeast Asia. The United States' commitment to South Vietnam had intensified during the Eisenhower years, with the administration proclaiming that the United States must "restore its prestige in the Far East . . . and prevent further losses to communism" in that region. Eisenhower not only drew a line in the sand regarding Vietnam; he also, as Chester J. Pach and Elmo Richardson have noted, "fasten[ed] American prestige to Ngo Dinh Diem." By elevating the survival of South Vietnam and the Diem government into a test of American resolve, the Eisenhower administration made it politically difficult for Kennedy to exit from Vietnam in a manner similar to Laos.[47] Any such exit would have to wait for after his presumed reelection in 1964. Kennedy believed the question of "Who Lost Vietnam?" would become the centerpiece of the 1964 campaign if he opted for a political solution in his first term.

As 1962 began, helicopters piloted by Americans seemed to knock the Viet Cong off their game for a time, all at a low price in terms of American lives. General Taylor reported "favorable trends in all military activities," while Secretary of Defense McNamara pledged that "we are going to win in Vietnam. We will remain until we do." Some members of the media echoed this optimism, with *Time* magazine celebrating the "remarkable U.S. military effort" by the Kennedy administration, which was determined "to hold South Vietnam at all costs."[48]

This optimism was not shared by everyone. An opinion piece written by James Reston on February 14, 1962, noted that "the United States is now involved in an undeclared war in South Vietnam. This is well known to the Russians, the Chinese Communists, and everyone else concerned except the American people." In a commencement address at Michigan State University in June 1962, Senate Majority Leader Mike Mansfield warned that "after years of enormous expenditures of aid in South Vietnam, that country is more, rather than less, dependent on aid from the United States." And he added ominously that South Vietnam's survival "is less rather than more secure than it was five or six years ago."[49] The following month, a report in *Newsweek* concluded that the war was "a losing proposition."[50]

Kennedy continued to hold out hope that the injection of enhanced American military and economic assistance would allow South Vietnam to remain an independent republic. In a commencement address at the United States Military Academy on June 6, 1962, the president appealed to the newly commissioned officers to embrace the world of unconventional warfare to counter "Mr. Khrushchev's . . . wars of liberation." This required a "wholly different kind of force," one capable of speaking in different tongues, and adept at countering "war by ambush" and war by "infiltration." This new challenge required soldiers to be "ambassadors of goodwill and good works around the globe." But, and there always was a qualifier whenever Kennedy talked about Vietnam, even opaquely, "the basic problems facing the world today are not susceptible of a military solution."[51]

The president seemed to suggest that the problems might be susceptible to a mix of military, political, psychological, and socioeconomic programs that would win popular support for the Diem government. At its core, this counterinsurgency effort would consist of "a combination of self-defense and civic action." The CIA and Army Special Forces units "provided medical help" and "educational programs" and promoted agrarian reforms for peasant farmers in rural areas. In addition to this, the American government persuaded Diem to adopt the Strategic Hamlet Program, which consisted of "fortified villages surrounded by barbed wire, bamboo parapets, and earthen ramparts bristling with spikes." All of this was part of a counterinsurgency strategy designed, as Roger Hilsman, one of its chief proponents put it, to win the "struggle . . . by cutting the Viet Cong off from their local sources of strength, i.e., by denying them access to the villages and the people."[52] The long-term objective of creating a "carefully developed network of interlocking hamlets" was undermined by government officials siphoning off money intended for various social, political, and economic reforms. The Diem government claimed it had established eighty-six hundred strategic hamlets, but only 20 percent lived up to American standards. Within a year, most of these hamlets had been overrun by the Viet Cong, who seized many of the weapons provided for self-defense.[53]

Many Defense Department officials were skeptical of the counterinsurgency campaign from the start, believing that victory could only be achieved through conventional applications of force. One of those who belonged to the latter camp was General Maxwell Taylor, who seemed to harbor few doubts about the American prospects in Vietnam. Taylor traveled to South Vietnam in September 1962, staying for three days and meeting with President Diem and several State and Defense Department figures. "Much progress has been accomplished since my visit in October 1961," Taylor reported in a memo he wrote after returning to Washington.[54] Shortly after his visit to Saigon, Kennedy replaced the Chairman of the Joint Chiefs of Staff, Lyman Lemnitzer, whom he disliked, with Taylor, whom he admired partly due to his status as a bona fide hero from World War II. From this point forward, Taylor, along with Walt Rostow, and Ambassador Frederick Nolting and his successor Henry Cabot Lodge Jr., became the chief proponents of escalating American involvement in Vietnam.

Robert McNamara, who would soon come to question the American entanglement in Vietnam, was positively buoyant about American prospects in Vietnam in 1962. In May, following a two-day visit where he explored the Vietnamese countryside, McNamara proclaimed, "I've seen nothing but progress and hopeful indications of further progress." Pressed by journalist Neil Sheehan to speak candidly off the record, the secretary of defense coldly stared at the reporter and observed, "Every quantitative measure we have shows we're winning this war." He repeated this rosy take in July, noting that he had seen "tremendous progress to date."[55] But at some point in 1963, it became apparent that McNamara's doubts about Vietnam were, to borrow a favored term from that era, escalating.

Senator Mike Mansfield remained skeptical about the buoyant assessments coming from the Pentagon and the American embassy in Saigon. Mansfield submitted a report about his trip to South Vietnam to the president on December 18, 1962, and then traveled to Palm Beach, Florida the day after Christmas to discuss his report with the president. Kennedy wasted little time and questioned Mansfield "minutely," revealing a "tremendous grasp of the situation." Mansfield's message to Kennedy was remarkably blunt: "Going to war fully by ourselves against the guerillas" and creating "some form of neocolonial rule in South Vietnam" was a course of action "I most emphatically do not recommend." South Vietnam, according to the majority leader, was neither an "essential" nor "vital" interest to the United States, but as the administration was increasingly inclined to label it as such, they were on a dangerous course of deepening American involvement. If American policymakers stopped overinflating South Vietnam's status, "we may well discover that it is in our interests to do less rather than more than we are now doing." By stepping back and acknowledging that South Vietnam was of little strategic import, Mansfield reiterated that it would be "in our interests to do less rather than more." It would follow then that the US should pursue a diplomatic settlement to the conflict that would be "designed to lighten our commitments."[56]

Kennedy initially rebuffed Mansfield's gloomy assessment and made it clear that it ran contrary to everything he was hearing from members of his own administration. Kennedy seemed almost offended by Mansfield's skepticism, prompting the majority leader to retort, "You asked me to go out there," leading Kennedy to concede that he would "read it [the report] again." But Mansfield was satisfied that "at least he got the truth as I saw it and it wasn't a pleasant picture that I had depicted for him." Kennedy aide Kenneth O'Donnell later recalled the president saying, "I got angry with Mike for disagreeing with our policy so completely, and I got angry with myself because I found myself agreeing with him."[57]

Mansfield's pessimism seemed borne out by a battlefield disaster that occurred less than seventy-two hours into the new year. The battle of Ap Bac on January 2 and 3, 1963, was designed to prove to the Viet Cong and their North Vietnamese benefactors that the Army of the Republic of Vietnam (ARVN) was capable of fighting and winning. As American advisors looked on, South Vietnamese forces allowed a large enemy force to slip away after the ARVN commander thought better of further committing his men to a battle where they might suffer substantial casualties. President Diem tended to punish Vietnamese generals whose forces suffered high casualties, thereby encouraging risk aversion to be the centerpiece of ARVN combat doctrine. One of Kennedy's key State Department officials, Roger Hilsman, was in Saigon at the time, and reported to the president that Ap Bac "was a stunning defeat," although General Paul Harkins, in charge of the Military Assistance Command–Vietnam (MACV), publicly declared, "I consider it a victory. We took the objective."[58]

Despite inflicting minimal casualties on the Viet Cong, three American advisors were killed at Ap Bac, and five helicopters, whose introduction was supposed to tip the scales in favor of the ARVN, were shot down and another nine were damaged.[59] In the midst of the official declarations of "victory," reporters such as David Halberstam and Neil Sheehan began to file jaundiced reports of the situation on the ground. Sheehan reported in the *Washington Post* after the battle at Ap Bac that "angry United States military advisers charged today that Vietnamese infantrymen refused direct orders to advance during Wednesday's battle at Ap Bac and that an American Army captain was killed while out front pleading with them to attack."[60] Key members of MACV grew increasingly frustrated with skeptical American news coverage, including General Harkins, who would later observe of David Halberstam's reporting that "Halberstam was a Jew, and he didn't like Diem" because of the latter's Catholicism.[61]

President Kennedy struck an optimistic tone regarding Vietnam in his State of the Union Address on January 14, 1963. "A settlement, though still precarious, has been reached in Laos," Kennedy declared to the nation, while "the spear-point of aggression has been blunted in Viet-Nam." The Pentagon continued to be a font of optimistic assessments, with the word "victory" (Kennedy defined victory as winning the war, containing the communists, and bringing American forces home) being tossed around loosely by officials who refused to listen to dissenting voices.[62] Army Chief of Staff Earle Wheeler reported that some eight million South Vietnamese were "safely tucked away" in hamlets protected by South Vietnamese forces, while those same forces were killing an average of three thousand Viet Cong guerrillas each month. These figures provided by the ARVN leadership were entirely fictional but often warmly welcomed by policymakers nine thousand miles away in Washington.[63]

Meanwhile, other critics of the war, including Army Lieutenant Colonel John Paul Vann, often found their pragmatic assessments dismissed by General Harkins and his command staff in Saigon. Vann worked closely with the South Vietnamese army and watched the entire disaster at Ap Bac unfold from an aircraft circling the battlefield. He later made the "mistake" of calling the event "a miserable damn performance." Vann was furious over what he considered to be falsified reports sent from Saigon to President Kennedy. After Ap Bac, Vann was allowed nowhere near General Harkins or the command center and was soon sent back to Washington and assigned to a desk job in the Pentagon.

Back in Washington, Vann persisted in lobbying on behalf of a realistic assessment of the South Vietnamese military and an acknowledgment of the corrupt nature of the Diem regime. He found some allies, including New Frontiersman Roswell Gilpatric, but his efforts to provide an unvarnished briefing to the Joint Chiefs of Staff were blocked by one of the biggest cheerleaders for continuation of the status quo, the chairman of the Joint Chiefs, Maxwell Taylor. A frustrated Vann resigned from the Army in July 1963 but continued to speak out against the misinformation surrounding the nation's efforts in Vietnam.[64]

During the summer of 1963, acts of civil disobedience by Vietnamese Buddhists complicated matters for both Diem and Kennedy. President Diem was a Catholic in a nation that was only 10 percent Catholic, and his policies and personnel appointments benefitted his Catholic brethren and slighted the nation's Buddhist majority. The trouble began in the ancient imperial capital of Hue, where Diem's brother served as the Catholic archbishop. The anniversary of the archbishop's ordination was publicly celebrated, while Buddhist attempts to celebrate Buddha's birthday were prohibited. Protests ensued and government forces killed nine protestors and beat hundreds of others with clubs.[65]

This event, and other acts of civil disobedience throughout the long hot summer of 1963, drove many American policymakers to consider removing Diem, whose authoritarian actions were seen as playing right into the hands of the Viet Cong. Diem was greatly influenced by his brother Ngo Dinh Nhu, who directed South Vietnam's security forces, and he in turn was influenced by his formidable wife, Madame Nhu, who also acted as the nation's First Lady. The Nhus were a power couple in the truest sense of the word; Machiavellian to the core, they concealed plots within plots.

Madame Nhu mocked a Buddhist monk who immolated himself in front of a crowd while protesting her brother-in-law's government on June 11, 1963 (the most significant day of Kennedy's presidency: it witnessed this event, the showdown in the schoolhouse door in Alabama, and JFK's address to the nation on civil rights). Kennedy responded to the photo of the burning monk by noting, "No news picture in history has generated as much emotion around the world as that one has." Madame Nhu referred to the highly publicized act as a "barbecue . . . with imported gasoline," invited American reporters to barbecue themselves, and encouraged dissenters to engage in further acts of immolation. "Let them burn and we shall clap our hands," she noted gleefully. Both Nhus rejected any compromise with South Vietnamese dissidents (although Ngo Dinh Nhu may have been secretly negotiating with the North Vietnamese and Viet Cong), and for all practical purposes they controlled President Diem, who was as far removed from the "Winston Churchill of Southeast Asia" as one could get.[66]

"No Nhus is Good News"

On August 21, 1963, President Diem declared martial law, which his brother enforced with a level of alacrity seldom seen in combat operations against the Viet Cong. Several Buddhist monks were killed during these raids and hundreds were arrested. The Diem administration persisted in conducting these raids despite American protests, and even over the objections of Madame Nhu's own father, who served as the South Vietnamese ambassador to the United States. Madame Nhu's father resigned in protest, arguing that there was no chance to save the republic while the Diem brothers controlled his country.

Ambassador Nolting had been a consistent supporter of Diem, but his pleas for restraint were rebuffed by the South Vietnamese president, who persisted in following the advice of his brother and sister-in-law. Diem had assured Nolting that he would halt his crackdown against the Buddhists, but instead the crackdown intensified.[67] The president removed Ambassador Nolting the same month the crackdown against the Buddhists began, replacing him with Kennedy's former senatorial opponent from Massachusetts, Henry Cabot Lodge Jr., who was Richard Nixon's running mate in 1960. The new ambassador was selected because of his known hostility to Diem's "police state administration," as he described it, and to give American policy in Vietnam a bipartisan character.[68]

Ambassador Lodge and other high-ranking administration officials concluded that Diem was not salvageable, that he was an authoritarian and, to make matters worse, an incompetent one at that. The key proponents of the "anybody but Diem" coalition were Averell Harriman; Harriman's protégé Michael Forrestal, the son of the nation's first secretary of defense, who served as an Asian specialist for the National Security Council; and Roger Hilsman, the assistant secretary of state for Far Eastern affairs. The latter became the driving force behind the effort to convince Diem to expel the destructive husband-and-wife team from his inner circle and, if Diem balked at this, to remove Diem as well.

On Friday, August 23, 1963, a group of South Vietnamese generals informed the US embassy that they were planning a coup against Diem. The next day, Harriman, Forrestal, and Hilsman made their move, contacting the president in Hyannisport and reaching out to other senior officials seeking approval for a message to Lodge to withdraw American support for Nhu and if necessary Diem as well. The cable stated that the American government could not tolerate a "situation in which power lies in Nhu's hands." It added, "Diem must be given a chance to rid himself of Nhu and his coterie," but if he remained "obdurate and refuses," then "we must face the possibility that Diem himself cannot be preserved." Ambassador Lodge responded quickly to the cable, noting that the chances of Diem meeting the American demands were "virtually nil" and suggesting that his embassy team begin to "go straight to [the] Generals with our demands, without informing Diem.

Would tell them we [are] prepared [to] have Diem without Nhus but it is in effect up to them whether to keep him."[69]

The president discussed this information and the broader situation in Vietnam with his national security team that Monday. Dean Rusk noted the gloomy prospects for stabilizing the "internal" situation in South Vietnam, and the likelihood that Diem and Nhu would not change their ways. "We're on the road to disaster," the normally mild-mannered Rusk observed. The only way out would be to "take it by our choice," apparently meaning to get rid of Diem promptly, "or be driven out by a complete deterioration of the situation in Vietnam, or move in such forces as would involve our taking over the country."

To the dismay of Lodge and others, the prospects for a successful coup quickly dissipated, and by the end of the week the plotters had abandoned their scheme.[70] Robert Kennedy had immediately engaged with the Vietnam issue after getting wind of the August 24 cable, and he alternated back and forth between staying the course in Southeast Asia, or, as he put it in his usual blunt manner, if there was simply no South Vietnamese government willing to fight to win, perhaps "now was the time to get out of Vietnam entirely, rather than waiting."[71]

On September 2, 1963, President Kennedy helped Walter Cronkite launch his newly expanded half-hour news broadcast with an interview on the lawn of "Brambletyde," a rented home a mile from the Kennedy compound that had the benefit of additional privacy and enhanced security. The president and First Lady had recently lost a child, Patrick Bouvier Kennedy, who lived for thirty-nine hours, passing away on August 9.[72] Patrick's death reinforced the First Lady's predisposition to shield her family, and this, plus the fact that she sought to distance herself from the chaotic atmosphere of Robert Kennedy's home at the compound, led to the choice of the hideaway.

Walter Cronkite was prompted by White House Press Secretary Pierre Salinger to ask Kennedy questions about Vietnam during the interview at Brambletyde. While the newscaster bridled at being managed by the White House, Cronkite ultimately did ask Kennedy about the situation in Southeast Asia. Determined to reinforce the message to the South Vietnamese military and to Diem himself, Kennedy noted, "I don't think that unless a greater effort is made by the Government to win popular support that the war can be won out there. In the final analysis, it is their war. They are the ones who have to win it or lose it. We can help them, we can give them equipment, we can send our men out there as advisers, but they have to win it—the people of Viet-Nam—against the Communists." Kennedy added that the United States was "prepared to continue to assist them, but I don't think that the war can be won unless the people support the effort, and, in my opinion, in the last two months the Government has gotten out of touch with the people." Kennedy hoped that it would "become increasingly obvious to the Government, that they will take steps to try to bring back popular support for this very essential struggle." He was cautiously optimistic that the South Vietnamese government would regain the support of its people, "with changes in policy and perhaps with personnel." Absent those changes, "the chances of winning . . . would not be very good."[73]

On September 6, Marine Corps general Victor Krulak and State Department official Joseph Mendenhall paid a whirlwind visit to South Vietnam, with both men briefing the president on their return four days later. Krulak presented an optimistic account of the durability of the Diem government and American prospects in Vietnam, while Mendenhall was decidedly pessimistic about the stability of the South Vietnamese government and the prospects for defeating the Viet Cong. Mendenhall noted, "The people I talked to in the government, when I asked them about the war against the VC, they said that is secondary now—our first concern is, in effect, in a war with the regime here in Saigon." The president, upon hearing these completely divergent assessments, asked, "The two of you did visit the same country, didn't you?" It was this meeting where Rufus Phillips, a counterinsurgency expert who had spent years in South Vietnam, broke with the bureaucratic tradition of dissembling and frankly informed the president that America was losing in Vietnam. Phillips later recalled that it was Michael Forrestal and Roger Hilsman who "corralled" him into attending this meeting. It was an auspicious move by these critics of Diem and his American supporters. Phillips bluntly told Kennedy, "I am sorry to have to tell you Mr. President, but we are not winning the war, particularly in the [Mekong] Delta." General Krulak was not amused, nor was Secretary McNamara, who the "whole time I was talking . . . was sitting there beside the President shaking his head."

Phillips further angered the Pentagon's optimists by noting, "When someone says that this is a military war and that this is a military judgment, I don't believe you can say this about this war. This is essentially a political war . . . for men's minds."[74] It was to Kennedy's credit that he understood the pathologies endemic to large bureaucracies and sought out dissenting voices, including allowing the participation of a mid-level civil servant in such a high-level meeting.

The conflicting viewpoints presented at the September 10 meeting led to the dispatch of another mission to Saigon, this time consisting of Secretary McNamara and General Maxwell Taylor. This mission departed on September 23, 1963, and was perhaps designed to convince two of Kennedy's more hawkish advisors of the dire situation in Vietnam. As a result, Kennedy slighted the State Department by selecting lower-level officials to accompany the secretary of defense and the chairman of the Joint Chiefs. An angry Roger Hilsman protested the hawkish, pro-Diem composition of the mission, prompting an even angrier Kennedy to silence Hilsman by noting, "I know all this Roger . . . I know all this. But we've got to keep the Joint Chiefs on board. . . . The only way we can keep the Chiefs on board is to keep McNamara on board and he wants to go. . . . That's the price we have to pay to keep the government together."[75]

As the authors of the *Pentagon Papers* would later observe, the McNamara and Taylor mission fell into a trap that marred previous high-level visits and would do so again in the future. "It is hard to believe that hasty visits by harried high-level officials with overloaded itineraries really add much in the way of additional data or lucid insight. And because they become a focal point of worldwide press coverage, they often raise public expectations or anxieties that may only create additional problems for the President."[76] However, one benefit from the McNamara and Taylor mission was that both men began to see through the rose-colored accounts provided by South Vietnamese and American officials and grasp that, as far as the political situation stood in 1963, South Vietnam was an unstable mess.

Nevertheless, the two men were less inclined to see the security situation in dire terms, arguing that the "military campaign has made great progress and continues to progress." The mission's report, released to Congress and the public, was a perfect specimen of bureaucratic politics, of "satisficing," of choosing a course of action minimally acceptable to all parties rather than an optimal course. Optimistic passages acceptable to those hoping Diem would see the light and hold on to power, were offset by more pessimistic comments expressing disappointment at Diem's failure to act and hinting at his removal. The withdrawal of one thousand US forces by the close of 1963 and the completion of America's military role by the end of 1965 were also added to the mix. The report had something for all the contending parties to cheer, including the small number of dissenters in Congress calling for withdrawal, but the essence of the report was to simply kick the can beyond the 1964 presidential election. President Kennedy approved McNamara's and Taylor's recommendations on October 5, 1963, which coincided with the day another Buddhist monk immolated himself on a Saigon street. This was the sixth monk since June to have taken his life in protest and reinforced the growing sentiment in Washington that "No Nhus is good news."[77]

Kennedy hoped that Diem's removal would restore some semblance of competence and reality to the Presidential Palace in Saigon, but if the coup succeeded and its leaders went on to fail, he would have reexamined America's commitment and likely decided to cut American losses. James K. Galbraith, whose father served as an ambassador for President Kennedy, has argued that in October 1963, John F. Kennedy "had formally decided to withdraw from Vietnam, whether we were winning or not. Robert McNamara, who did not believe we were winning, supported this decision. The first stage of withdrawal had been ordered. The final date, two years later, had been specified. These decisions were taken, and even placed, in an oblique and carefully limited way, before the public."[78]

Galbraith's view, which is supported by the work of scholars John M. Newman and Howard Jones, deserves greater attention than it receives.[79] Critics have condemned it as "Camelot-mythmaking," but the documentary evidence and presidential recordings make for a compelling case.[80] After a series of contentious meetings at the White House during the first week of October 1963, the secretary of defense, at the direction of the president, ordered the planning for the removal of one thousand American soldiers from South Vietnam by December 31, 1963, and a complete withdrawal by December 31, 1965. McNamara later noted that "the President endorsed our recommendation to withdraw 1,000 men . . . because objections had been so intense and because I suspected others might try to get him to reverse the decision, I urged him to announce it publicly. That would set it in concrete."[81] This was not, as some have argued, a bargaining chip to force Diem to reform his ways; the withdrawal order was not contingent on the situation on the ground. During one of the meetings, McNamara stated, "We need a way out of Vietnam, and this is a way of doing it." As McNamara prepared to brief reporters to announce the withdrawal timetable, President Kennedy caught the secretary just before he began his briefing and said, "Tell them that means all the helicopter pilots too." For both domestic political reasons and to avoid influencing internal affairs in South Vietnam, the initial withdrawal was to be a low-key affair without any bands or fanfare.[82]

It is my belief that those scholars who promote the October 1963 withdrawal thesis are correct in their conclusion that Kennedy had decided to withdraw from Vietnam. This thesis is in accord with Kennedy's aversion to armed conflict and with the president's determination to pursue détente with the Soviet Union, as outlined in his American University address of June 1963. All that stood in the way of this, it was thought, was the 1964 election where Kennedy would be attacked from the Right for his "appeasement" of communism. If he could win that fight, his second term held the promise of significant foreign policy corrections.

As historian Howard Jones has noted, on Thursday, November 21, 1963, Michael Forrestal spoke with the president just before his departure for Texas. Kennedy told him, "I want you to come and see me because we have to start to plan for what we are going to do now in South Vietnam. I want to start a complete and very profound review of how we got into this country, and what we thought we were doing, and what we now think we can do. I even want to think about whether or not we should be there." The forthcoming election prevented any "drastic changes of policy, quickly," but Kennedy wanted to consider "how some kind of a gradual shift in our presence in South Vietnam [could] occur."[83]

While much has been made of the Kennedy administration's role in removing Diem, encouraging various ARVN Generals to proceed with this coup required little effort. The generals had been ready to do this for some time, and the temptation in Washington to act in the face of Diem's repeated intransigence and inept governance was irresistible. American lives and treasure had been sacrificed to bolster a government which acted as if the United States were an interloper. Without American assistance, Diem would have been executed in the courtyard of the Presidential Palace by the Viet Cong rather than killed in the back of an armored personnel carrier by his own military. He never grasped this cold, hard truth.

Throughout the month of October, the American embassy in Saigon and policymakers in Washington cabled one another with conflicting assessments regarding the odds of a successful coup, expressing concern over protecting the "plausible deniability" of the president. If the attempt failed, it was possible that Diem might expel the United States from Vietnam. As

Robert Kennedy put it, "This risks so much . . . if it fails, Diem throws us out." At one point, President Kennedy echoed the same argument, noting, "If we miscalculate, we could lose our entire position in Southeast Asia overnight."[84]

Comments from Kennedy such as these render my thesis that a full withdrawal was likely to occur after the 1964 election problematic. However, Kennedy was not above playing the role of devil's advocate by injecting statements like this into a discussion for purposes of generating a response. He may have also been making a statement designed to resonate with a particular member of his audience. Additionally, this was a president who was always pushing the envelope in terms of weighing all the angles. This could be a case of Kennedy attempting to encourage dissenting voices in the room to speak up, a tactic he often employed when dealing with issues where he was so obviously conflicted.

Despite the arguments of critics both then and now who are convinced of American omnipotence, the Diem coup, which was both encouraged and discouraged by American officials depending on which day you choose to examine, was for the most part an indigenous South Vietnamese affair. This was not a repeat of the Bay of Pigs, in which the planning, training, and resources were all made in America. The White House was fairly consistent on this point, instructing Lodge on the eve of the coup that he was to "reject appeals for direct intervention from either side . . . aircraft and other resources will not be committed . . . without authorization from Washington. But once a coup under responsible leadership has begun, and within these restrictions," it was in the interest of the US government that it succeed.[85]

The coup against Diem occurred on November 1, 1963, despite continued misgivings in Washington about its prospects for success. As the authors of the *Pentagon Papers* would later note, "the coup itself was executed with skill and swiftness," one of the few times that description was bestowed on the South Vietnamese military. The coup plotters secured the Presidential Palace that day, but Diem and his brother managed to flee the palace grounds through an underground tunnel, evading capture until early on the morning of November 2. Allowing the brothers to flee the country and live their lives in exile was not a priority for the coup plotters, although there seems to have been an assumption on the part of some Americans that this is how the coup would unfold. Nevertheless, President Diem and his brother were murdered by South Vietnamese soldiers who shot and stabbed them multiple times while their hands were tied behind their backs in an American-made armored personnel carrier.

An apparently shaken President Kennedy abruptly left a meeting with his national security team after he was handed a cable sent by Ambassador Lodge containing the news that the brothers were dead. Maxwell Taylor muttered under his breath, "What did he expect?" A few days later, on November 8, 1963, the United States government formally recognized the new military regime in Saigon.[86]

"We're Not Going to Have Three Hundred Thousand Men in Asia"

It would become part of the conventional narrative, particularly in conservative circles and among supporters of President Richard Nixon, that the Kennedy administration's support for the coup against President Diem on November 1, 1963, marked a fatal turning point in America's involvement in Vietnam. This narrative claimed that Diem was the only person capable of governing South Vietnam. In order to come to this conclusion, one has to ignore the record of the South Vietnamese government and its woeful military throughout 1963. Diem had alienated every constituency in Vietnam except the Catholic minority that he and his corrupt brother bought through an array of preferential policies. While President Diem himself may have been a feckless but somewhat clean leader, his brother and sister-in-law were the personification of corruption leavened by a heavy dose of authoritarian, one might even say borderline totalitarian, excess. This was a government that refused to truly fight for its independence, or to accord the majority of its citizens any sense of belonging to the new republic.

The notion that South Vietnam could have been saved if Diem had been left in place is a fantasy used to justify the misguided policies that were enacted by Kennedy's successors Lyndon Johnson and Richard Nixon, and by an array of diplomats and generals who presided over this epic disaster. Diem's regime was out of control throughout 1963, with looming (non-American-sponsored) conspiracies to remove him from office hatched by his own military, including the plot previously mentioned that percolated in late August 1963 but was quickly aborted. Diem had also lost the confidence of South Vietnam's civilian political leadership, to the extent that this entity existed.[87] This was an isolated president increasingly detached from reality, egged on by a conniving brother and his Rasputin-like wife.

The war in Vietnam War was lost regardless of whether Ngo Dinh Diem stayed in place or not. Kennedy's "green light" for the coup was designed to install a more competent government with broader public support, but instead it led to further instability and popular disenchantment. At the point at which that became clear, which was after his death, Kennedy would likely have cut his losses, rather than taken over a war that he believed "in the final analysis" was "their war." It was Lyndon Johnson's decision to completely Americanize the war, or as Dean Rusk bluntly put it, "tak[e] over the country," that turned it into an American quagmire.

When Lyndon Johnson took the first steps toward Americanization of the struggle in March 1965 by deploying American combat troops to Vietnam, John F. Kennedy had been dead for sixteen months. That decision, along with Johnson's push for the Gulf of Tonkin Resolution in August 1964, was the tipping point. The Gulf of Tonkin Resolution provided the legal cover Johnson felt he needed to expand the war, and this occurred nine months after Kennedy's death. Considering the speed with which American policy evolved in Vietnam, nine months, certainly sixteen months, was the equivalent of a lifetime, and to assume that Kennedy would have followed a similar course of action is the height of speculative folly. Up until the day he died, Kennedy was doing everything he could, for better or worse, to minimize the American footprint. His critics cannot, or at least should not, be allowed to have it both ways—that he did not do enough to win the war, but that he also did too much to expand it.

It is possible that a reelected Kennedy might have pursued some type of covert campaign against the Viet Cong and the North Vietnamese and continued to provide economic assistance and military supplies to the South. It is also possible that he would have persisted in a kind of rhetorical barrage against communist nationalist movements in Southeast Asia of the type he engaged in with Cuba. This is plausible, as John F. Kennedy was no George McGovern, and the Democratic Party had not moved leftward yet on the Cold War. But there would not have been close to 550,000 troops in Vietnam by the time a reelected John F. Kennedy watched his successor take the oath of office in January 1969.

The argument for continuity between Kennedy's and Johnson's Vietnam policies hinges primarily on the fact that Johnson kept Kennedy's national security team in place. But this ignores one glaring absence from that team: President Kennedy. Johnson believed he was continuing Kennedy's policies in Vietnam, but when Kennedy was killed, the Rubicon had yet to be crossed. The notion that this president, who cut his losses at the Bay of Pigs, opted to neutralize Laos, settled with Khrushchev over the status of Berlin in 1961, made significant concessions to Khrushchev during the Cuban missile crisis, and negotiated the Nuclear Test Ban Treaty with the Russians in 1963, intended to Americanize the war in Vietnam requires something beyond a leap of faith. As James K. Galbraith observes, Kennedy "subordinated the timing of these events [gradual disengagement] to politics: he was quite prepared to leave soldiers in harm's way until after his own reelection. His larger goal after that was to settle the Cold War, without either victory or defeat—a strategic vision laid out in JFK's commencement speech at American University on June 10, 1963."[88]

Galbraith's assumption, and mine, that Kennedy would not have Americanized the war, is not, to borrow a word from another foreign policy fiasco, "a slam dunk." But the evidence seems to indicate that Kennedy would have followed a different path than Lyndon Johnson, and in fact had begun to do so in October 1963. The most striking feature from Kennedy's brief presidency was his aversion to an overt, traditional American combat presence in Vietnam. He has been widely criticized for this from conservative critics who viewed his halting actions in that nation, and elsewhere as well, as contributing to the failure of the Diem regime to quell the insurgency. Tougher, more overt actions, this critique goes, including combat troops and air strikes against the North, conducted at this time, would have prevented the war from becoming the long, inconclusive slog that it became. The American war in Vietnam, according to these critics, was lost between 1961 and 1965. Had Kennedy and Lyndon Johnson acted in a more decisive and ruthless manner the way Richard Nixon did between 1970 and early 1973, using heavy bombers against the North, attacking sanctuaries in Laos and Cambodia, mining Haiphong harbor, the Vietnam War would have evolved differently. This is a legitimate argument to make, and one that this author has made in the past.

But this was not Kennedy's way, which makes it even more difficult to believe that he would have ignored George Ball's warning and deployed hundreds of thousands of American troops to fight in Vietnam. Ball had warned in 1961 that three hundred thousand men would be necessary to quell the insurgency; instead, President Johnson sent over five hundred and thirty-six thousand troops by 1968. Kennedy reacted sharply to Ball's prediction with the comment, "George, you're just crazier than hell! This decision doesn't mean that. We're not going to have three hundred thousand men in Asia."[89]

As noted, several credible scholars and prominent American policymakers have taken it as a given that Lyndon Johnson's policies in Vietnam were simply an extension of Kennedy's policies. While Kennedy's grasp of international affairs was far greater than Johnson's, and his interest in those affairs was far greater as well, the policies of the two presidents are frequently lumped together for convenience under the label "Kennedy and Johnson." This view is shared by scholars on the Far Left such as Noam Chomsky and legions of critics on the Right who accuse both men of pursuing synonymous policies. President Johnson encouraged this take by claiming that he was merely continuing Kennedy's policies in Vietnam. One of Johnson's key advisors during the war, Walt Rostow, repeatedly emphasized the continuity of policy between Kennedy and Johnson. Journalist and historian Stanley Karnow reinforced this theme in his critically acclaimed *Vietnam: A History* (1983), arguing that when Johnson succeeded Kennedy in the White House, he "essentially signaled a continuation of Kennedy's policy" in Vietnam.[90]

Even Robert Kennedy provided ammunition for those arguing that Johnson did exactly what John F. Kennedy would have done. In a 1964 oral history interview, Bobby Kennedy answered "no" to the question of whether President Kennedy considered pulling out of Vietnam, and "yes" to the statement that President Kennedy was convinced we "had to stay in there" and "couldn't lose it." (It should be noted that Robert Kennedy was determined to remain politically viable at the time of this interview, and went to great lengths not to alienate Lyndon Johnson, especially in 1964 when he hoped to be selected as a vice presidential running mate. It was not until 1967 that Kennedy began to move decisively to break with Johnson over Vietnam). But at the same time, Robert Kennedy answered "no" to the question of whether President Kennedy's was planning on "going all in." He added, "everybody including General MacArthur felt that land conflict between our troops, white troops and Asian, would only . . . end in disaster. . . . We went in as advisers, but to try to get the Vietnamese to fight themselves, because we couldn't win the war for them. They had to win the war for themselves."[91]

In dealing with Vietnam, and other issues, Kennedy compartmentalized matters in a way that elicits comparisons to Thomas Jefferson or Franklin Roosevelt, men who kept those around them intentionally off balance, calculated every decision through a political lens, and often deceived those closest to them.[92] John M. Newman argues that Kennedy deceived members of his own administration and members of Congress, not to mention the American public, regarding his intentions in Vietnam.[93] For instance, Kennedy claimed that the October 1963 withdrawal order was the result of improved performance of the South Vietnamese military, which he knew was not the case.[94] This tactic of keeping his advisors off-balance was second nature to Franklin Roosevelt, as it was for Kennedy. Two of these presidents deceived their wives for years, while Jefferson lived a "forbidden" life atop his mountain hideaway for decades. These men tended to be conflict averse and preferred surrogates to conduct the rough and tumble business of politics for them. For the most part, Kennedy does not belong in the same category as Thomas Jefferson or Franklin Roosevelt except for this shared complexity of character. But this complexity makes the crudely simplistic assumption that Kennedy would have followed the same path as Lyndon Johnson the least credible speculation of all.

But this we know from the record: John F. Kennedy was a conflict-averse commander in chief who agonized over the prospect of mass casualties. At the height of the Cuban missile crisis, when he was badly outnumbered by his hawkish advisors urging some type of military response, Kennedy noted acerbically, "We all know how quickly everybody's courage goes when the blood starts to flow."[95] To believe that Kennedy would have stayed the course in Vietnam as body bags began arriving first by the tens and then by the hundreds week after week in the latter half of the 1960s reveals a complete misunderstanding of the man.

7

No Assassins to the Left

When I was six years old and a student in the first grade, I overheard two of my teachers on November 22, 1963, discussing the shooting of the president as we waited to board our school buses to take us home. When I returned home, my mother was seated next to our television set monitoring the news from Dallas, and she was crying. On Sunday, November 24, 1963, I watched the same footage over and over of Dallas strip club owner Jack Ruby executing Lee Oswald (as he was known then; the "Harvey" became commonplace later) for killing President Kennedy or, as many believed, in order to silence him.

Just as Presidency Kennedy's policies have been distorted by ideologues hoping to advance their political agenda, so too has his death. The birth of modern America's obsession with conspiracy theories began at approximately 12:30 p.m. central standard time on November 22, 1963. Long before Donald Trump's presidency, an omnipotent "Deep State" was accused of being the perpetrator of one of the greatest crimes of the twentieth century. Trump himself would contribute to the endless proliferation of unsupported theories about Kennedy's killing, suggesting that the father of Senator Ted Cruz (R-TX) was one of Kennedy's murderers.

The Warren Commission's conclusion that Lee Harvey Oswald acted alone was accepted by 87 percent of Americans when the report was released on November 23, 1964. But decades of microscopic parsing of the commission's report, aided and abetted by the American government's effort to conceal Operation Mongoose, led to a complete turnaround in public support for the idea that a lone gunman killed Kennedy. On the fiftieth anniversary of Kennedy's murder, nearly two-thirds of the American public believed that Oswald was part of a broad conspiracy.[1]

Many of these conspiracy theories have withered away upon further review but are quickly replaced by others. The gunman or gunmen on the grassy knoll, the "Umbrella Man," the "Babushka Lady," "the Three Tramps," Oswald's body double, the gunman who popped out of a manhole cover in Dealey Plaza, the FBI, the CIA, Fidel Castro, organized crime, the KGB, the "military-industrial complex," Vice President Lyndon Johnson, an errant shot fired by a Secret Service agent in a follow-up vehicle, or the shot fired by the agent driving the president's limousine have all been part of the ever-shifting list of suspects of who killed Kennedy.

In addition to this infinite list of suspects, there are allegations that Kennedy's body was switched somewhere between Dallas and the site of his autopsy at the Bethesda Naval Hospital. As author Vincent Bugliosi has observed, "With both feet planted firmly in the air, the conspiracy theorists created a cottage industry that thrives to this very day, and whose hallmark, with noted exceptions, has been absurdity and silliness." There is simply no room in the conspiracy world for "mistakes, human errors, anomalies, or plain incompetence, though the latter, from the highest levels on down, is endemic in our society."[2]

The tragic event in Dallas would elevate conspiracy theories on the Left to something akin to a secular gospel. This development has been remarkably destructive, as it represents an abandonment of what Kennedy himself was scheduled to say at the Dallas Trade Mart on November 22, 1963. In his prepared remarks, the president noted that America must be "guided by the lights of learning and reason." And, he added, "but today other voices are heard in the land—voices preaching doctrines wholly unrelated to reality . . . we can hope that fewer people will listen to nonsense."

The Road to Dealey Plaza

It is ghoulishly fitting that John F. Kennedy was murdered in Dallas, Texas, a city that was and is a hotbed of conspiracy theorists. Dallas had approximately thirty-five chapters of the John Birch Society, whose members believed that Dwight Eisenhower and John F. Kennedy were communist agents seeking to subordinate American sovereignty to an international order, or to the Kremlin itself. Issues such as fluoridation of the water supply were seen as central to a plot to destroy America from within, a popular conspiracy theory Kennedy publicly condemned in 1961.[3]

These opinions were held not only by extremists on the fringes of society, but by Dallas's community leaders. President Kennedy referred to the city and its environs as "nut country," although Kennedy had in mind the Birchism that permeated Dallas's country clubs, segregated salons, and its main newspaper, not outliers like Lee Harvey Oswald, whose extremist views were of the left-wing variety.[4] As author Max Holland has noted, Oswald was "the only Marxist in a hundred-mile radius of Dealey Plaza," a fact that immediately raised doubts about his culpability for the president's murder.[5]

The events of November 22, 1963, in Dallas hold an equivalent place in the American mind, for those of a certain age, to December 7, 1941, or September 11, 2001. Arguably, the Kennedy assassination shocked the American people even more than September 11, for never before had the nation been able to view, in close to real time, the shocking events as they unfolded. The major television networks of the day interrupted their regularly scheduled programming and stayed with the story over the course of that long, mournful weekend, something they had never done before. The American people were able to tune in and watch the aftermath of the tragedy play out, including the murder of Lee Harvey Oswald as the Dallas Police Department paraded him in front of the cameras once again, thereby earning the distinction of broadcasting the first murder ever committed on live television.

Jack Ruby's televised execution of Lee Harvey Oswald on November 24, 1963, launched a decades-long quest to uncover the "conspiracy" behind Kennedy's murder and that of his murderer. Something resembling a cottage industry formed around this assassination, with books, films, countless articles, and websites devoted to revealing the president's "real" killers. Over time, most Americans rejected the conclusion of the Warren Commission that Lee Harvey Oswald acted alone. On the fiftieth anniversary of the assassination in 2013, 61 percent of Americans believed that Oswald had not acted alone, concluding that the president was the victim of a conspiracy.[6] "Grassy knoll" quickly became a synonym for the subterfuge practiced by the "Deep State," while the "magic bullet" became the catchphrase for those dismissive of the idea that Lee Harvey Oswald acted alone.

Few Americans in November 1963 would have been familiar with the last successful presidential assassination which had occurred over sixty-two years earlier. The nation experienced a wave of grief after President William McKinley's murder, but what made John F. Kennedy's death especially hard to accept was the fact that it happened to such a young man who was murdered beside his thirty-four-year-old wife. The dead president left behind the nation's second youngest First Lady and two children, John, who turned three on November 25th, and Caroline, who turned six on November 27th.[7] The fact that the First Lady was even on this trip was unusual, since she tended to avoid the domestic political trips required of a president. That she witnessed the horror unfold at close range added to the tragedy of it all, and her ability to retain her poise and composure throughout the state funeral helped the nation deal with the trauma. It seemed almost superhuman that she was able to conduct herself the way she did while most of the world looked on.

The Cult of Conspiracy

Much of the blame for the proliferation of Kennedy conspiracy theories rests with Lyndon Johnson and his creation, the Warren Commission, officially known as "The President's Commission on the Assassination of President Kennedy." Johnson and the members of the commission were determined to protect certain covert operations authorized by President Kennedy that were still underway on November 22, 1963, particularly the effort to kill Castro. For this reason, coupled with Johnson's desire to prevent the emotional reaction to Kennedy's death from spiraling out of control and leading to war, the commission did its best to pin the blame on Oswald, where it rightly lay, while ignoring other avenues that might prove embarrassing to President Kennedy, Robert Kennedy, the FBI, and the CIA, or hint at possible Cuban or Russian involvement.

Lyndon Johnson feared that revelations of Cuban or Russian involvement in Kennedy's assassination would generate demands for retaliation that could lead to a nuclear exchange. While this concern may seem overwrought to modern Americans, it did not seem so in 1963, with Kennedy's death occurring barely a year after the Cuban missile crisis. President Johnson's concerns were legitimate.[8] As a result, the Warren Commission conducted an incomplete investigation with restrictions imposed on it, some externally imposed, others self-imposed. When these restrictions were later revealed, they fueled one of the most enduring conspiracy theories in American history.

Punching holes in the Warren Commission report requires little in the way of intellect or imagination, but naming President Kennedy's real killers presents a tougher challenge, although not for those with vivid imaginations. Some sixty years after the fact, no one has uttered a deathbed confession (with one possible hearsay exception), nor has anyone yet produced a credible suspect or suspects beyond "the CIA," "the Mafia," "disgruntled Cubans," and "the military-industrial complex." Most conspiracists are unwilling or unable to name names, although they have cited amorphous elements within various corporate, criminal, or government entities. The "Deep State" is a prime suspect, which is usually presented as a composite of the CIA, the FBI, and the National Security Agency, with other government entities added into the mix depending on the partialities of the conspiracy theorist.

This American "Deep State," which is accepted as an article of faith by President Donald Trump, was originally a favored theory on the American Left among those who believed Kennedy was the victim of a vast right-wing conspiracy. Oliver Stone's film *JFK* (1991) is perhaps one of the best examples of this perspective. Stone himself admitted that he was attempting to spin history, not report the facts of the matter. "I'm shaping history, to a degree," he observed on the set of the film. To clarify the point, in another venue he observed, "Who owns reality? Who owns our history? He who makes it up so that most everyone believes it. That person wins."[9] As Steven M. Gillon observed, Stone's movie "makes it seem that First Lady Jacqueline Kennedy was the only person in Dealey Plaza that day who was not planning to murder the President."[10] Another commentator captured the paranoia that dripped from the film: "It was hard to leave the theater without momentarily double-checking your own whereabouts on 22 November 1963."[11]

The following account of the various conspiracy theories in circulation is by no means a comprehensive listing of the sixty years' worth of "plots" circulated by those knowing that the name "Kennedy" continues to sell and that any material labeled "Kennedy assassination" has a devoted audience of cultists who will pay any price and bear any burden to purchase and disseminate the latest "revelation." It should be noted that conspiracy theorists tend to fall into two distinct ideological camps: those leaning in the conservative direction finger Castro and the KGB as suspects, while those on the left point to the US government, "right-wing Cubans," or an alliance of the latter with the mob. The Kennedy assassination is yet another victim of the hyperpolarization of America; one's ideological stance is a generally reliable predictor of who you think killed JFK.

The most credible conspiracy theories focus on the role of organized crime or of Cuban involvement, either those Cubans opposed to Castro and irked at the "surrender" at the Bay of Pigs, or those working for Castro. Some theorists combine the anti-Castro Cubans with organized crime, as the two shared the same goal of regime change in Cuba. The motive for those angry at Kennedy's "betrayal" of Brigade 2506 was clear enough, as the House Assassinations Select Committee, created in 1976, concluded. Formed in the wake of Vietnam and Watergate, when the United States government was considered untrustworthy at best, the committee concluded that Castro's Cuban opponents "had [the] motive." And they had "the means, since they were trained and practiced in violent acts," and had "the opportunity" since President Kennedy "appeared at public gatherings." Additionally, some of Lee Harvey Oswald's "associations . . . were, or may have been with anti-Castro activists."[12]

Oswald did know individuals who were anti-Castro around the same time he was distributing leaflets calling for "Hands off Cuba!" and seeking to form a New Orleans chapter of the "Fair Play for Cuba Committee," a chapter he created but whose only member was its founder. Yet Oswald also expressed interest at one point in aiding anti-Castro Cubans in New Orleans in their fight, as he told Carlos Bringuier, a New Orleans–based Cuban exile and anti-Castro activist. Bringuier came to believe that Oswald was seeking to infiltrate the anti-Castro community and that when the Oswald killed the President, he did so at Castro's behest.[13]

In Lee Harvey Oswald's fantasy world, a world without true friends or even lasting acquaintances, a world upon which this self-professed Marxist desperately sought to leave a mark, any human interaction was welcomed if he had an attentive audience. Infiltrating anti-Castro Cuban organization addressed his need for attention and his desire to become a figure of importance. Whether pro- or anti-Castro, the individuals Oswald interacted with were inclined toward zealotry, and their zeal was matched by a conviction that they were far better informed than their peers, although most were engaged in a constant struggle to maintain their sanity.

The idea that Fidel Castro got to Kennedy first is also widely accepted,

again mostly on the American Right, although Democrats who held important government positions and had some knowledge of Operation Mongoose
also belonged to this camp. Kennedy's successor in the White House, Lyndon Johnson, and his ally and mentor Senator Richard Russell (D-GA), a
member of the Warren Commission, believed Castro was behind Kennedy's
murder. Russell mentioned this to President Johnson in a recorded conversation between the two in 1964 while discussing the creation of the Warren
Commission.[14] On several occasions, Johnson claimed that "Kennedy tried
to kill Castro, but Castro got Kennedy first." Johnson had no inside information supporting this claim, other than the fact that he was well aware of
Operation Mongoose years before his fellow citizens.

The fact that the Kennedy administration's effort to eliminate Castro was
directed by his hated rival Robert Kennedy, the underboss of what Johnson
called a "Murder, Inc." in the Caribbean, was too tantalizing a piece of information for Johnson to keep from those he trusted, like Richard Russell.[15] It
may be, at the risk of engaging in armchair psychology, that Johnson took a
certain satisfaction from knowing the agony that Mongoose caused Robert
Kennedy.

Lyndon Johnson's conjecture was bolstered by the fact that Oswald visited
the Cuban and Soviet embassies in Mexico City in late September and early
October 1963. These visits ended in a refusal of his request to travel to Cuba,
where the soon-to-be assassin hoped to meet with Fidel Castro. Oswald even
told his wife that he might be able to secure an appointment in Castro's government. This is further evidence of the delusional state of this pathological
fantasist.[16]

Those who see a link between Castro and the assassination also refer to the
testimony of the American ambassador to Mexico in 1963, Thomas Mann.
The ambassador was convinced that Oswald was likely doing the bidding of
Cuban operatives he had met in Mexico City. When Mann was interviewed
by staff members for the Warren Commission in 1964, he told them that he
"still has the 'feeling in his guts' that Castro hired Oswald to kill Kennedy."
In 1977, Mann repeated this allegation to the House Select Committee on
Assassinations, a charge that was echoed by the CIA station chief in Mexico
City in 1963, Winston Scott, who believed that Oswald acted under the influence of a foreign power.[17] Mann and others who see Castro's hand in this cite
the dictator's interview with an Associated Press correspondent on September 7, 1963, in which he vowed to retaliate against American plots to kill him.

This was a clear warning to the Kennedy administration, as Castro pledged that "we are prepared to fight them and answer in kind." He added, "United States leaders should think that if they are aiding terrorist plans to eliminate Cuban leaders they themselves will not be safe."[18] Castro's remarks were widely reported by the New Orleans *Times-Picayune* during the time Oswald lived in that city, and he was apparently an avid reader of that newspaper.[19]

The notion of possible Cuba involvement was bolstered by the confession of Fiorentino Lombard, a former Cuban intelligence official who defected to the United States in 1987. Lombard told American officials that Castro was aware that Oswald told Cuban authorities on his visit to their embassy in Mexico City several weeks prior to the assassination that he intended to shoot the president. After being rejected in his request to visit Cuba, Oswald stormed out of the embassy saying he would kill Kennedy to prove his pro-Castro bona fides.

Author Brian Latell, a former CIA officer, noted in 2012 that Fiorentino Lombard claimed that he was instructed on the morning of Friday, November 22, 1963, to focus all of Cuba's listening devices on Texas. "Fidel knew of Oswald's intentions and did nothing to deter the act," Latell noted. Latell did not claim that Castro ordered the assassination, nor did he claim that Oswald was under his control. "He might have been," Latell noted, "but I don't argue that, because I was unable to find any evidence for that." Another source, a CIA spy, confirmed that Castro had told him Oswald had "stormed into the embassy, demanded the visa, and when it was refused to him headed out saying, 'I'm going to kill Kennedy for this.'"[20]

Author Philip Shenon, a former *New York Times* reporter, has tracked down several witnesses who claimed that Cuban intelligence operatives were more involved with the assassin in Mexico City in late September and early October 1963 than was previously believed. Shenon's book, *A Cruel and Shocking Act: The Secret History of the Kennedy Assassination* (2013) focused on discovering the truth behind Oswald's visit to Mexico City. Shenon noted that "Lee Harvey Oswald was invited by Silvia Duran [a Cuban embassy official] to a dance party in Mexico City attended by Cuban diplomats and spies, as well as Mexican supporters of Castro's government, and that some of the guests had spoken openly of their hope that someone would assassinate President John F. Kennedy, if only to ensure the survival of the revolution in Cuba that Kennedy had been so desperate to crush." "The fact is we saw Lee Harvey Oswald at the party," one witness told Shenon. "We met and saw and spoke with someone who then went and killed the President of the United States." According to Shenon, Oswald was more warmly received by the Cubans in Mexico City than the Castro government, and many members of the conspiracy movement, tend to acknowledge.[21] Nonetheless, Shenon has made it clear that "there is no credible evidence that Castro was involved personally in ordering the assassination."[22]

The suggestion that Castro or his intelligence operatives may have been involved in Kennedy's killing is rejected by left-leaning members of the conspiracy movement. They consider right-wing Cubans and American militarists as the only truly "legitimate" forces behind the Kennedy assassination. Brian Latell's and Philip Shenon's carefully researched work and their circumscribed assessment of Castro's role in the assassination—in other words, he and his intelligence service may have known it would happen, but Castro did not order it, nor do anything to stop it—has been rejected by some conspiracy activists simply on the ground that it offends their ideological inclinations.

The reluctance of the conspiracists to pursue the Castro angle is odd to say the least, as Oswald's trip to Mexico City several weeks before the assassination (not to mention the little over two years and seven months he spent in the Soviet Union) and his repeated effort to convince Cuban embassy officials to let him travel to Havana is more damning than many of the more popular theories circulating within the conspiracy movement. As journalist Ron Rosenbaum observes, authors like Philip Shenon point "to a far more salient reason for Oswald's act, one that most conspiracy theorists have shuddered at contemplating because they can't bear the idea that there might be even a hint of Cuban involvement."[23]

On multiple occasions, Fidel Castro went out of his way to deflect the blame for Kennedy's killing onto Cubans who opposed his regime, or on American government entities who worked to overthrow him. Even in the final years of his life, Castro would lecture visiting Americans about his and his intelligence service's innocence. As late as 2013, Castro noted, "There were people in the American government who thought Kennedy was a traitor because he didn't invade Cuba when he had the chance, when they were asking him. He was never forgiven for that."[24]

Scholars who study left-wing movements have noted a tendency within leftist movements to operate under the principle of "no enemies to the left." This statement has been attributed to the moderate socialists of the Russian

Revolution, some of whom had a blind spot when it came to the threat presented by the more extreme Bolsheviks in 1917. These organizational blind spots are rooted in loyalty to an ideology and can infect entire organizations or movements. It seems appropriate to borrow from this aphorism when analyzing the Kennedy conspiracy movement, in that "no assassins to the left" dominates the thinking of too many conspiracy activists. Fidel Castro, perhaps more than any other twentieth-century revolutionary, became an admired figure for many Western liberals, and the thought that he would do harm to another figure admired by many liberals was simply unfathomable.

James Pierson has argued, correctly, that if President Kennedy had been killed by a right-wing gunman, "there never would have been any serious speculation about conspiracies" if that right-winger's guilt "was confirmed by the same evidence as condemned Lee Harvey Oswald."[25] A right-wing Oswald would have fit within the Dallas as a "city of hate" template, and also within the larger compelling narrative that Jacqueline Kennedy had expressed—that if her husband had to be taken, it would be as a martyr for the cause of civil rights.

Fidel Castro or his operatives may not have ordered the hit on Kennedy, but Lee Harvey Oswald shot President Kennedy in defense of El Comandante. Despite Oswald's blatant fealty to Marxism, the "city of hate" template took root within hours of Kennedy's death. Television host David Brinkley proclaimed, "The act which killed the President was spawned out of bigotry and extremism." The authorized chronicler of the Kennedy assassination, William Manchester, named a key co-conspirator in the Kennedy assassination, the city of Dallas, composed of citizens who bore a "plural responsibility for the tragedy."[26] All of this even though no one was more out of step with the ethos of Dallas, Texas in November 1963 than the man who pulled the trigger, Lee Harvey Oswald.

"Like a Russian Matryoshka Doll"

While many conspiracy theorists are quick to dismiss allegations of foreign involvement, they are far less reticent when it comes to blaming domestic American sources as the key to unlocking the "mystery" of who killed Kennedy. American organized crime figures are frequently cited as prime suspects, and these figures certainly had the motive, the means, and the opportunity to kill the president. Robert Kennedy's Justice Department had aggressively pursued the mafia and did so despite the government recruiting some of the mob's leaders to eliminate Fidel Castro. Robert Kennedy's contempt for the mob was deep and abiding, as he made clear in 1960 when he wrote, "If we do not attack organized criminals with weapons and techniques as effective as their own, they will destroy us."[27]

Santo Trafficante Jr. from Florida, Carlos Marcello of New Orleans, and John Roselli, a former protégé of Al Capone who went on to manage affairs in Hollywood and Las Vegas, are all frequently mentioned as leading suspects in the assassination of the president. Roselli was involved in varying degrees with the CIA's efforts to kill Fidel Castro. Also, as many conspiracy theorists are quick to point out, Oswald's assassin Jack Ruby had ties to several shady crime figures, a somewhat common phenomenon in the world of "adult entertainment."

Another prominent organized crime figure mentioned as a possible suspect is Sam "Momo" Giancana of Chicago, who was sharing the same girlfriend with President Kennedy. Robert Kennedy had pursued Sam Giancana with a vengeance, as William Hundley, a Justice Department official, remembered. "Robert Kennedy was always out to get him. . . . He would raise hell about him. . . . Bobby pushed to get Giancana at any cost." Complicating all of this was the president's relationship with Judith Campbell Exner, who was also Giancana's mistress. When the FBI uncovered this information, it undoubtedly delighted J. Edgar Hoover, who brought it to the president's attention on March 22, 1962, at which point Kennedy terminated contact with Exner.[28] But the situation was even more complicated due to the CIA's recruitment of Giancana to assist in the effort to kill Castro. Nevertheless, the FBI pursued Giancana, even after the CIA had recruited him for "wet work" in Cuba. Both Giancana and John Roselli seemed to have concluded that their work for the CIA entitled them to a "get out of jail card."[29] The resentment these two allegedly felt when they discovered these cards were useless fueled their desire to "get even" with the Kennedys.

Teamsters Union president Jimmy Hoffa's ties to organized crime and his relationship with Trafficante and other mob bosses also offers a compelling angle for those contending that the mob murdered Kennedy. David Kaiser, in his reputable book *The Road to Dallas: The Assassination of John F. Kennedy* (2009), flatly concluded that the mob bosses recruited by the CIA turned on President Kennedy due to Robert Kennedy's "effort to put the mob out of business." In essence, Attorney General Kennedy's pursuit of these mobsters, coupled with his celebrated "war" with Jimmy Hoffa, led to the shooting of President Kennedy.

Lee Harvey Oswald was the perfect foil to carry out this plot, as his alleged Marxist inclinations threw investigators and the public off the trail of the real perpetrators. According to this account, in May 1963, a lawyer who represented both Hoffa and Trafficante, Frank Ragano, passed the word from Hoffa to Trafficante and Carlos Marcello that "it was time to execute the contract on President Kennedy." While the CIA did not kill President Kennedy, Kaiser argued, it created a web of underworld intrigue that led to Dallas and to Lee Harvey Oswald killing the president. Oswald was an "extraordinarily useful assassin" who was quickly silenced by Jack Ruby, making it "much harder for the truth to emerge."[30]

Those who believe organized crime killed the president rely heavily on Ragano's account from his memoir, *Mob Lawyer: Including the Inside Account of Who Killed Jimmy Hoffa and JFK* (1994). Ragano claimed that he served as Hoffa's liaison with the mobsters and that Trafficante personally confessed to him four days before the mob leader died in 1987 that he was behind the plot to kill Kennedy. G. Robert Blakey, who served as the counsel to the House Assassinations Committee, argued in 1994 that Ragano was credible: "I have carefully studied his story and I think he is telling it as he remembers it." Others are less certain, including Trafficante's widow and daughters, who claim Trafficante was in no condition to be riding around in a car with Ragano four days before he died.[31]

The essential elements of the plot outlined by David Kaiser and others were tentatively endorsed by the House Select Committee on Assassinations in 1979. The committee concluded that "President John F. Kennedy was probably assassinated because of a conspiracy. The committee is unable to identify the other gunman or the extent of the conspiracy." But while the committee suggested in its final report that President Kennedy was "probably" killed in a conspiracy, there was no evidence to support the claim that the CIA, the FBI, the Russians, the Cubans, or anti-Castro Cubans killed the president. But regarding the anti-Castro Cubans and organized crime, "the available evidence does not preclude the possibility that individual members may have been involved."[32]

The committee's suggestion of a conspiracy was based on the transmission from a Dallas motorcycle patrolman's radio microphone. The patrolman's radio switch remained stuck in an "on" position for some five minutes, and the sound was recorded by the Dallas Police Department. But as Gerald Posner has observed, the "evidence" was nothing but a jumble of static that experts claimed contained discernible "impulse patterns" that had a 50 percent chance of being gunfire (later upped to 95 percent), and as a result they concluded that four shots instead of three were fired at the president's motorcade, more than originally thought. If this evidence were true, then Lee Harvey Oswald did not act alone.[33]

These acoustic findings were later discredited due to forensic advances and to evidence indicating that this recording took place outside of Dealey Plaza, removed both in time and place from the shooting. The Dallas patrolman whose radio allegedly captured the "evidence" was denied permission to listen to the recording, which turned out to be likely from an entirely different vehicle.[34] It was apparent that some members of the committee, or their staffers, rushed to judgment on this "evidence" in their determination to discover a new "smoking gun."

The findings of the House Select Committee on Assassinations succeeded only in further muddying the waters surrounding the crime of the century. Author Ron Rosenbaum encapsulated the never-ending quest to bring closure to the Kennedy murder, and the inevitable disappointment that follows. As with "almost every other piece of 'definitive' evidence in the case," it ends up "lost in that limbo of ambiguity, that endless swamp of dispute that swallows up any certainty in the Kennedy case."[35] But for conspiracy devotees, there is always a new lead to pursue once older "leads" turn to dust.

Those who plumb the depths of the Kennedy assassination quickly discover there is no bottom. "Depths" is an inadequate word to describe the world inhabited by Lee Harvey Oswald, Jack Ruby, David Ferrie, Jim Garrison, and others figures from this vile saga. The ugliness of this world was best captured by the American novelist Don DeLillo, whose 1988 novel *Libra* evokes the tawdry underside of American life and Oswald's place within that underside. As one chronicler of the Kennedy conspiracy universe has observed, "There is a world within the world. That is the refrain that Don DeLillo weaves throughout his classic novel *Libra*; the real story is always just underneath the surface." The Kennedy case is "like a Russian matryoshka doll, it has stories nested within stories, small plots within larger."[36] This world consumes many of those who enter it, for the "real story" never emerges.

DeLillo's *Libra* posits that CIA and anti-Castro elements were plotting

Kennedy's death, and Oswald was caught up in these plans but did not deliver in the manner designed by two of the three main plotters. DeLillo noted at the time of *Libra*'s release that he considered Oswald to be the first of a new sort of assassin. "After Oswald, men in America were no longer required to lead lives of quiet desperation," a chillingly concise statement that is all too accurate.[37]

"History is the sum total of the things they're not telling us," DeLillo added in *Libra*, a book that at its core was about "unknowable plots being worked out in hidden corners."[38] DeLillo was haunted by the Kennedy assassination and gave a concise and compelling explanation as to why that event continues to stalk the American imagination. "I think that what's been missing since the assassination is a sense of coherent reality . . . We seem to have entered a world of randomness, confusion, even chaos. We're not agreed on the number of gunmen, the number of shots, the time span between shots, the number of wounds on the president's body, the size and shape of the wounds. . . . And, beyond this, I think we have developed a sense of the secret manipulation of history: documents lost or destroyed, official records sealed for 50 or 75 years, a number of extremely suggestive murders and suicides."[39]

As one of DeLillo's characters calmly observed in *Libra*, "Here is a crime that clearly yields material for deep interpretation." The persistence of the Kennedy assassination conspiracy complex reflects, as DeLillo once noted, "a particular type of nostalgia: the nostalgia for a master plan, the conspiracy which explains absolutely everything."[40] This complex emerges in the spotlight every November 22, as scholar Tim Cloward notes, although crowds come to Dallas "all year round" but "especially around November 22, when the conspiracy conventions convene." These conventions "have been reliable and steady business" in Dallas for decades. The participants at these conventions "take pains to honor the pantheon of earlier searchers, the giants upon whose shoulders they stand—people like Mark Lane. . . . whose 1966 book *Rush to Judgment* is generally credited with transforming JFK conspiracy talk from random chatter into the beginnings of a movement."[41]

The mysteries surrounding the events in Dealey Plaza are catnip for countless authors and website tinkerers, some of whom seamlessly segued from Dallas in November 1963 to another disastrous sunny day, this one in September 2001. Prominent members of the Kennedy conspiracy movement jumped on the 9/11 "truther" bandwagon, seeing both events as compelling evidence of the existence of the "Deep State." Author Jim Marrs's book *The*

Terror Conspiracy (2006) claimed that "in many ways, the aftermath of the 9/11 attacks fit the same template as the assassination of President Kennedy in 1963." As Jonathan Kay noted in his book on America's perennial penchant for conspiracy theories, those convinced that everyone from George W. Bush, the Israelis, Dick Cheney, Haliburton and assorted neoconservatives brought down the Twin Towers frequently engaged in flights of fancy regarding Dealey Plaza. "Scratch the surface of a middle-aged 9/11 Truther, and you are almost guaranteed to find a JFK conspiracist," Kay observed.[42] For those on the outer limits of the conspiracy movement, including followers of the extremist QAnon online movement, the existence of a nefarious "Deep State" is a given, but they also claim that John F. Kennedy Jr. did not die in a plane crash in 1999 but is alive and well in the Pittsburgh area and will reappear sometime soon.[43]

To the generation known as the Baby Boomers, a generation that happened to be demographically enormous, Kennedy's death represented the precise moment America lost its way. As Jim Marrs put it in his preface to his book *Crossfire: The Plot that Killed Kennedy* (2013), "Not only do I seek the killers of President Kennedy, I seek the persons who planned the probable coup against Camelot—those who killed the confidence and faith of the American people in their government and institutions."[44]

The desire to imbue Kennedy's murder with a deeper meaning clearly motivates the endless search for his "real killers." William Manchester, the author of *The Death of a President* (1967), perfectly summed up this quest:

If you put six million dead Jews on one side of a scale and on the other side put the Nazi regime—the greatest gang of criminals ever to seize control of a modern state—you have a rough balance: greatest crime, greatest criminals.

But if you put the murdered President of the United States on one side of a scale and that wretched waif Oswald on the other side, it doesn't balance. You want to add something weightier to Oswald. It would invest the President's death with meaning. He would have died for something. A conspiracy would, of course, do the job nicely.[45]

Jacqueline Kennedy fell into this trap, despairing that her husband was killed by a "silly little communist." "He didn't even have the satisfaction of being killed for civil rights,"[46] she added. Mrs. Kennedy was not alone; within hours of President Kennedy's death, the assumption among many

Americans was that right-wing elements, "big oil," or "white supremacists" had murdered Kennedy in the "city of hate."

Premonitions of Dallas

There is one government agency that bears partial culpability for the death of the president—the United States Secret Service. The events in Dallas came close in 1962 to having an eerie trial run in Springfield, Illinois, during the famous thirteen days of the Cuban missile crisis. This event should have prompted a reassessment of the security protocols surrounding the "leader of the free world."

On October 19, 1962, President Kennedy kept a commitment to speak in both Springfield and Chicago, Illinois. Kennedy's visit to Springfield was a rather perfunctory one, with the president expected to lay a wreath at the tomb of one of his assassinated predecessors, Abraham Lincoln, and then deliver a campaign address at the Illinois State Fair. The 1962 off-year elections were a little over two weeks away, and Kennedy had made a commitment to campaign for Democrat Sidney Yates, who was running for the United States Senate against the Republican senate minority leader, Everett Dirksen.

While traveling from the airport in Springfield to Lincoln's tomb, Kennedy's open motorcade traveled through downtown on its way to Oak Ridge Cemetery. As the motorcade passed through the heart of Springfield, a rifle with a scope emerged from the second floor of a building and was spotted by an Illinois public safety officer. No shots were fired, but the presidential motorcade was scheduled to quickly return using the same route through downtown Springfield. The local police took two men into custody and handed them over to the United States Secret Service.

Despite having a rifle and a box full of ammunition, the men were released after the motorcade passed on its return trip. The two men, aged twenty and sixteen, claimed they were using the scope to get a better look at the president, a somewhat unique manner of trying to improve one's line of sight. These men were young, but the twenty-year-old, who held the rifle, was not much younger than Lee Harvey Oswald, who had just turned twenty-four on October 18, 1963. A brief report of the event was submitted to the president in late November 1962, although it is not clear that he read it.

No changes were made to presidential security despite this close call in the shadow of Lincoln's tomb, nor does it appear that any information related to this event was ever relayed to the Warren Commission. Had the president been murdered or wounded during the Cuban missile crisis, decision makers in Washington would have likely assumed Russian or Cuban involvement and taken steps that could have easily led to a confrontation with the Soviet Union and Cuba.[47]

The United States Secret Service was underfunded and undermanned during the Kennedy years. Despite an attempt on President Truman's life that came close to succeeding in November 1950, at the time of Kennedy's death there were only thirty-four agents serving on the presidential protection detail assigned to President Kennedy. Additionally, the Kennedy detail was sleep-deprived and stretched to its limits due to the president's frenetic pace, a pace that far exceeded that of his immediate predecessors.[48] There was also an undisciplined, one might say reckless element to Kennedy's presidential travels, in that women of unknown provenance were repeatedly granted access to service the president, giving his travels the character of a fraternity house on wheels.

Nevertheless, the Secret Service was negligent in both covering up the near miss discussed above (this item was listed on page three of a Treasury Department report, below a notice about "Important Watch Smuggler Convicted at New York"), and in their conduct on the trip to Dallas in November 1963. While the allegation is strongly resisted by some agents on the Kennedy detail, including Gerald Blaine and Clint Hill, it appears that many of the agents had been drinking until the early hours of the morning on November 22, 1963, and were not in top condition when it came to protecting the president as he traveled through Dallas.

The House Select Committee on Assassinations concluded that "a lack of discipline and bad judgment by some members of the Secret Service protective detail in Dallas, who were drinking on the night before the assassination" contributed to the tragedy in Dallas. One critic of the Secret Service's performance that day, Donald E. Wilkes Jr., a professor of law at the University of Georgia, decried the fact that "six of the nine agents stayed out until around 3 a.m., while the seventh did not return to his room until 5 a.m. [on November 22]. It is nearly unbelievable that despite multiple recent reports of sinister plans to shoot the president in his limousine, agents were drinking and partying late on the night before a visit to a dangerous place like Dallas."[49]

"Hunter of Fascists"

Any objective account of the assassination of President Kennedy must acknowledge the animus toward Kennedy from the mob, from the anti-Castro Cuban community, from Fidel Castro, and from right-wing elements in Dallas, not to mention the failures of the Secret Service. But if one can move beyond ideological predispositions and the desire to make use of the murder victim as a martyr for a great cause, then all the evidence points to Lee Harvey Oswald as President Kennedy's lone assassin. The evidence against Oswald is overwhelming, yet despite this the Kennedy assassination will likely remain an "unsolved" mystery in the minds of most Americans.

The main counts in the indictment against Lee Harvey Oswald include the following: After returning from Russia in 1962, he created secret identities for himself, and ordered a rifle under an assumed name, A. Hidell, that he would use to shoot at both retired General Edwin Walker and President Kennedy. Oswald staked out General Walker's house and included photos of the home in his "book of operations." Oswald attempted to assassinate Walker on April 10, 1963, and having failed to kill Walker, he latched on to a new cause—defending Castro from American sponsored assaults on Cuba.

He hoped to add a dramatic entry to his self-proclaimed "Historic Diary" that he kept for a time, dreaming about leaving a mark on the Cold War struggle between Marxism and capitalism. Inscribed on the back of a photograph taken by Marina Oswald in April 1963 of Lee holding the rifle that killed President Kennedy were the words "Hunter of Fascists," written in Russian. Throughout the last year of his life, Oswald was determined to travel to Cuba and meet with Cuban officials and impress them with his actions in defense of their regime.

On the morning of Friday, November 22, 1963, he brought a package of "curtain rods" into the Texas School Book Depository, and immediately after the shooting, his rifle, with his palm print, was found on the sixth floor of the building. One eyewitness in Dealey Plaza, fifteen-year-old Amos Lee Euins, tried to convince Dallas Police to direct their attention to the book depository rather than the grassy knoll, for he saw a man firing a rifle from the sixth floor of that building.[50] Even the House Select Committee on Assassinations, no friend of the Warren Commission, concluded that "the shots that struck President Kennedy from behind him were fired from the sixth floor window of the southeast corner of the Texas School Book Depository building," although they conjectured based on the faulty acoustics evidence mentioned earlier that there may have been another gunman firing from the grassy knoll.[51]

Additionally, the House Committee noted that a number of the Dealey Plaza witnesses, in addition to Amos Lee Euins, said they saw either a rifle or a man with a rifle in the vicinity of the sixth floor southeast corner window.[52] Three employees watching the motorcade from the fifth floor of the building testified that the shots were fired from above them; one of the men yelled, "It's coming right over our heads," while another recalled the sound of shell casings hitting the floor, and "three shots" so loud they shook the building; "Cement even fell on my head," one of the men stated.[53] Several eyewitnesses saw Oswald, the only depository employee to flee the building after the assassination, shoot Dallas Police Officer J. D. Tippit.[54]

The claim that there was a second shooter in Dealey Plaza has weakened over time, as researcher Max Holland has made a compelling case that it was actually over eleven seconds that Oswald, a former Marine marksman, had to shoot at a starkly exposed president. Holland has convincingly argued that the Zapruder film, a home movie of Kennedy's murder taken by Dallas businessman Abraham Zapruder, has misled investigators and researchers for years; by piecing together additional photographs taken at the scene of the crime, it becomes apparent that Oswald fired earlier than the Zapruder film seemed to indicate. The Warren Commission, the FBI, and the American people, through the efforts of *Life* magazine which bought the film, came to believe that Abraham Zapruder had captured the entirety of the Kennedy shooting. He did not. As Holland notes, for decades Americans were "Zaprudered." Investigators were "so mesmerized by the footage that it lost perspective. Merely seeing should not be believing, yet the bureau [FBI] accepted *Life's* claim that the film was a full time-clock of the shooting sequence."[55]

The heinousness of Kennedy's murder permanently seared the nation's conscience, even though the country was spared the more graphic images of the head shot that killed the president until the 1970s. While the infamous Zapruder film would remain under lock and key for some time, still photos from the assassination appeared in the November 29, 1963, issue of *Life* magazine, without the frame containing the shocking head shot. A copy of the Zapruder film aired on a syndicated television show in five American cities in 1970, but it was not until March 6, 1975, that Geraldo Rivera of ABC's

Good Night America first broadcast the footage of Abraham Zapruder's 26.6-second assassination film to a national audience.

"That's the most horrifying thing I've ever seen in the movies," Rivera blurted out, as if he were watching a Hollywood production. Minutes later, after recovering from his horror, Rivera then showed a close-up of Kennedy's head at the moment of impact. One of the guests who narrated the film boasted that Rivera had defied executives and lawyers at ABC who did not want him to the air the film. Rivera "stood up for it and we showed it. And it was the highest ratings he had ever gotten. Ever!" Another guest on Rivera's show that night was the author of a book on the paranormal mysteries of the Bermuda Triangle that sold over fourteen million copies. Speculative theories about the Kennedy assassination were frequently as forensically sound as those claiming the existence of an underwater alien base off the coast of Bermuda.[56]

This not to say that the Kennedy case is completely closed. There remain questions about Oswald's time in New Orleans in the summer of 1963 and his association with anti-Castro activists. Some witnesses swear that he was seen with some of these activists, and his whereabouts on certain days cannot be determined. One of the most credible witnesses to attest that Oswald was consorting with these activists was Sylvia Odio, the daughter of an imprisoned Cuban dissident, who stated that Oswald and two other men visited her at her Dallas home on September 25, 1963, seeking her assistance in putting them in touch with anti-Castro forces inside Cuba.[57]

If Oswald was consorting with anti-Castro activists, it does not require a great leap of imagination to conclude that he wanted to "infiltrate" these organizations for mention in his "Historic Diary" and to bolster his case that the Castro government needed his clandestine assistance. But while these questions continue to linger, the refusal of many members of the assassination movement to place the blame on Oswald seems less rooted in a desire for the truth and more about propagating a scenario to suit their ideological preferences. Max Holland noted that the Warren Commission did not receive complete cooperation from the CIA about Operation Mongoose and about Robert Kennedy's direction of the operation. At the height of the Cold War, this was standard operating procedure. But in so doing, the CIA and Robert Kennedy weakened the explanation for Oswald's motive, and thus "set the stage for later revelations that condemned the Warren Report to disbelief. . . . If the word conspiracy must be uttered in the same breath as

'Kennedy assassination' Holland concluded, "the only one that existed was the conspiracy to kill Castro and then keep that effort secret after November 22nd."

The bottom line regarding the Kennedy assassination is that there was a cover-up, and it was designed to conceal the existence of Operation Mongoose. This distorted the Warren Commission's report to the nation, but they got it right when it came to who killed the president. For Lee Harvey Oswald, "fair play for Cuba" meant, as Holland chillingly notes, "subjecting [President] Kennedy to the same dangers plaguing Castro."[58]

Despite the overwhelming evidence that Lee Harvey Oswald killed the president, the Kennedy assassination conspiracy complex continues to flourish. Priscilla Johnson McMillan, the only person who knew both President Kennedy and Lee Harvey Oswald and concluded that the latter was the assassin, noted in 1975 that "the killing of a President, or a king or father, is the hardest of all crimes for men to deal with . . . it is this crime that stirs the deepest guilt and anxiety. . . . No matter what steps are taken, what investigation may be authorized or what autopsy material made public, I suspect that the doubts about President Kennedy's murder are going to be with us forever."[59]

8

Legacy

During my time at the John F. Kennedy Library (1979–1985) and during my later involvement with the Edward M. Kennedy Oral History Project (2004–2007), I saw countless examples of the Kennedy family's efforts to protect the family "brand." This was done to assist the electoral aspirations of assorted family members, including two of President Kennedy's brothers and countless nieces and nephews. JFK's legacy was frequently repackaged to keep his record in sync with the prevailing sentiment in the Democratic Party as it evolved over the decades, thereby enhancing the political prospects of his heirs. My former colleague at the John F. Kennedy Library, David F. Powers, used to privately observe that none of the family members who rode to political office on JFK's coattails possessed the latter's talents and political skills. Unfortunately, their misdeeds in the ensuing decades affected JFK's legacy and contributed to a distorted view of his record.

The Kennedy Library was ground zero for the family's efforts to shape the image of the thirty-fifth president. The library's museum, particularly in its earlier incarnation, embodied the Schlesinger and Sorensen heroic conception of Kennedy's "thousand days" in office. Uncomfortable issues such as the Vietnam War were, and continue to be, slighted. But the most egregious form of family manipulation involved efforts to limit archival access to those scholars who might question the sanitized version of John F. Kennedy or Attorney General Robert Kennedy. This required keeping the lid on embarrassing material on matters such as Operation Mongoose, where Robert Kennedy's family made sure that documents related to that event were kept closed long after legitimate secrecy considerations had expired. Historians cleared by the family, such as Doris Kearns Goodwin or Arthur Schlesinger Jr., were granted special access because they could be trusted, while more objective historians such as Herbert Parmet were kept at arms' length. These decades-long efforts to spin the historical record regarding John F. Kennedy and his heirs did untold damage to the truth and in the long run fueled a counter-narrative that was equally at odds with the facts.

Postmortem Polling

Sixty years after his murder, John F. Kennedy remains a revered figure in the American mind, yet his real record remains shrouded in either myth or misinformation, captive to memorialists or to those who deride him and his policies. Both camps promote a slanted account of Kennedy's presidency; the memorialists in the service of keeping brothers and nieces and nephews politically viable, while Kennedy's detractors hope to prevent the rise of Kennedy's familial or ideological heirs. These distorted accounts did considerable damage to the president's place in history, and arguably to the entire American body politic. It is well past the time to move beyond the myths of both the idolaters and those who revile him. As Kennedy said during another underrated address, the dedication of the Robert Frost Library at Amherst College in October 1963, it is time to "let the chips fall where they may."[1]

President Kennedy was a politician and he was proud of it, but unlike many of his peers, he was remarkably open to new ideas and possessed a probing intellect that challenged the canned responses of bureaucrats and risk-averse political colleagues. He understood that politics is the art of compromise, and compromise was essential for the survival of republican government. He trimmed and tacked when he deemed it necessary, as do all effective political leaders. But this did not translate into a lack of principles; instead, he refused to be confined and defined by ideology or partisanship. This contributed to the tensions he had with some of the liberal ideologues in his own party. As I have outlined in this book, on the major issues of the day he revealed himself to be set apart from the conventional thinking of his time. And that elevates him to a somewhat unique position in comparison to many of his presidential predecessors and successors.

Public opinion polls asking Americans to retrospectively rank their presidential favorites consistently show Kennedy at the head of the pack. For some older Americans, the Kennedy of Camelot remains alive and well, particularly those who identify as Democrats and live in the northeast, where admiration for Kennedy is stronger than in other parts of the nation. But it is remarkable that Kennedy's hold on the American imagination persists sixty years after his presidency. Warren Harding, William McKinley, and James Garfield all died before their time, two by assassination, yet sixty years after their passing most Americans could not identify them, never mind revere them. That is not true when it comes to John F. Kennedy.

Kennedy continues to poll well even though those who remember where they were on November 22, 1963, are rapidly shrinking in number. A poll from 2000 revealed that most Americans believed Kennedy was "the greatest President ever," while a 2008 Gallup poll ranked Kennedy at the top of the list of chief executives you wished "you could bring back" to the presidency. Three years later, Americans ranked Kennedy higher than George Washington, Franklin Roosevelt, and Thomas Jefferson on a list of great American presidents.[2]

Another Gallup poll, this one taken on the fiftieth anniversary of Kennedy's death in 2013, revealed that a remarkable 74 percent of the American public ranked Kennedy as an outstanding or above-average president. His closest competitor for that honor, among the modern presidents, was Ronald Reagan at 61 percent. The Gallup organization noted Kennedy's consistently favorable public approval in polls taken between 1963 and 2013, where he won the highest retrospective approval rating of any president measured during the organization's history.[3] There is something more at work here than the tragic, premature death of a young president with a beautiful wife and two attractive young children. Even in our remarkably jaundiced times, where cynicism is the order of the day, Kennedy continues to be seen as the personification of hope in the promise of America.

Kennedy is also admired by the nation's historians and political scientists in those polls of presidential greatness that emerge with some regularity, although there is a growing gap between the public's reverence for Kennedy and the praise he receives from scholars. Academics tend to cast a more skeptical eye on Kennedy's policies, particularly his dealings with Cuba, his "brinksmanship" with Khrushchev, and as we have also seen, his "cautious" approach to civil rights. Nevertheless, Kennedy was ranked eighth overall in a C-SPAN survey of presidential historians in 2021, behind Thomas Jefferson and ahead of Ronald Reagan. In the twenty-first century, Kennedy has come in no lower than eighth on these C-SPAN rankings, and no higher than sixth. His highest ranking was in the category of "public persuasion" (sixth), and his lowest rankings were in the category of "moral authority" (sixteenth) and "administrative skills" (eighteenth).[4]

In the years immediately following his assassination, he was the subject of near uniform adulation, shaped in good part by Jacqueline Kennedy's directives regarding his state funeral and her comments drawing comparisons between the Kennedy presidency and Camelot. It was at Mrs. Kennedy's direction that the most memorable scenes emerged from those mournful "days of drums." She asked the chief White House usher, J. B. West, to follow the same procedures that had been used for Abraham Lincoln's funeral ninety-eight years earlier. Working around the clock, West's team transformed the East Room of the White House, with black silk crepe draped over the chandeliers and the president's remains resting on Lincoln's catafalque. An unruly member of the funeral procession was a riderless horse with a pair of boots reversed in the stirrups named "Black Jack." The horse repeatedly balked as he was led through the streets of Washington, a sign that some poetically inclined observers claimed was indicative of the nation's refusal to part with the president. Mrs. Kennedy insisted on walking behind the caisson to the funeral in St. Matthew's Cathedral instead of riding in a "fat black Cadillac," and requested that the Scottish Black Watch Regiment and the Navy hymn, "Eternal Father, Strong to Save," be added to the program. She coached her young son John to salute his father's casket as the family stood outside the cathedral. And it was Jacqueline Kennedy's idea that an "eternal flame" grace his grave in Arlington National Cemetery.[5]

The Keepers of the Flame

Just one week to the day after her husband's murder, Jackie Kennedy called journalist Theodore White of *Life* magazine and invited him to Hyannisport for an interview. It was in this interview that the term "Camelot" was first used to describe the abbreviated term of the nation's thirty-fifth president. The former First Lady said that her husband loved to listen to a recording of the musical *Camelot*, and "the lines he loved to hear were 'don't let it be forgot, that once there was a spot, for one brief shining moment that was known as Camelot.'"[6] She told White that "I'd get out of bed at night and play it for him when it was so cold getting out of bed." The music appealed to Kennedy because as a sickly child Jack would "devour [stories of] the knights of the Round Table." Mrs. Kennedy was determined to convey the "magic" of those one thousand days, although less than two months later, she admitted to British prime minister Harold MacMillan that the "Camelot" appellation was "overly sentimental." However, she also believed there was an element of truth to it, in that her husband's presidency was a "brief shining moment" the likes of which would not be seen again. As she had told Theodore White on November 29, "there will be great presidents again, but there will never be another Camelot."[7]

Jackie Kennedy was afraid of what the "bitter old men" who wrote history would have to say about her husband, but she also came to appreciate that "history made Jack what he was . . . this little boy, sick so much of the time, reading in bed, reading history." And she added, to a barely composed White, "Jack had this hero idea of history, the idealistic view." While White dictated his story over the phone to the editors at *Life,* Mrs. Kennedy made sure the story appeared just as she wanted it, overruling the suggestion to remove the Camelot references. There is no more pronounced example of a political spouse helping to shape the image of a dead statesman than that of Jacqueline Kennedy.[8] With this one late evening interview in Hyannisport Jacqueline Kennedy set the tone for decades worth of analysis of President Kennedy's time in office. The zeal with which Jackie Kennedy promoted this image, assisted by a bevy of former White House aides who published flattering memoirs, must be considered one of the most successful public relations campaigns in over two centuries of American life.

Theodore White would later observe, "So the epitaph on the Kennedy administration became Camelot—a magic moment in American history." This was, as White argued in 1978, "a misreading of history. The magic Camelot of John F. Kennedy never existed." He added that his sympathy for the young widow led him to do her bidding in the piece he wrote for *Life,* and thus he became "her instrument in labeling the myth."[9]

Another such instrument was author William Manchester, who was selected to write an "authorized account" of the events surrounding the death of the president. Manchester believed he was recruited for the task because "she [Jackie Kennedy] thought I would be manageable." The former First Lady noted in September 1964 that "I hired William Manchester—to protect

President Kennedy and the truth." She also insisted that she would be the one to decide if and when the book was to be published. If it were not published, "Mr. Manchester would be reimbursed for his time." Almost everyone involved in the events surrounding Dallas agreed to be interviewed by Manchester, including Jackie Kennedy. The only two holdouts were Lyndon Johnson and Marina Oswald, the assassin's wife, although President Johnson did answer some written questions. The assassin's deranged mother was also interviewed, and at their last meeting, her final words to Manchester were "you can't say my son wasn't a good shot."[10]

Robert Kennedy, acting at the behest of his sister-in-law, quickly became involved in a brutal battle for editorial control over the completed manuscript. Author Thomas Mallon referred to the actions of Bobby and Jackie Kennedy in the Manchester imbroglio as "grief-entitled arrogance." Their actions were motivated by a desire to protect RFK's presidential prospects within the Democratic Party and by Jackie Kennedy's hypersensitivity to her public image (for instance, she wanted passages deleted related to her cigarette habit). Mallon's harsh verdict, and it is harsh, ignores the fact that the First Lady was suffering from an extreme case of post-traumatic stress syndrome, and the attorney general was doing his best to protect his widowed sister-in-law. But their reaction was also of a piece with a family dedicated to controlling John F. Kennedy's legacy. That William Manchester worshipped President Kennedy and agreed to a deal that awarded the bulk of his earnings to the Kennedy Library was not enough for the image-obsessed Kennedys. At bottom, their treatment of Manchester became the very definition of cruelty.

Mrs. Kennedy had been very candid with Manchester during several late-night sessions, totaling ten hours in all (sealed until 2067), where daiquiris helped ease the pain and fuel the conversation. *Look* magazine agreed to pay the author for serialization rights to the book in the spring of 1966, and later that year, Mrs. Kennedy filed a lawsuit seeking an injunction to block publication. At one point prior to the suit, according to Manchester's son, Jackie whispered to his father, "'I'm going to ruin you.'" The suit was settled out of court on January 16, 1967. "Ultimately," as Sam Kashner has noted, "Manchester agreed to cut 1,600 words out of the *Look* serialization and 7 pages out of the book's 654 pages of text—changes he later deemed 'harmless.'" But in the interim, Manchester was reduced to something of a physical and emotional wreck. Manchester later described his dealings with the Kennedys and their surrogates as comparable to dealing with officials in Nazi Germany.[11]

In a way, the dispute over *The Death of a President* came to define the Kennedys' approach to JFK's legacy. Jackie Kennedy, Robert Kennedy, and later Edward Kennedy, frequently working through surrogates, usually ex-New Frontiersmen such as Arthur Schlesinger, Ted Sorensen, and Dave Powers at the John F. Kennedy Library in particular, would play favorites with sympathetic chroniclers and deny access to others, and withhold information.

One nemesis for the Kennedy family was Nigel Hamilton, a British biographer whose *Reckless Youth* (1992) drew the ire of the family for its hostile portrait of Joseph P. Kennedy and its account of the future president's hijinks. Hamilton recalled that "the family leaned upon well-known historians such as Arthur Schlesinger Jr. and Doris Goodwin to write protest letters to the press. . . . I was warned that no Kennedy-era official or friend would be 'allowed' to speak to me for my proposed sequel." Hamilton decided to abandon the sequel in the face of this ostracism. A former Kennedy Library Director noted that Hamilton was kept at a distance because of the "family . . . ma[king] those decisions." Hamilton publicly fired back after he was ostracized, noting that "thousands of documents have been removed or sanitized over the years to avoid the wrath of the Kennedys."[12]

Ted Sorensen flatly confessed to his role in the airbrushing of history, noting in 2008, forty-five years after the President's murder, that he "felt it prudent to limit my criticisms of LBJ, the Democratic Party, and the Kennedy family to avoid burning any bridges" when he wrote his bestselling *Kennedy* in 1965. In effect, Sorensen admitted that his book was accurate other than his account of the two presidents he worked for and of the party to which he belonged. At the time Sorensen wrote the book, "I thought I might soon return to government," and this led him to trim his sails.[13] Many New Frontiersmen looked forward to a Kennedy restoration and believed it would occur with Robert Kennedy's assumption of the presidency in 1968 or perhaps 1972.

The necessity of protecting the family brand kept public recollections of President Kennedy duly circumspect, as one's career prospects depended on it. Long after Robert Kennedy's murder, the same phenomenon could be seen in the loyalty given to Senator Edward Kennedy by members of JFK's circle. Distorting history for the short-term political gain of the slain president's brothers seemed to many members of the Kennedy circle to be a worthwhile cause. As with any human endeavor, the motives for doing so were often mixed. Some did so simply for career advancement, others wished to protect a young widow with two small children, while some acted out of a genuine sense of loyalty to the enduring "cause . . . and the dream [that] shall never die." as Edward Kennedy put it at the 1980 Democratic National Convention.

Paul "Red" Fay, one of the president's PT boat buddies and his under-secretary of the navy, earned the wrath of the Kennedy family by writing a partially candid account of his friendship with the president in *The Pleasure of His Company* (1966). Jacqueline and Robert Kennedy reviewed the manu-script prior to publication, and Fay bowed to their demands, and according to one account removed ninety thousand of one hundred and eighty thou-sand words. His publisher later claimed that they balked at another request to remove an additional thirty thousand words, which would have rendered the manuscript unpublishable.

Robert Kennedy demanded the removal of passages dealing with Frank Sinatra, and told Fay that President Kennedy's father "shall not be called Joe, Big Joe, but Ambassador Kennedy or Joseph K." The former First Lady insisted that she be referred to as "Jacqueline," not "Jackie," even though Fay always called her "Jackie" in his personal interactions with her. She also objected to Fay's statement that the president and Arthur Schlesinger "weren't close." According to Fay, President Kennedy distanced himself from Schlesinger after the latter overstated his role to the press in the wake of the Cuban missile crisis: "That goddamn Artie. I'll tell you who he's going to advise. He's going to advise Jackie on the historical significance of the furniture that goes in the White House, period." That quote was removed.

At times Paul Fay resisted Robert Kennedy's interventions, prompting the latter to allegedly retort, "You mean to tell me as the senior member of the family I don't have the right to clear that book?" Even after Fay agreed to numerous deletions, Robert Kennedy gave him the silent treatment, refusing to acknowledge his presence at a funeral for a mutual friend. The royalties from Fay's book were donated to the Kennedy Library, but Jacqueline Ken-nedy returned them, claiming that the contribution was "hypocritical."[14]

Arthur Schlesinger and Ted Sorensen contributed to the Camelot leg-end by publishing the first insider accounts of the Kennedy presidency. *A Thousand Days* and *Kennedy* were both released in 1965, with each author celebrating the Kennedy presidency as a brief but shining moment in the na-tion's history. As Richard Reeves would later observe, the accounts provided by Schlesinger and Sorensen "looked like Leonardo's Last Supper—without

Judas at the end of the table."[15] Although they competed with one another in 1965 to be the first to get their book released, Schlesinger and Sorensen were basically on the same page when it came to Kennedy's greatness. The problem was that their accounts of major events were woefully incomplete, or downright distorted, as we saw in the chapter examining President Kennedy and the Cuban missile crisis, where Schlesinger and Sorensen's version of Robert Kennedy's role turned the truth on its head to enhance Bobby's electoral prospects.[16]

Arthur Schlesinger rose to Mrs. Kennedy's defense in her conflict with William Manchester, noting disingenuously that this was a conflict between a gifted writer, Manchester, and "the Kennedy family, which more than most presidential families has scrupulously tried to meet its obligations to the historians of the future." Serious scholars should never examine the private lives of public figures, Schlesinger went on to observe, noting that "the public lives of public officials is thus one thing. But—and this is surely just as self-evident—the invasion of private life and sensibility is a wholly different question, at least for the professional historian." Over time, Schlesinger "kind of set himself up as the oracle for the family," as Paul Fay put it, causing some New Frontiersmen to recoil. "He kind of started to speak for the family. I just didn't think he ever had the right," Fay noted in 1970.[17]

It is not necessarily surprising, and perhaps somewhat admirable, that loyal aides would remain loyal. What is surprising as well as troubling is that members of the media and some scholars abandoned their objectivity to prop up elements of the Camelot myth. This was unfortunate on so many levels, in that it prolonged a tottering Camelot façade for far too long, which in turn led to the rise of a counter-Camelot narrative that overcorrected and was equally inaccurate. It also contributed to the antagonism felt by many conservatives toward the mainstream media, who believe, with some justification, that a double standard was, and is, applied to political candidates depending on whether there is a (D) or an (R) after their name.

The keepers of the Kennedy flame had friends in the media who often seemed averse to challenging the mythological version of Kennedy's life. As the publication of Arthur Schlesinger's *Journals* revealed, he fostered a network of luncheon and dinner companions that reads like a *Who's Who* of late twentieth century media personalities: Robert Manning of the *Atlantic Monthly;* John Chancellor and Sander Vanocur of *NBC News;* Art Buchwald of the *Washington Post;* author George Plimpton; presidential election chronicler Theodore White; syndicated columnist Tom Braden; Ben Bradlee, editor of the *Washington Post*; Katherine Graham, publisher of *the Washington Post*; James Wechsler, editor of the *New York Post*; and David Burke, president of CBS News and a former staff member for John and Edward Kennedy; among many others. Ben Bradlee became the object of some concern when he wrote a memoir which revealed that JFK was prone to use salty language, prompting members of the Kennedy circle to condemn the book as "mischievous and damaging."[18]

There were a few media and literary figures who called into question Sorensen's and Schlesinger's version of events, most of whom emerged in the mid-1970s after revelations of the role the Kennedys played in attempting to eliminate Fidel Castro. Author Christopher Hitchens, Seymour Hersh of the *New York Times*, Joan Didion ("a viperish . . . little creature") and her husband John Gregory Dunne ("this dreadful couple") all made Schlesinger's list of deplorables. Academics occasionally appeared on Schlesinger's enemies list, including Thomas C. Reeves, whom Schlesinger dismissed as a "so-called historian," whose book *A Question of Character: A Life of John F. Kennedy* (1991), focused on Kennedy's character issues.

Schlesinger was also dismissive of Michael Beschloss, author of *The Crisis Years: Kennedy and Khrushchev, 1960–1963* (1991), who published unflattering information about Kennedy's Cold War miscalculations and his reckless private life, including enlisting the help of his secretary of state to arrange a tryst on a presidential visit to Italy in July 1963. Beschloss, according to Schlesinger, "knows better" but was exploiting the "same lode" as Reeves, the "sexual stuff on JFK." Schlesinger was particularly indignant with Bill Moyers, a former Lyndon Johnson aide who went on to produce documentaries for CBS News and for the Public Broadcasting System. Moyers served as the writer and host of a CBS documentary, *The CIA's Secret Army* (1977), which documented President Kennedy's efforts to remove Fidel Castro.[19]

When Operation Mongoose was exposed by the Church Committee in 1975, Arthur Schlesinger quickly dismissed the idea that the Kennedy brothers were involved. When CBS broadcast Moyers's documentary, Schlesinger referred to it as "an extraordinarily shabby and tendentious polemic." On the other hand, during the administration of "Old Ike," the CIA had recruited "gangsters to murder Castro," although Schlesinger continued to deny that "any of the three presidents [Eisenhower, Kennedy, and Johnson] authorized or were aware of these plots." The hated Lyndon Johnson had in fact terminated the assassination plots against Castro in the aftermath of the events in Dallas.[20]

Remarkably, Schlesinger asserted in 1985 that "Cuba was not a major concern for U.S. policy-makers" during the Kennedy years. In Schlesinger's assessment, "revisionist" historians who portrayed JFK as a Cold Warrior and an advocate of operations such as Mongoose were possessed by an "obscure and sour envy of Kennedy." They were "paying [him] back" for being "too handsome, too popular, too rich" and having "too beautiful a wife." In the annals of Camelot mythmaking, the notion that Kennedy's critics were possessed by jealously over good looks and money represents the pinnacle of Schlesingerian excess. As recently as 2008, Ted Sorensen was adhering to the party line that the CIA misunderstood JFK's interest in "deposing" Castro, for "that did not mean he wanted him [Castro] murdered."[21]

Unfortunately, Ted Sorensen served on a three-person committee that reviewed requests to open materials held by the John F. Kennedy Library. Sorensen saw his role as the gatekeeper ensuring that the official account offered by himself and Schlesinger remained intact. Both Richard Reeves and historian Robert Dallek encountered roadblocks created by the family's appointed guardians, Ted Sorensen, Burke Marshall, and Harvard professor Samuel Beer. Dallek's book *An Unfinished Life: John F. Kennedy, 1917–1963*, which was released in 2003, caused a bit of sensation when it revealed JFK's affair with a nineteen-year-old White House intern.[22] But Dallek was primarily interested in Kennedy's myriad health issues and ended up writing a very sympathetic account of the president's medical problems, portraying a courageous man who refused to let his health define his life and who rarely complained to anyone about the constant pain he experienced.

Sorensen balked at first but eventually consented to allow Dallek to examine the records. When Dallek's book was published, Sorensen was "angry" because he was caught unaware of some of the important information that had been concealed for years. Sorensen told Dallek "there was no cover up," but there had been a cover up since the 1960 election. According to Dallek, "Sorensen was the keeper of the flame. . . . He was somewhat a prickly character, very defensive about Kennedy as if he were the, you know, keeper of the flame."[23]

The John F. Kennedy Presidential Library and Museum developed a reputation for playing favorites in the archives and for fostering the Camelot myth in its public exhibitions. Richard Reeves noted thirty years after the

President's death that the library existed not "to serve history" but to "serve the Kennedys," The problem with doing books like the one Reeves wrote was that the Kennedys "run the library. . . . And it is less user-friendly and less research-friendly" than the other presidential libraries. Reeves added, correctly, that "Arthur Schlesinger . . . has been allowed to see things that no one else has ever been allowed to see because the family trusts him. . . . There is an obvious and visible attempt to control what information comes out."[24]

Both the National Archives and Robert Kennedy's confidant Burke Marshall urged Senator Edward Kennedy and Jackie Kennedy not to grant Schlesinger and others privileged access to the library's archives; the materials should be open to all or closed to all. The family rejected this advice and followed its favoritism policy for decades, leading critics to observe that it was, as *Washington Post* reporter Paula Span noted, "the library scholars denounce most, hands down."[25] Sorensen's three-member review committee was the subjected of frequent criticism from scholars for its tight-fisted approach to releasing material. While the staff may be US government employees, Richard Reeves claimed that they acted as if the American people "had no right to see this stuff."[26] The archival staff in fact was loyal to the idea that they serve history, but their hands were tied by the controlling influence the family exerted through the John F. Kennedy Library Foundation and through the family's continued political clout in Washington, DC.

Archival materials were placed under "deed of gift restrictions" that sealed materials relating to "personal, family, and business affairs," including President Kennedy's medical records and private correspondence. An additional restriction was placed on material that could "injure, embarrass, or harass" the Kennedy family. Audio-visual materials fell under the rubric of the deed of gift, with the screening committee instructed to label as "non-available" all items that show "aspects of a person's character which in some way contradict the image of that person held by the general public."[27] The instruction to abide by the prevailing public image as the standard by which to open historical materials runs completely counter to the purpose of any archive or library, and is deeply troubling in a political order dependent on the free flow of information.

The family's efforts to preserve the Schlesinger and Sorensen take on the Kennedy presidency persisted well into the twenty-first century. In January 2011, the History Channel announced that it was canceling *The Kennedys*, a film the channel had commissioned in 2008. A concerted effort to abort the series began before the film was even cast, led by Ted Sorensen and other keepers of the flame who were given access to the script. Sorensen described the script as "vindictive" and "malicious," while objections were also raised by family members, allegedly including Caroline Kennedy and Maria Shriver, both of whom wielded considerable clout within the media and entertainment industry.

The family had good reason to be suspicious, as the driving force behind the film was a friend of conservative radio host Rush Limbaugh, although the main scriptwriter was characterized by the producer as "a Kennedy loving liberal from New York." The series itself was hardly high art, and as with all Hollywood productions dealing with historical matters, it fictionalized some scenes and frequently altered the chronology.[28] Nevertheless, it is troublesome that Hollywood, or Broadway, or an author would be subject to cancellation due to objections raised by descendants of historical figures. At the very least, the statute of limitations should run out on family control over who gets to tell their story long before the passage of half a century.

"He Knew It Was Wrong"

One of the more awkward issues confronting Schlesinger and Sorensen, an issue that the *Kennedys* miniseries highlighted, was the persistent allegation that the president had engaged in multiple extramarital affairs. His lovers included a nineteen-year-old intern who had been on the job for four days when she was summoned by the president (Kennedy later shared her with one of his aides, and watched while the teenager serviced the aide), two White House "secretaries" codenamed "Fiddle and Faddle," and the First Lady's secretary, Pamela Turnure.[29] And that is by no means a complete list.

The scale of Kennedy's philandering is simply hard to fathom. Perhaps it was due to the amphetamine concoction he took to ward off Addison's Disease and other ailments. The theory that he had been near death so often and decided to throw all caution to the wind for the short time he had left has also been broached. Kennedy's friend K. LeMoyne Billings noted that the president treated "each day as if it were his last, demanding of life constant intensity, adventure, and pleasure" due to repeated brushes with death in war or on the surgeon's table, and being told Addison's disease would lead him to die young.[30] Perhaps he consciously modeled himself after his father or was so emotionally stunted from being raised by a cold and distant mother, or perhaps his behavior was the result of elements of all the above. This will never be conclusively settled. All we can say with certainty is that his behavior was reprehensible. The First Lady obliquely acknowledged this behavior when she noted in an oral history interview with Arthur Schlesinger Jr. in 1964 that "one side of Jack" was "a rather, I always thought, sort of crude side." Then catching herself so as not to violate her usual self-censorship regarding her husband's flaws, she quickly injected "not that Jack had the crude side."[31]

The "me too" movement is here to stay, and Kennedy's behavior will likely hold greater weight in future assessments of him. His conduct, as Mimi Alford has noted, was not far removed from the fictionalized depiction of television's Don Draper in *Mad Men*. One could argue that it is unfair to criticize Kennedy for behavior somewhat typical of the times, that to retrospectively condemn him for his actions is to engage in a form of "presentism," of applying the standards of today and unfairly judging the actions of those in the past. But as Ted Sorensen noted, not everyone behaved as Kennedy did, and he knew what he was doing was wrong and therefore went to great lengths to conceal it.[32] This behavior was President Kennedy's deepest character flaw, and it will continue to serve as a serious blot on his reputation as the twenty-first century unfolds.

Kennedy's remarkably irresponsible behavior presented a challenge to those who sought to deify him. Ted Sorensen initially endorsed the position of "the greatest Kennedy historian of them all, Arthur Schlesinger Jr." who proclaimed that "questions which no one has a right to ask are not entitled to a truthful answer."[33] Nevertheless, as Sorensen neared the end of his life, he was clearly troubled by the revelations regarding Kennedy's affairs that had emerged over time. He wrote in 2008, "At this stage, it does not honor JFK for me to attempt to cover up the truth. All my life, the principle of loyalty has been important. But sometimes blind loyalty is trumped by overriding principles of truth and decency." Sorensen termed Kennedy's behavior "self-indulgent" and noted that it did "not reflect well on his attitude toward his public office, the sacred trust." Sorensen added that the "everyone does it" defense was an insufficient defense, because "not everyone does it" and the stakes involved are far greater when it involves the president. The "scale" of Kennedy's cheating was unique, and "he knew it was wrong, which is why he went to great lengths to keep it hidden." Kennedy should have been aware, Sorensen argued, that his misconduct would eventually be revealed and would diminish the "moral force and credibility" of all that he achieved.[34]

John F. Kennedy presents a challenge for those who contend that the private life of an elected official is none of the public's business. Unfortunately, some of JFK's private affairs seeped into the public arena. It is simply not true, as Sorensen claimed in 1980, that Kennedy "never permitted the pursuit of private pleasure to interfere with public duty," a remark he repeated with a slightly different twist in 2008: "I know of no occasion where his private life interfered with the fulfillment of his public duties."[35] Kennedy's affairs included, but were not limited to, a woman whom the president was sharing with Sam Giancana, the Chicago mob boss who was providing assistance to Operation Mongoose; the ex-wife of the CIA's covert operations planning division; and, allegedly, a suspected East German spy, Ellen Rometsch, who was quickly deported after word reached Robert Kennedy that J. Edgar Hoover believed the president was sleeping with her. As Larry Sabato dryly observes, "Records related to Rometsch's deportation have either vanished or were never created in the first place." All of this information, and more, ensured that Hoover, whose time had already passed, would not be removed as director of the FBI.

One member of Kennedy's Secret Service detail recalled "morale problems" among his fellow agents, due to their jobs being reduced to guarding a john and his prostitutes: "You were on the most elite assignment in the Secret Service, and you were there watching an elevator or a door because the president was inside with two hookers."[36] There were eyewitness accounts provided by frustrated Secret Service agents regarding a drunken orgy at Bing Crosby's home involving the president, his brother-in-law Peter Lawford, and other members of the presidential party having their way with a group of European airline stewardesses.[37]

This book did not focus on John F. Kennedy's multiple affairs, but that should not be interpreted to mean that they were of no importance to his presidency. At any moment, his presidency could have imploded due to his repeated tendency to place himself in compromising positions. Needless to say, the damage he did to his wife is beyond imagining.[38] In the public sphere, at the very least, his serial adultery, and FBI director J. Edgar Hoover's knowledge of it, kept the increasingly paranoid and dangerously autonomous Hoover in a position of power long past his time, and may have contributed to Robert Kennedy's decision to approve electronic surveillance of Martin Luther King.[39]

Character matters in the presidency, for the chief executive serves as the nation's head of state. He, eventually she, is the personification of the American nation, its national figurehead. The office should be treated with due respect by its occupants. While Kennedy's rhetoric often appealed to the "better angels of our nature" and highlighted the best America had to offer, his own conduct fell far short of what one should expect from a genuinely great president.

"The Dream Shall Never Die"

One of the final steps in securing President Kennedy's legacy occurred on October 20, 1979, when the long-delayed John F. Kennedy Presidential Library and Museum was opened at Columbia Point, next to the University of Massachusetts at Boston. As with all matters related to President Kennedy's legacy, the library opening, from its timing to the content of its exhibits, was subsumed by the ambitions of the family's most recent contender for political office, in this case Edward Kennedy.

President Kennedy had hoped that his library might be affiliated with his alma mater, Harvard University, and had examined two potential sites for his library in Cambridge, Massachusetts in October 1963. After Kennedy's assassination, fundraising for the president's library began in earnest, with money raised from around the world. The proposed Harvard site generated opposition, with many of the denizens of Cambridge fearful of the traffic the institution would generate in an already cluttered Harvard Square, and of the potential for "gum-chewing, paper-throwing, sneaker-wearing" tourists overwhelming the University "like Goths overwhelming the intelligentsia."[40] Years of fruitless negotiations ensued, including a proposal to split the archives from the museum. In the end, the library's foundation and Jacqueline Kennedy opted to move the entire project to Columbia Point.

By 1979, Senator Edward Kennedy had emerged as the spokesman for the liberal wing of the Democratic Party, whose nominal leader was incumbent president Jimmy Carter. The Kennedy Library was rushed to completion that October to ensure a nationwide platform for Edward Kennedy, and to conjure up the ghosts of Camelot before he announced his campaign just weeks later. Kennedy's rival, Jimmy Carter, accepted the library on behalf of the federal government, and spoke movingly about his reaction to the news that John F. Kennedy had been killed. Robert Kennedy's eldest son, Joseph P. Kennedy II, gave a fiery speech condemning the Carter administration for its mean-spirted approach to the nation's downtrodden, adding a sour note to an occasion intended to celebrate the life of President Kennedy and the belated completion of his presidential library.

At one point during the dedication ceremony, Jacqueline Kennedy recoiled at a kiss planted on her cheek by President Carter, a moment captured in a photograph that dominated the tabloids the following day. "I started to kiss her on the cheek and she flinched away ostentatiously," Carter recalled later. This was taken as a sign of the low regard members of the family felt toward the pretender on the throne. After Carter finished his well-received remarks, a member of the White House advance team rushed to the podium and removed the presidential seal so that Edward Kennedy would not be photographed with the seal.[41]

Ted Kennedy's speech noted that the New Frontier had transformed America. "It was all so brief," he added, "the thousand days are like an evening gone. But they are not forgotten." And he noted the "special bond" that existed between himself and his brother, "despite the 14 years between us. When I was born, he asked to be my godfather. He was the best man at my wedding. He taught me to ride a bicycle, to throw a forward pass, to sail against the wind." The senator not-so-obliquely committed himself to completing his older brother's unfinished work, noting that "in dedicating this library to Jack, we recall those years of grace, that time of hope. The spark still glows. The journey never ends. The dream shall never die."[42]

Ted Kennedy's presidential campaign disintegrated almost immediately, when the American embassy in Iran was seized three days before his formal announcement on November 7, 1979. Equally damaging to Kennedy was the airing of an hour-long television interview on CBS called "Teddy" that ran the same night as the embassy seizure. Kennedy struggled throughout the interview with questions dealing with his personal life and with the Chappaquiddick incident ten years earlier, and stumbled over the question of why he wanted to be president.[43] Kennedy lost to Carter in many of the early caucuses and primary states but ended up winning a number of states in the later rounds, some twelve in all to Carter's thirty-six states.

In fact, considering that he was challenging an incumbent president,

Kennedy's performance was somewhat impressive, carrying delegate-rich states including California, New York, Pennsylvania, and New Jersey, victories which allowed him to fight for the nomination all the way to the convention. Kennedy fell short in the end, but delivered his most impressive speech of the campaign, and perhaps of his life. While conceding the nomination to Carter, he movingly invoked the memory of his lost brothers.

A campaign that began with Jackie Kennedy rebuffing a presidential kiss ended with Ted Kennedy rebuffing a presidential handshake on the stage after conceding to Carter. Or so the legend went. Kennedy did shake Carter's hand, "two or three times" he later insisted, but there was no celebrating with raised arms.[44] From this point on, Edward Kennedy would devote his time to the United States Senate, where he served until 2009, amidst the occasional speculation that he might make another attempt to run for president and fulfill the yearnings of those hoping for a Kennedy restoration.

The Counter-Camelot Myth

The United States bicentennial celebration of 1976 came on the heels of Vietnam, Watergate, and the aftereffects of the 1960s cultural revolution. During the bicentennial year, much of the nation was in no mood for the usual cheerleading versions of American history. In fact, American morale was arguably lower in the 1970s than at most times in American history. Few American historical figures emerged unscathed from the attacks of skeptical revisionists, and John F. Kennedy was no exception. These skeptics tended to view the history of the United States as a recurring story of exploitation and unceasing violence. When it came to John F. Kennedy, revisionists tended to focus on his "reactionary" Cold War policies and his foot-dragging on civil rights.

A year earlier, the first details of "Operation Mongoose" and Kennedy's involvement with Judith Campbell Exner were revealed by a Senate Select Committee in 1975 looking into abuses of power by the nation's intelligence entities. Chaired by Idaho senator Frank Church (D-ID), the committee put the first serious dents in the "Camelot" myth.

During that same bicentennial year, Joan and Clay Blair published *The Search for JFK*, a popular history that was nonetheless a groundbreaking book that anticipated future work by Robert Dallek and Herbert Parmet.

The Blairs were stymied in terms of gaining access to the materials in the John F. Kennedy Library, becoming some of the earliest victims of the family's penchant for stonewalling. But the Blairs conducted their own interviews and focused on puncturing Kennedy's reputation as something of an intellectual and the personification of youth and vigor. Regarding the latter, they were well ahead of their time in outlining Kennedy's battles with Addison's disease and his degenerative back issues.

The most problematic aspect of the book was its critical focus on Kennedy's World War II exploits, as the authors apparently believed they could have handled PT-109 in a more effective manner than Lieutenant Kennedy. This is a topic that should be approached with some humility and restraint, as second-guessing a person's actions while in combat seems the height of authorial arrogance. As one commentator on the Blairs' book charitably put it, they assumed "a standard of performance that demands a lot of people in combat." According to the Blairs, Kennedy was "in effect, a 'manufactured' war hero."[45] The PT-109 incident was undoubtedly exploited by Kennedy's ambitious and image-conscious father, but Kennedy's rescue of his crew members was truly heroic. Kennedy swam with a life jacket strap clenched between his teeth for hours on end to save a severely burned crew member, an action that clears the heroism threshold for fair-minded observers.

In 1984, two former 1960s radicals turned authors, Peter Collier and David Horowitz, published *The Kennedys: An American Drama*, which highlighted every foible and every scandal, as well as some of the accomplishments, committed by America's "royal family."[46] Part of this lengthy tome was devoted to Ted Kennedy's character flaws, with Chappaquiddick serving as the centerpiece of the indictment. The authors were correct to note that Chappaquiddick was "one of the crucial moments of the Kennedy saga. All during the development of the Legacy a sort of shadow legacy of doubt and suspicion had moved along in lock step, waiting for an opening." This "shadow legacy of doubt" was held in check for a lengthy period due to sympathy for a family that had experienced far more than their share of tragedy. But Chappaquiddick and the damage control efforts that took place in its aftermath gave "credence" to those who claimed that the family's mastery of public relations and its "reckless" and "arrogant" flaunting of the laws and rules led to their rise to power. "The family which before had been the victim of conspiracies now stood accused of perpetrating one," and Chappaquiddick made that plain for all the world to see.[47]

One of the many downsides of attempting to sustain a narrative for the benefit of relatives of political figures is that those relatives can damage the coattails of those they ride, in this case President Kennedy. Allegations of misbehavior against Edward Kennedy would persist long after Chappaquiddick, alongside numerous allegations against various presidential nephews for drug-related and other offences. "Camelot" was an unsustainable myth from the start, but the actions of many members of the "clan" made the myth all the more difficult to perpetuate and fed a desire to undermine the founder of it all, President Kennedy.

One author determined to do just that was Thomas C. Reeves, the author of well-received studies on Senator Joseph McCarthy and President Chester Alan Arthur. Reeves's *A Question of Character: A Life of John F. Kennedy* (1991) portrayed a president who was "all dazzle and no substance," a man who would not have been president were it not for a domineering father. John F. Kennedy lacked "any guiding intellectual, philosophical, or moral vision in his pursuit of office. Politics, like life, was about winning, and little else."[48] But as Sorensen and Schlesinger and other family acolytes had overreached, so did Thomas Reeves and others who sought to dismantle the entirety of Kennedy's record. Everything John F. Kennedy accomplished was seen by Reeves as nothing more than a constant attempt at self-aggrandizement. Even regarding the issue of civil rights, where Kennedy took great political risks putting the full weight of his presidency behind the movement for equal treatment under the law, Reeves managed to find a jaded rationale: Kennedy's civil rights initiatives were designed solely to win more votes and suppress demonstrations during the 1964 election. Reeves ignored the fact that the president's support for civil rights cut deeply into his poll numbers in the American South; had Kennedy been thinking only about his political future, he would never have embraced the cause of civil rights.

Reeves contended that there was nothing genuine about John F. Kennedy, that his public image, which first took hold when he a United States senator, was the result of Ted Sorensen's tutoring. The latter was "largely responsible for the wit, sophistication, and literary prowess linked in the public's mind with JFK," an assertion not borne out by the Cuban missile crisis tapes and by Kennedy's impressive handling of live televised press conferences.[49] While Kennedy had some idea of the questions he would likely be asked at these press conferences, they were for the most part unscripted affairs where his wit and sharp mind were readily apparent.

President Kennedy's policies against Castro's Cuba stemmed from his pathological obsession to win at all costs, a trait he inherited from Joseph P. Kennedy, according to Reeves. Following the maxim of "don't get mad, get even," the Kennedy brothers decided to settle the score with Fidel. "If an open invasion of Cuba would not get rid of its jeering Communist dictator, then clandestine efforts, however immoral, were resorted to." Kennedy, who publicly took full responsibility for the Bay of Pigs fiasco, was accused by Reeves of engaging in a "cover-up" and eagerly sought "to blame others."[50]

If Kennedy's clandestine efforts in Cuba were "immoral" and the result of a dysfunctional father, then how does one explain Dwight Eisenhower's plots against Castro? Eisenhower and Kennedy believed that it was in the national interest to undermine that regime, and this drove their policy toward Cuba. Kennedy's predecessor, as well as his successors, were not raised by Joseph P. Kennedy, yet they viewed Castro as an enemy and took steps to weaken his regime.

The notion that Kennedy's father was responsible for the "sins" of his son received its most over-the-top treatment in Nancy Gager Clinch's *The Kennedy Neurosis* (1973).[51] Clinch argued that Kennedy's policies in Cuba and Vietnam were rooted in his never-ending quest to impress his father and demonstrate his virility. Kennedy was deeply neurotic, as were the American people who believed in this "pseudo-sorcerer."[52] The "controlling" Joseph P. Kennedy, it should be noted, had a stroke in December 1961, rendering him a non-participant for almost two years of Kennedy's presidency.

Nancy Clinch and Thomas C. Reeves were not alone in condemning Kennedy for practicing a macho foreign policy driven by character flaws and a domineering father. While Reeves and Clinch were two of the leading lights of the counter-Camelot school, they had plenty of allies. One was historian Thomas G. Paterson, who suggested that President Kennedy pursued "a strategy of annihilation."[53] Kennedy's American University speech discussing a "strategy of peace" was an aberration, and not truly reflective of the man's approach to the Cold War, Paterson argued. These sweeping judgments were made at a time when there was limited access to archival materials due to government secrecy restrictions and family stonewalling, but this should have been cause for circumspection, not sweeping judgments, about Kennedy's "belligerent foreign policy." The period between 1961 and 1963 was an era which "seemed to court nuclear cremation," Paterson argued, and one of the main drivers courting cremation was President Kennedy.

A persistent tactic animating the works of members of the Counter-Camelot school was its psychoanalysis of the dead president and "discovering" the source of his neuroses. Paterson suggested that Kennedy was "aroused" by "stings of anti-Catholic bias" and by allegations of being soft on communism and was thus "eager to prove his toughness once in office." Paterson's Kennedy "strove to win" and "thought [he] could lick anything." In the aftermath of the Bay of Pigs he "nurtured a sense of revenge"; thus he backed Khrushchev into a corner by choosing a televised address during the missile crisis "rather than a direct approach to Moscow . . . choosing public rather than private diplomacy . . . thereby significantly increasing the chances of war." Paterson accused Kennedy of an unwillingness to understand Khrushchev's motivations, impairing the possibility for negotiation, and seemingly "willing to destroy, in Strangelovian fashion, millions in the process."[54] Paterson's description of Kennedy's foreign policy was inaccurate history coupled with a tendency to assume the worst about the president's motives.

The notion of Kennedy's nuclear recklessness, of flirting with the apocalypse, would be adopted by scholars as diverse as the British-born commentator Christopher Hitchens, who accused this "high risk narcissist" of almost killing him during the Cuban missile crisis. Hitchens noted his sense of "mild relief" when the news arrived from Dallas a year later. Hitchens also claimed that Kennedy's policies in Southeast Asia were the result of having been bested by Khrushchev at Vienna, leading him to "abruptly . . . pick a macho fight in Indochina."[55]

Author Garry Wills echoed the argument that the quest for virility drove Kennedy's foreign policy. Kennedy's desire to project a "macho appearance" was the motive behind his "reckless" actions during the Cuban missile crisis. Wills also downplayed any contribution on Kennedy's part to advancing the cause of civil rights, giving all credit to Martin Luther King Jr., whose eloquence outlasted Kennedy's "tinny" rhetoric. King traveled further than JFK, according to Wills, ignoring the fact that the millionaire from Hyannisport and Palm Beach had come quite a distance by 1963, and had cleared a discriminatory hurdle in becoming the nation's first Catholic president.[56]

Journalists and commentators I. F. Stone and Henry Fairlie, along with scholars such as Bruce Miroff, Barton Bernstein, and Richard J. Walton, all argued that Kennedy overreacted to the Cuban missile crisis by making it more of a threat than it needed to be. Henry Fairlie argued that Kennedy generated foreign crises to distract from his domestic political problems, claiming that "he turned us to foreign policy confrontations when he could not win any domestic policy victories here at home."[57] For Bruce Miroff, Kennedy's inferiority complex in regard to his father led him to push himself, and the Soviet Union, to the brink to prove his courage and slake his thirst for greatness, although upon the release of additional information Miroff modified this assessment.[58]

These commentators were all critical of Kennedy's handling of the missile crisis and were inclined to put the onus for Khrushchev's missile gambit on Operation Mongoose. Another somewhat consistent criticism was that Kennedy transformed the missiles of October into a test of his personal prestige. Remarkably, Khrushchev's role in bringing the world to the brink is often downplayed in these accounts. The analogy does not entirely hold, but had Khrushchev's standard been adopted by the Kennedy administration, the United States would have been justified in stationing nuclear weapons in any allied nation that the Soviet Union sought to clandestinely topple.

The main theme of key members of the Counter-Camelot school was that Kennedy took the world to the edge of thermonuclear war without due cause. Some went so far to suggest that because of his "victory" in the Cuban missile crisis, the use of force became Kennedy's default position in Southeast Asia. Many of these discredited theories were based on incomplete history, which was not necessarily the fault of the authors, but these theories continue to appear in far too many accounts despite ample evidence to the contrary.

The one book that could have done more damage than it did to Kennedy's reputation was Seymour Hersh's *The Dark Side of Camelot* (1997), a lurid tale of lust and depravity within the Kennedy White House. The book's launch was marred by the news that Hersh had been fleeced by someone claiming to have correspondence between President Kennedy and Marilyn Monroe proving conclusively that an extramarital affair had occurred between the two and that arrangements were made to buy Monroe's silence. Hersh should have known that entering the realm of the alleged dalliance between Monroe and either John or Robert Kennedy is akin to entering a wilderness of mirrors; a world inhabited by assorted hucksters and the mentally unhinged.

Despite the Monroe fiasco, the book was catnip for millions of Kennedy haters eager to toss the Camelot legend onto the ash heap of history. Hersh claimed that he was simply trying to "help the nation reclaim some of its

LEGACY [201]

history," but one review accurately noted, "this warts-and-more-warts bio is so determined to kill off the Kennedy mystique it should be subtitled *The Second JFK Assassination*." It was all here—by page two we are told that the president was briefly married for a few days to a Palm Beach socialite in 1947 but had destroyed any evidence of the marriage. It should be noted that the woman involved in this story repeatedly denied there was any marriage, and the source, a seventy-nine-year-old man with memory problems, was recounting an event fifty years prior and had never mentioned this to anyone except Hersh.

But that was only the beginning of this tale of debauchery and cover-up. Hersh devoted a large portion of his massive book to the role organized crime played in electing John F. Kennedy. The candidate's father allegedly secured cash from mobsters for use in the critical West Virginia primary in May 1960, and this made all the difference in buying votes in that poverty-stricken state. Joseph Kennedy was also influential in winning Illinois for his son in the general election that fall, holding, according to Hersh, a "dramatic and until now unrevealed summit" meeting with Sam Giancana to secure critical electoral support in Chicago. (Kennedy's critics frequently point to the "stolen" election in Illinois in 1960 as evidence of the family's corruption. The work of Edmund F. Kallina Jr. and Paul Von Hippel refutes many of the core arguments surrounding this persistent rumor. The one uncontestable fact regarding Illinois in 1960 is that Kennedy did not need to carry the state to win the presidency).[59]

Building on his claim of close ties between the Kennedys and organized crime, Hersh recounted Sam Giancana's role as a major player in the CIA's efforts to eliminate Fidel Castro. John F. Kennedy was in deep with these mobsters, Giancana especially, as he and his friend Frank Sinatra gave Kennedy the gift of a girlfriend in the form of Judith Campbell Exner. Giancana allegedly boasted to Exner, "Listen, honey, if it wasn't for me your boyfriend wouldn't even be in the White House." Kennedy was also guilty of financial corruption, as General Dynamics was accused by Hersh of successfully extorting the president for a federal contract after executives at the company got wind of the Kennedy's relationship with Exner.

Hersh found Exner to be credible, despite her repeatedly evolving story. After first denying that she served as a go-between for cash payments to Giancana and for payments back to the White House to assist in the president's reelection effort, and of carrying messages back and forth dealing with

Operation Mongoose, Exner changed her story. She had originally claimed under oath that she was only the president's lover, but as time went on, she expanded her role to include her services as a secret courier of presidential money and assorted missives. Hersh even attributed the tragic event in Dallas to the President's inability to control himself, in that Kennedy's errant attempt to pinch the backside of a woman forced him to wear a back brace that kept him propped up in the seat of the limousine in which he was murdered.[60]

Responses to Hersh's book varied. Thomas Powers rightly noted that "again and again we are told that so-and-so 'said in an interview for this book' or 'told me' thus-and-such or that certain documents were 'obtained for this book' and are here 'published for the first time,'" although Powers saw this as Hersh's attempt to highlight his own investigatory diligence and make it clear that he was not "smuggl[ing] things in from other books." But consequently, Hersh was almost as much a part of *The Dark Side of Camelot* as Sam Giancana.

Garry Wills, no admirer of President Kennedy, found some of Hersh's claims difficult to believe, including the mob ties between Joseph P. Kennedy and Sam Giancana. "In his mad zeal to destroy Camelot," Wills observed, "Hersh has with precision and method disassembled and obliterated his own career and reputation." A reviewer in the *New York Times* observed that many of Hersh's allegations came "from secondary sources, the children, widows and mistresses of the now-deceased."[61]

Edward Jay Epstein, a political scientist and frequent author, offered the most penetrating assessment of Hersh's work in a review in the *Los Angeles Times*. Epstein raised questions about the provenance of some of Hersh's allegations, including the author's ability to divine Robert Kennedy's thoughts in the immediate hours after his brother's assassination. Hersh claimed that the attorney general knew he had to "hide all evidence of Kennedy's secret life from the nation," an allegation that appeared on the very first page of the book. Hersh alleged that "Bobby Kennedy understood that revelation of the material in his brother's White House files would forever destroy Jack Kennedy's reputation as president" and that "as Bobby Kennedy knew, President Kennedy and Sam Giancana shared . . . a stolen election and assassination plotting" and "Bobby Kennedy knew . . . that Jack Kennedy had been living a public lie." Hersh "must have invented these facts," Epstein argued, because he did not interview Robert Kennedy, who had been killed in 1968, nor did he cite any source for the remarkable claims that open the book.[62] All of this was, at best, an act of literary license.

As Edward Jay Epstein rightly observed, this type of "license" might "serve to expand the universe of creative journalism, but it unfortunately does not produce credible history. When the pretensions of 'helping the nation reclaim some of its history' fade away on scrutiny, this book turns out to be, alas, more about the deficiencies of investigative journalism than about the deficiencies of John F. Kennedy."[63] Seymour Hersh, along with Bob Woodward and a host of young reporters, had developed a new post-Watergate form of journalism that encouraged such flights of fancy including divining the thoughts of key figures from history, or sometimes even their deathbed confessions. It was morbidly entertaining reading, but not the stuff of history. But Hersh was fine with this; as he told the *New York Times* when asked about the absence in his book of "rigorous footnoting favored by historians," he replied, "who wants to write a book for historians?"[64]

Seymour Hersh delighted in puncturing American myths, in discovering the inevitable conspiracy underlying every action of the United States government.[65] His work was the seminal expression of the Counter-Camelot school, and perhaps its most unreliable. But partial responsibility for the misguided assessments of the Counter-Camelot school rests with the excesses propagated by the Kennedy idolaters. The latter's fictionalized accounts of the Cuban missile crisis, the heroic thirteen day "eyeball to eyeball" showdown where Khrushchev blinked first, led to the distorted counter-narratives of Paterson, Miroff, Walton, Bernstein, and many others.

Beyond the missile crisis, the idolaters created an image of a president who did not exist, a president who was a combination of a knight in shining armor with elements of sainthood thrown into the mix. In so doing, the idolaters opened Kennedy up to the most jaded interpretations of his actions. Compounding this was the Kennedy family's decision to play favorites with those given access to presidential materials. This was a prescription for an incendiary reaction, a counter-narrative that only further blurred Kennedy's record. Thankfully, closer to our time, popular histories and scholarly works by authors including James Giglio, Mark White, Michael O'Brien, Robert Dallek, Robert Rakove, and Fredrik Logevall offer a more nuanced account of the Kennedy presidency, one that was long overdue.

Kennedy's Place in the American Mind

While John F. Kennedy remains highly regarded among the American public, and even to an extent among scholars, it is possible that his behavior toward women will erode his standing in the future. A piece by Timothy Noah in the *New Republic* in 2012 might reveal a foreshadowing of things to come. Entitled "JFK, Monster," the essay focused on Mimi Alford, the nineteen-year-old intern who had an affair with Kennedy, who recalled the president asking her to fellate Dave Powers in the White House swimming pool while the president watched. Alford noted that later, "President Kennedy apologized to us both." She wrote that Kennedy tended to display "his darker side . . . when we were among men he knew. That's when he felt a need to display his power over me." She also stated she did not regret her affair with the president and that she loved him.[66]

Kennedy's cruel side was also observed, from a far remove, by Richard Reeves, who in working on his Kennedy book for six years came across episodes where the president had humiliated people close to him, including "friends and staff right up to Secretary of State Dean Rusk" who were asked to "pimp for him and handle the complicated logistics of his sex life." Reeves was "put off by the fact that most of them [Kennedy's circle of aides] considered humiliation an honor, a sign that they were close to the center." Ted Sorensen later remarked that he was never asked to do such things, nor were Arthur Schlesinger and countless other high-ranking officials. But some were, and some did, in order to get "close to the center." This phenomenon is commonplace among powerful, attractive leaders, which does not make it any less repulsive. If there is one element of Kennedy's character that could lead to a decline in his posthumous standing, it is this element, particularly regarding his treatment of scores of "girlfriends" and the effort it took to feed this frenzy.

But an exclusive focus on Kennedy the sexual libertine offers an incomplete picture of the thirty-fifth president. A member of the California delegation to the United States House of Representatives, Thomas Rees, campaigned with John F. Kennedy in 1960 and had this to say about him: "I've read all the books, and they get everything down but the most important thing: the magic. The man was magic. He lit up a room. He walked in, and the air was lighter, the light was brighter."[67] Rees's comment is something that I heard repeatedly during my time at the Kennedy Library from those who knew the man.

For some, meeting Kennedy seems to have been the highlight of their life. John Seigenthaler, a journalist who would go on to join Robert Kennedy's Justice Department, recalled his first meeting with Kennedy while a Nieman Fellow at Harvard University. "Everybody wanted to be close to him, wanted to talk to him, wanted to sort of just feel a piece of . . . Jack."[68] One of JFK's girlfriends from the 1940s observed that "he had the charm that makes birds come out of their trees," a verdict echoed by Senator George Smathers of Florida, who said of his friend and frequent party companion, "the most charming man I ever knew." Reporter and family friend Charles Bartlett said of Kennedy, "Anyone . . . who knew him briefly or over long periods, felt that a bright and quickening impulse had come into their life."[69]

While Kennedy's repeated affairs are often cited as evidence of a deep streak of narcissism, he was no Donald Trump. Part of Kennedy's charm was his ability to laugh at himself and not take himself seriously. He dismissed some of the praise he received, whether it was for his wartime heroics ("It was involuntary. They sank my boat") or for his presidency ("It's just like Eisenhower, the worse I do the more popular I get").[70] When Robert Mc-Namara argued that he did not have the necessary training to be secretary of defense, claiming, "Mr. President, it's absurd; I'm not qualified," Kennedy responded, "Look, Bob, I don't think there's any school for Presidents, either."[71] When asked if he was enjoying his job, Kennedy replied, "I have a nice home, the office is close by, and the pay is good."[72] Ted Sorensen noted that the president "would work diligently for the right opening witticism, or take as much pride the next day in some spontaneous barb he had flung, as he would on the most substantive paragraphs in his text."[73]

Kennedy mocked his family wealth and his father's alleged Rasputin-like control over him: "I just received the following wire from my generous Daddy. 'Dear Jack, don't buy a single vote more than is necessary. I'll be damned if I am going to pay for a landslide. Love, Dad.'"[74] When his younger brother Edward Kennedy ran for JFK's former seat in the United States Senate against Speaker of the House John McCormack's nephew, Edward Mc-Cormack, the president converted a popular phrase at the time from "better dead than red" to "we'd rather be Ted than Ed."[75]

He responded to a newspaper story describing one of his White House aides as "coruscatingly brilliant" by mocking the skills of his Ivy League coterie, the so-called "best and the brightest." He joked that journalists "should never forget: 50,000 votes the other way and we'd all be coruscatingly stupid."[76] And on a return visit to Columbus, Ohio in January 1962, after losing the Buckeye State to Nixon in 1960, he remarked, "There is no city in the United States in which I get a warmer welcome and less votes than Columbus, Ohio." Speaking to a group of industry executives in February 1961, he observed "that it would be premature to ask for your support in the next election, and it would be inaccurate to thank you for it in the past."[77] When his friend and potential opponent in 1964, Barry Goldwater, took a photo of the president and asked him to sign it, Kennedy wrote, "For Barry Goldwater, whom I urge to follow the career for which he has shown much talent—photography."[78]

Kennedy would occasionally use his rapier wit to skewer those guilty of hypocrisy, as when New York Times columnist Arthur Krock criticized Kennedy for delaying a visa for Moise Tshombe, the leader of a Congolese separatist movement. Krock was a member of the segregated Metropolitan Club of Washington, one that Kennedy had resigned from due to its race-based membership policy. Kennedy proposed a deal: "I'll give Tshombe a visa and Arthur can give him dinner at the Metropolitan Club."[79]

And he could mock some of his own memorable lines, as he did at a fundraiser for the Democratic Party on the first anniversary of his inauguration: "We are sworn to pay off the same party debt our forebears ran up nearly a year and three months ago. Our deficit will not be paid off in the next hundred days, nor will it be paid off in the first 1,000 days, nor in the life of this administration, nor perhaps even in our lifetime on this planet, but let us begin." The night before he was assassinated, he delivered a speech in Houston in which he flubbed a line and quickly corrected himself, "When this new series of rocket is launched, it will carry the largest payroll, excuse me, payload in history. Well, it will be the largest payroll too, and who knows that better than the folks in Houston."[80] Kennedy loved a good laugh, and unlike some of his dysfunctional presidential peers, he knew how to laugh at himself. He gave Dave Powers a silver mug for a birthday gift in 1962 with this inscription: "There are three things which are real: God, Human Folly and Laughter. The first two are beyond our comprehension, so we must do what we can with the third."[81]

This devotion to laughter was understandable for a man who had seen the horrors of war, had lost two siblings to violent deaths, and had himself been given the last rites of the Catholic Church on more than one occasion. When his sister Kathleen, who was a favorite of his, was killed in an airplane crash in 1948, Kennedy's friend Billy Sutton observed later that "when they say that the Kennedys never cry, don't believe that. They do. . . . He cried that morning for his sister Kathleen." Cardinal Richard Cushing of Boston recalled that after the funeral mass for Kennedy's son Patrick Bouvier, who died after living for only thirty-nine hours in August 1963, the president cried "copious tears." Cushing added that JFK "was the last of the family to leave the little chapel. I was behind him. The casket was there. It was in a white marble case. The president was overwhelmed with grief that he literally put his arm around that casket as though he was carrying it out. I was right behind him. I said, 'Come on, Jack. Let's go. God is good.'"[82]

Kennedy wondered aloud to his friend Lem Billings as to how a loving God could permit his brother Joe and his sister Kathleen to be taken long before their time. He later mused, "The thing about Kathleen (Kick) and Joe was their tremendous vitality . . . For someone who is living at the peak, then to get cut off—that's the shock." The impact of these deaths contributed to his seemingly insatiable desire to push every day to the limit, or at least the limits of his remarkably frail body. Another friend, Chuck Spalding, noted, "Death was there—it had taken Joe and Kick and it was waiting for him. . . . So whenever he was in a situation, he tried to burn bright. . . . He had something nobody else did. It was just a heightened sense of being; there's no other way to describe it."[83]

I mention these points not to resurrect the Camelot image of Kennedy the saint, but to round out the portrait of a man who some have argued could be remarkably cruel, a hard man who was incapable of emotional attachment, perhaps even a "monster." Hard at times, thoughtless when it came to his wife, yes, but devoid of humanity, no. In 1962, a year when he had to fight for every available vote in Congress, a Democratic representative from California, Clem Miller, was killed in a plane crash. Kennedy was told that the district generally voted conservative, and the only way the party could hold the seat was to run Miller's widow, who was reluctant to do so, and who made it clear that only a direct request from the president would lead her to run. "She's got five children, doesn't she? . . . I can't ask that. We'll just have to give up the seat."[84] Congressman Miller was elected posthumously, forcing a special election in January 1963, when the seat was lost to a Republican.

Politics was not everything to John F. Kennedy, as it seemed to be for some presidents, including his two immediate successors. Kennedy's understanding that there was more to life than politics was a healthy attribute that sets him apart from those whose obsession with wielding power caused them to overreach. This was a president who was interested in history, journalism, language, and a good joke, all infused with an awareness of the razor-thin nature of life itself.

This is not to suggest that he did not approach his job with the respect it was due, at least while on business, if not in the White House swimming pool. In a professional setting, the president kept his easygoing jocularity on a leash and expected his friends to do the same. Paul "Red" Fay recalled Kennedy's ability to draw a line. "You knew just exactly how far you could go with the President. He had a reserve to him. He enjoyed an awful lot of fun, but when he was, say, in his role as the President of the United States among other people, why, his friends knew exactly what their role was." They were not his peers, nor were they on par with senior government leaders. "In other words," Fay noted, Kennedy's pals were not to "be front row center when he was dealing with the Cabinet, or when he was dealing with other people. And I think this is one thing that all his friends certainly observed . . . that this was a time for government business and not a time for camaraderie."[85]

"We Choose to Go to the Moon"

While John F. Kennedy's record in the realm of civil rights, Cuba, and the Cold War generates continued controversy, his commitment to landing a man on the moon before the end of the 1960s stands taller with each passing decade. This remarkable scientific and engineering achievement, using primitive technology by today's standards, has become the benchmark against which Americans weigh every endeavor. If we can land a man on the moon, the cliché goes, then surely we can do "X."

President Kennedy packaged the race to the moon in the language of his "New Frontier," appealing to the abiding American commitment to progress and exploration. As he noted in 1962 while arguing in favor of a manned mission to the moon, "The United States was not built by those who waited and rested and wished to look behind them. This country was conquered by those who moved forward." The very name "the New Frontier" recalled

America's pioneering spirit, and as Kennedy said the day before he was murdered, the 1960s would be a time for "pathfinders and pioneers."[86] This appeal to the nation's pioneering past, coupled with Kennedy's ability to transform the race to the moon into a competition with communism, was truly a masterstroke.

Kennedy's commitment to winning the space race unified the American people at a time when prosperity was the order of the day, at least for a majority of Americans, and the tendency in times of prosperity is to turn inward, away from common endeavors. This national endeavor, the race to the moon, captured the imagination as much as any earlier American crusade, including the opening of the West or the creation of the "arsenal of democracy." All baby boomers can recall the excitement not only of the moon landing itself, but of various space missions and space walks carried out by those with "the right stuff." Schools would shelve the curriculum for the day and carry "blast offs" and ocean landings on grainy television sets, and at night, spaced-themed programming, much of it remarkably vapid, would fill the airwaves. *Life* and *Look* magazines, which helped craft the Kennedy image, made heroes out of obscure mid-level military officers such as Alan Shepard, John Glenn, Virgil "Gus" Grissom, Wally Schirra, Neil Armstrong, and countless others.

Americans, as George Patton proclaimed, "love a winner and will not tolerate a loser. Americans play to win all the time." And Americans particularly hated the idea of losing to a regime that they believed was intrinsically backwards. One correspondent covering the space race summed up the American attitude toward the Soviet Union as "these people couldn't build a refrigerator . . . how can they get into orbit?"[87] General Patton's comments may fall on deaf ears to contemporary Americans, or even induce a sense of unease, but they would not have during the Kennedy years, when all seemed possible. This president personified the notion of limitless possibilities, that "man can be as big as he wants." It was John F. Kennedy more than any other American who made the moon landing a reality and understood the powerful appeal of adventure and of the insatiable thirst for heroes.

During the Kennedy years, the notion that the "money would be better spent here at home" had not yet emerged as the standard riposte to racing the Russians to the moon. Critics who accused the United States of wasting billions on an effort designed to simply "beat the Russians" ignore the fact that Kennedy had hinted at a joint Soviet and American space effort in his inaugural address and made an explicit proposal for such an effort in a speech to the United Nations General Assembly in September 1963. Kennedy noted that "the United States and the Soviet Union have a special capacity—space," where "there is room for new cooperation, for further joint efforts. I include among these possibilities a joint expedition to the moon." These joint space endeavors would have the benefit of "require[ing] a new approach to the Cold War." This somewhat remarkable offer caught many Americans and Russians by surprise but elicited a firm "no" from Soviet leader Nikita Khrushchev.[88]

At the time of his special message to Congress on "Urgent National Needs" on May 25, 1961, where Kennedy proposed landing a man on the moon, an American had been in space for a grand total of fifteen minutes. Nevertheless, Kennedy argued that an American triumph in space was necessary "if we are to win the battle that is now going on around the world between freedom and tyranny." Events since Sputnik in 1957 had demonstrated the impact of space adventure "on the minds of men everywhere," the president argued, adding that the ability of free men to triumph in space "may hold the key to our future on Earth." The goal, which he acknowledged would be "difficult" and "expensive" to achieve, was to land "a man on the Moon and return him safely to the Earth" before "this decade is out." The reference to "this decade" was inserted by Kennedy himself as a way of pressuring the National Aeronautics and Space Administration to step up their game. Not every member of Congress was impressed by Kennedy's clarion call to shoot for the moon; as one Republican member remarked, "President Kennedy's deficit is going to reach the Moon before we do."[89]

Contemporary Americans forget that Kennedy was "committing the nation to do something we couldn't do," as Charles Fishman has noted. The nation had none of the equipment, nor any of the computer capability or space suits or launchpads or rocket thrust capable of taking a man to the moon. "We didn't even know what we would need" to go to the moon, Fishman added. Christopher Columbus Kraft, creator of the mission control facility for NASA, noted that "when [Kennedy] asked us to do that in 1961, it was impossible."[90] Gene Kranz, the flight director for Apollo 11, echoed this assessment, likening the early days of the effort to "learning to drink from a fire hose. . . . We had to virtually invent or adapt every tool that we used."

One essential tool was money, and when Kennedy set the moon landing goal, NASA's budget for that year was one million dollars. A measure of his success in altering the nation's priorities can be seen in the fact that five years later, NASA would be spending one million dollars every three hours, all day, every day.[91]

NASA had been created in 1958 during the Eisenhower years, but Kennedy had been critical of his predecessor for "losing" the space race, for standing idly by while Russia was beating the United States. "The first vehicle into space was called Sputnik . . . the first passengers to return safely from a trip through space were named Strelka and Belka, not Rover or Fido," Kennedy observed. The space program during the Eisenhower years had been widely ridiculed, fair or not, for its repeated delays and launch pad disasters. But Kennedy was on to something that Ike seemed to find frivolous if not outright childish, and that was the perennial American desire to finish in first place. "I can't understand why the American people have got so worked up over this thing," Eisenhower mentioned to White House aides after Sputnik; "it's certainly not going to drop on their heads."

When asked for his response to Soviet cosmonaut Yuri Gagarin's historic flight on April 12, 1961, when Gagarin became the first human being to travel into space, the former president replied, "It is not necessary to be first in everything." This kind of talk was anathema to Kennedy, who argued that America's second-place performance in space was eroding one of the nation's selling points around the globe—an educational system that produced remarkable scientific and technological achievements. As a result of American complacency regarding the space race, the people of the world were no longer certain "as to which way the future lies."[92]

While Kennedy sought to downplay expectations at times during his presidency, partly to cover his backside if NASA failed, he continued to push for landing an American on the moon even as other issues pressed in on him. He was the program's biggest cheerleader and gave Vice President Lyndon Johnson the assignment of overseeing the effort, for which Johnson deserves ample credit. But Kennedy was more than just a cheerleader, becoming, as Charles Fishman notes, "the nation's poet laureate of space."[93]

On September 12, 1962, Kennedy traveled to Rice University in Houston, Texas to deliver one of the most moving speeches of his presidency. The president criticized those reluctant to take the leap into space, comparing them to "those who resisted the horseless carriage and Christopher Columbus." He cited explorers and adventurers including George Mallory, a British mountaineer who, as Kennedy noted, "was to die on Mount Everest. When he was asked 'why did he want to climb it?' He said, 'because it is there.' Well, space is there, and we're going to climb it." And he invoked the blessings of God on the forthcoming adventure, in a manner that John Winthrop or the architects of "manifest destiny" would have approved. "Therefore, as we set sail we ask God's blessing on the most hazardous and dangerous and greatest adventure on which man has ever embarked."[94]

Kennedy's appeal to God and to the spirit of American exceptionalism roused his Texas audience, as did his appeal to local passions to make the case for this national initiative. Critics of the race to the moon, Kennedy claimed, were defeatists. "But why, some say, the moon? Why choose this as our goal?" then ad-libbing, "why does Rice play Texas?" In the midst of thunderous applause, the speech reached its crescendo: "We choose to go to the Moon in this decade and do the other things, not because they are easy, but because they are hard; because that goal will serve to organize and measure the best of our energies and skills, because that challenge is one that we are willing to accept, one we are unwilling to postpone, and one we intend to win."

The Rice University speech did not receive prominent coverage in its day but has since gone on to become one of the most notable orations of Kennedy's presidency. The address electrified those who were at Rice stadium that day, including a young journalist named Dan Rather, who later recalled, "It was a thrilling moment." A high school sophomore rode his bike to the stadium and found the moment close to life-altering: "John F. Kennedy did something. He took the horror of the Cold War and made something beautiful, a dream for all of us." On his way out of the stadium, the president turned to NASA director Jim Webb and his staff, smiled and said, "All right. Now you guys do the details."[95]

Director Webb proved to be an obstacle when it came to fulfilling Kennedy's goal of landing a man on the moon before the end of the decade. Webb supported a broader effort to explore space for purposes of gathering scientific data. Just over two months after the Rice University speech, a contentious meeting was held in the White House where Webb and Kennedy sparred over NASA's priorities. Kennedy asked Webb if he believed "this program [a manned mission to the moon] is the top-priority program of the Agency?" Webb responded that it was not *the* top priority but one of many top priorities. The president rejected Webb's assessment, noting that "I think it is *the* top priority. I think we ought to have that very clear . . . this is important for political reasons, international political reasons. This is, whether we like it or not, in a sense a race. If we get second to the Moon, it's nice, but it's like being second any time. . . . Everything that we do ought to really be tied into getting onto the Moon ahead of the Russians."[96]

John F. Kennedy's last public words about the space program were delivered in San Antonio, Texas, the day before he was killed. The President dedicated an aerospace medical facility and cited the work of Frank O'Connor, an Irish writer whose 1961 autobiography *An Only Child* described how he and his boyhood friends managed to surmount certain obstacles as they ambled across the Irish countryside. "When they came to an orchard wall that seemed too high and too doubtful to try and too difficult to permit their voyage to continue," Kennedy observed, "they took off their hats and tossed them over the wall—and then they had no choice but to follow them." And he added that the United States "has tossed its cap over the wall of space, and we have no choice but to follow it. Whatever the difficulties, they will be overcome. . . . We will climb this wall . . . and we shall then explore the wonders on the other side."

Following Kennedy's assassination, Frank O'Connor remarked that it was "a very brilliant use of the quotation, and I would never have thought of it myself." O'Connor was delighted when he heard the news in Ireland that night that Kennedy had quoted him in far-away Texas. "On Thursday night I was called to the telephone to hear: 'President Kennedy is quoting you in San Antonio, Texas'; on Friday night I was called to the telephone to hear: 'President Kennedy is dead.'" O'Connor went on to add, "I wept, partly for ourselves [the Irish], who have lost a man that represented not only his own country but ours."[97]

Kennedy's support for winning the race to the moon drew the ire of leading members of the Republican Party. Barry Goldwater believed that the administration's effort distracted from the more important goal of winning the race to militarize space. Former President Dwight Eisenhower, always alert to excessive government spending, considered the effort to be something of a wasteful public relations gambit. Ike noted, "I frankly do not see the need for continuing this effort as such a fantastically expensive crash program" he wrote in 1962. Kennedy's "mad effort" was intended to "win a stunt race." Meeting with a group of Republican congressmen in June 1963, Ike opined that "anybody who would spend $40 billion in a race to the Moon for national prestige is nuts." As late as 1965, Eisenhower was still referring to the race to the moon as a "stunt."[98]

President Kennedy was always deferential to his predecessor, understanding the hold that Ike had on the American imagination. But Kennedy clearly bridled over Eisenhower's repeated public and private denunciations of the space program. At a press conference on April 3, 1963, Kennedy responded to Eisenhower's criticism of "enormous sums" of money going to the space program. Kennedy responded that the space program was not just his program but was authorized by an "almost unanimous" Congress. That Congress agreed with him that "the United States would not continue to be second in space." President Eisenhower's criticism was "not a new position for him," Kennedy argued, "from the time of Sputnik on," Ike had been making the same point, and this was "a matter on which we disagree."

Kennedy concurred with Eisenhower that if there was any "waste in the space budget" then cuts should be made, but he was not going to accept second place. "I think having made the decision last year, that we should make a major effort to be first in space. I think we should continue to do so. . . . If we are going to get into the question of whether we should reconcile ourselves to a slow pace in space, I don't think so."[99]

Dwight Eisenhower was a remarkable president in many ways, but was afflicted with a kind of green-eyeshade, Rotarian Republicanism of limited horizons. This child of the nineteenth century was an unusually skilled leader when it came to planning and coalition building, but his unwillingness to see the moral implications involved in the struggle for racial equality and his cramped imagination regarding the space program offers an unflattering distinction between himself and John F. Kennedy.

John F. Kennedy's ambitious goals for the American space program were realized on July 20, 1969, after the successful launch of Apollo 11 from Cape Kennedy. An American had set foot on the moon only sixty-six years after the Wright brothers' flight at Kitty Hawk. This accomplishment could well be what Americans in the centuries to come remember most about Kennedy's brief presidency.

Kennedy and Reagan

All unreconstructed ideologues will perish at the thought, but Ronald Reagan and John F. Kennedy shared many leadership qualities. Americans are instinctively drawn to the power of positive thinking, attracted to the perennial optimist who assures them of their special place in the world and that, as the epitaph on Ronald Reagan's grave reads, "What is right will always eventually triumph."[100]

Kennedy's conservative critics need to consider the fact that much of their condemnation of Kennedy can also be applied to Ronald Reagan. Arguably, their similarities outweighed their differences. While they disagreed profoundly on the proper role of the federal government, both men personified the spirit of the "can do" American and shared a love of a good off-color joke. Both men had a heroic conception of American history and celebrated courage. As Reagan said of Kennedy, and of himself, "History is, as young John Kennedy demonstrated, as heroic as you want it to be—as heroic as you are."[101]

Both were men of cheerful demeanor, and each man was charming, in his own different way. Both men took language and rhetoric seriously, and they were good editors of the product produced by their speechwriters. Both men believed in American exceptionalism and in the gospel of progress (Ronald Reagan served as the host of television's *General Electric Theater*, signing off of each show with "here at General Electric progress is our most important product.")[102] While Reagan perpetually quoted Thomas Paine's clarion call to Americans, "We have it in our power to begin the world over again," Kennedy echoed a similar theme in 1963 when he proclaimed that "never before has man had such capacity to control his own environment . . . we have the power to make this the best generation of mankind in the history of the world—or to make it the last."[103] Kennedy's American University speech, his inaugural address, and his speech announcing the nation's commitment to land a man on the moon all revealed his belief in America's inherent greatness and its unique ability to accomplish whatever it chose to do.

Both Kennedy and Reagan ran insurgency campaigns and refused to "wait their turn," setting a new standard in terms of running for president. "You are qualified to run for President if *you* think you are qualified to run for President," as Scott Farris insightfully observed. Kennedy was, as Farris noted, "America's first 'movie star-President,'" while Reagan was "the first movie star to become President." Both men, for better or worse, cemented the link between Hollywood and power brokers in Washington, both in terms of fundraising and in policy formulation and political marketing.[104]

Both Reagan and Kennedy were fond of quoting John Winthrop's "City on a Hill" speech—"For we must consider that we shall be as a City Upon a

Hill," the forty-three-year-old Winthrop said to his fellow Puritans as they migrated to Massachusetts Bay Colony, "the eyes of all people are upon us." This chosen people, Winthrop said, must abide by the precepts of Christian charity. The forty-three-year-old Kennedy cited Winthrop's remarks 331 years later during his only public speech between his election in 1960 and his inauguration in 1961, an address to the Massachusetts state legislature.[105] Neither president properly understood Winthrop's remarks, but for Kennedy and Reagan, the notion of the United States as a beacon of hope to the rest of the world was a truism.

In an underappreciated speech President Reagan delivered at a fundraising event for the John F. Kennedy Library Foundation in 1985, "the Gipper" captured the essence of Kennedy's appeal. "Everything we saw him do seemed to betray a huge enjoyment of life . . . you have to enjoy the journey, it's unfaithful not to. I think that's how his country remembers him, in his joy. And it was a joy he knew how to communicate." Kennedy was, as Reagan said, "quintessentially, completely American."[106]

Americans want to look up to their president and admire the nation of which he, eventually she, serves as head of state. This reason more than any other explains why these two presidents score the highest approval ratings when Americans are asked to rank their favorite presidents. They made Americans feel good about themselves, their country, and their future. They offered a message of hope and optimism, not the snarling message of hate and fear that dominated American politics during the Trump presidency.

Conclusion: Coming Full Circle after Sixty Years

The real Kennedy presidency was obscured for decades by those who transformed him into a saintly icon, as well as by those who saw nothing but hair and teeth concealing a destructive ambition and a frenzied libido. The presidency of John F. Kennedy mattered in ways that affect us to this day and will continue to do so. He contributed to an exaggerated sense of what the American presidency and the federal government could be expected to deliver. In that sense, he was on par with all his twentieth-century progressive peers.

Nonetheless, Kennedy understood that the president is the keeper of the nation's tablets and can play a vital role as a unifying head of state. Critics who claim that he emphasized rhetoric over legislative legwork are guilty of denigrating the power of ideas, particularly those enunciated to an audience of millions through the medium of television and radio. As the nation's head of state, the president possesses an extraordinary platform to educate and ennoble his fellow citizens. Abraham Lincoln grasped this fact better than any president before or since, as he demonstrated at Gettysburg in 1863 or in his second inaugural address. Lincoln understood that a president can appeal to "mystic chords of memory" and help bind the nation's wounds. Abraham Lincoln is rightly celebrated for his words, not his legislative scorecard. John F. Kennedy also understood the power of words, and he and his speechwriter Ted Sorensen did their best to equal the rhetoric of Kennedy's greatest predecessors.

John F. Kennedy's complex character contributed to a misunderstanding of his presidency. His expansive rhetoric, brimming with patriotic calls to action, concealed his abiding pragmatism. Additionally, this multifaceted man kept his own counsel and compartmentalized his life with remarkable and sometimes disturbing ease. He rejected ideology and ideologues and the canned solutions they offered, grasping the nuanced nature of the issues confronting him. Kennedy encouraged dissenting perspectives, and often was a font of dissent when meeting with his own advisors. John F. Kennedy became an eloquent defender of the principle that all men are created equal, and his commitment to this principle, along with his moving rhetoric on the superiority of liberal democracy over totalitarianism and his devotion to controlling, and eventually eliminating, nuclear weapons, led to some of the most moving rhetoric in the history of the presidency.

Like some of his celebrated predecessors, Thomas Jefferson and Franklin Roosevelt for instance, Kennedy was Machiavellian to the core, and his approaches to issues like Vietnam, civil rights, and the Cold War confrontation with the Soviet Union, were marked by feints and misleading rhetoric. Grasping Kennedy's true intentions requires digging well below the superficial accounts offered by friends and foes, or his own public rhetoric. On top of this, the brevity of his presidency denied us the fuller picture of the man and his policies that would have emerged in a second term. Thankfully, we have the secretly recorded White House conversations that allow us a deeper insight into the man in the Oval Office.

After "living" with the Kennedy presidency for over six decades, I have come to the conclusion that he deserves more than just a second look, that in fact he deserves the status of a "near-great" president. President Kennedy challenged the American people, sometimes belatedly, asking them to deliver on the nation's promise. He appealed to their "better angels," urging them to devote themselves to something higher, the Peace Corps being one of the primary examples of his call for service before self. Kennedy was not far removed from his immigrant forebears, who came to America because they considered it the "last, best hope of mankind." Kennedy encapsulated this spirit, both for his fellow citizens and for those watching from abroad. Like Thomas Jefferson, he fell far short in his own personal conduct of living up to the best, but like Jefferson, his aspirations for the nation point the way for all of us. And for that reason alone, his place in the American mind should be secured.

INTRODUCTION

1. Jimmy Dean, "P.T. 109," https://genius.com/Jimmy-dean-p-t-109
-lyrics.

2. Jenna Johnson, "Mike Pence Says It's 'Inarguable' that Putin is a Stronger Leader than Obama," *Washington Post*, September 8, 2016, https://
www.washingtonpost.com/news/post-politics/wp/2016/09/08/mike-pence
-says-its-inarguable-that-putin-is-a-stronger-leader-than-obama/; Matthew Nussbaum, "Trump Publicly Sides with Putin on Election Interference," *Politico*, July 16, 2018, https://www.politico.com/story/2018/07/16/trump
-russia-putin-summit-722418; Brook Seipel, "Trump Defends Putin: 'You Think Our Country Is so Innocent?'" *The Hill*, February 4, 2017, https://
thehill.com/blogs/ballot-box/317945-trump-defends-putin-you-think-our
-country-is-so-innocent.

3. William F. Buckley, Jr., "Worshipping JFK," *National Review*, November 21, 2003, https://www.nationalreview.com/2003/11/worshipping-jfk/; Jonah Goldberg (@JonahDispatch), "JFK's endurance on these lists is one of the longest lived triumphs of style over substance in American culture," Twitter, June 30, 2021.

4. Nick Bryant, *The Bystander: John F. Kennedy and the Struggle for Black Equality* (New York: Basic Books, 2006); Michael Kazin, "Ending the Kennedy Romance," *New York Review of Books*, May 27, 2021, 19.

5. The figure of forty thousand titles is taken from Jill Abramson, "Kennedy, the Elusive President," *New York Times*, October 22, 2013, https://
www.nytimes.com/2013/10/27/books/review/the-elusive-president.html.

6. I am indebted to the anonymous reviewer of this manuscript for suggesting that I include this passage.

CHAPTER 1. REFOUNDING THE PRESIDENCY

1. Neustadt quoted in Michael Nelson, "James David Barber and the Psychological Presidency," *Virginia Quarterly Review*, 56, no. 4 (Autumn 1980), https://www.vqronline.org/essay/james-david-barber-and-psychological
-presidency.

2. See Stephen F. Knott, *The Lost Soul of the American Presidency: The Decline into Demagoguery and the Prospects for Renewal* (Lawrence, KS: University Press of Kansas, 2019); Jeremy Suri, *The Impossible Presidency: The Rise and Fall of America's Highest Office* (New York; Basic Books, 2017); and John Dickerson, *The Hardest Job in the World: The American Presidency* (New York: Random House, 2020).

3. Larry Sabato, *The Kennedy Half-Century: The Presidency, Assassination, and Lasting Legacy of John F. Kennedy* (New York: Bloomsbury, 2013).

4. Stephen F. Knott, "What Might Have Been," *Review of Politics* 76, no. 4 (Fall 2014): 661–670. This piece offers a critical view of Kennedy's presidency; perhaps too critical.

5. Stephen F. Knott and Tony Williams, *Washington and Hamilton: The Alliance That Forged America* (Naperville, IL: Sourcebooks, 2015), 179–180.

6. Ellen Fitzpatrick, *Letters to Jackie: Condolences from a Grieving Nation* (New York: Ecco, 2010). Much of this correspondence was destroyed simply for a lack of archival space to house the over one million letters received. See also Katie Zezima, "Letters Capture Grief for President Kennedy," *New York Times*, March 8, 2010, https://www.nytimes.com/2010/03/09/us/09kennedy.html; John F. Kennedy Presidential Library and Museum, "Jacqueline Kennedy Onassis Condolence Mail," https://www.jfklibrary.org/asset-viewer/archives/JBKOCM.

7. Christopher Matthews, *Jack Kennedy: Elusive Hero* (New York: Simon & Schuster, 2011).

8. Ron Simon, "See How Kennedy Created a Presidency for the Television Age," Time.com, May 30, 2017, https://time.com/4795637/jfk-television/.

9. David Nasaw, *The Patriarch: The Remarkable Life and Turbulent Times of Joseph P. Kennedy* (New York: Penguin Books, 2013), 542.

10. Ted Sorensen, *Kennedy: The Classic Biography* (New York: Harper Perennial Modern Classics, 2013), 311.

11. Matthews, *Jack Kennedy*, 10.

12. John F. Kennedy Presidential Library and Museum, "The President and the Press: Address before the American Newspaper Publishers Association, April 27, 1961," https://www.jfklibrary.org/archives/other-resources/john-f-kennedy-speeches/american-newspaper-publishers-association-19610427.

13. Jeff Himmelman, *Yours in Truth: A Personal Portrait of Ben Bradlee, Legendary Editor of the Washington Post* (New York: Random House, 2017), 306.

14. Michael Schudson, *The Power of News* (Cambridge, MA: Harvard University Press, 1995), 146; Sean J. Savage, *JFK, LBJ, and the Democratic Party* (Albany, NY: State University of New York Press, 2006), 85.

15. Himmelman, *Yours in Truth*, 82–83.

16. Don Gonyea, "How JFK Fathered the Modern Presidential Campaign," *National Public Radio*, November 16, 2013, https://www.npr.org/2013/11/16/245550528/jfk-wrote-the-book-on-modern-Presidential-campaigns; Steven Levingston, "JFK on TV, Trump on Twitter," *Washington Post*, May 18, 2017, https://www.washingtonpost.com/lifestyle/magazine/jfk-on-tv-trump-on-twitter-and-the-shaping-of-two-Presidential-legacies/2017/05/15/08c60ed8–1eed-11e7-be2a-3a1fb24d4671_story.html.

17. Gonyea, "How JFK Fathered."

18. Gonyea, "How JFK Fathered"

19. *Primary*, directed by Robert Drew, (Drew Associates, 1960), 53 minutes. https://drewassociates.com/films/primary/.

20. Gonyea, "How JFK Fathered"

21. Emma Green, "The Forgotten Joy of 1960 Presidential Campaign Jingles," *At-*

lantic, October 31, 2013, https://www.theatlantic.com/politics/archive/2013/10/the-for gotten-joy-of-1960-Presidential-campaign-jingles/281015/; "Click with Dick," Cornell University Library Digital Collections, https://digital.library.cornell.edu/catalog /ss:10638586.

22. Simon, "How Kennedy Created a Presidency"

23. I am indebted to the anonymous reviewer of this manuscript who suggested the inclusion of this passage.

24. Trip Gabriel, "50 Years into the War on Poverty, Hardship Hits Back," *New York Times,* April 20, 2014, https://www.nytimes.com/2014/04/21/us/50-years-into -the-war-on-poverty-hardship-hits-back.html.

25. Daniel K. Williams, *God's Party: The Making of the Christian Right* (New York: Oxford University Press, 2010), 54.

26. Dave Roos, "How John F. Kennedy Overcame Anti-Catholic Bias to Win the Presidency," *History,* November 20, 2019, https://www.history.com/news/jfk-catho lic-President; Paul Schwartzman, "How Trump Got Religion—And Why His Legendary Minister's Son Now Rejects Him," *Washington Post,* January 21, 2016, https:// www.washingtonpost.com/lifestyle/how-trump-got-religion—and-why-his-leg endary-ministers-son-now-rejects-him/2016/01/21/37bae16e-bb02–11e5–829c-26ffb8 74a18d_story.html; Savage, *JFK, LBJ, and the Democratic Party,* 79.

27. Thomas J. Carty, *A Catholic in the White House? Religion, Politics, and John F. Kennedy's Presidential Campaign* (New York: Palgrave MacMillan, 2004), 11.

28. James T. Fisher, "The Second Catholic President: Ngo Dinh Diem, John F. Kennedy, and the Vietnam Lobby," *U.S. Catholic Historian* 15, no. 3 (Summer 1997): 134.

29. Savage, *JFK, LBJ, and the Democratic Party,* 79; Roos, "How John F. Kennedy Overcame Anti-Catholic Bias."

30. Williams, *God's Party,* 56. For a thoughtful account of Kennedy, Catholicism, and the impact of his presidency on the politics of church and state, see Patrick Lacroix, *John F. Kennedy and the Politics of Faith* (Lawrence, KS: University Press of Kansas, 2021).

31. Ruth Igielnik, Scott Keeter, and Hannah Hartig, "Behind Biden's 2020 Victory," Pew Research Center, June 30, 2021, https://www.pewresearch.org/politics /2021/06/30/behind-bidens-2020-victory/.

32. Quoted in Jason K. Duncan, *John F. Kennedy: The Spirit of Cold War Liberalism* (New York: Routledge, 2014), 198.

33. Garry Wills, *The Kennedy Imprisonment: A Meditation on Power* (Boston, MA: Mariner Books, 2002), 188.

34. Matthew J. Dickinson and Elizabeth A. Neustadt, eds., *Guardian of the Presidency: The Legacy of Richard E. Neustadt* (Washington, DC: Brookings Institution Press, 2007), 15, 41.

35. James N. Giglio, *Presidency of John F. Kennedy* (Lawrence, KS: University Press of Kansas, 1991), 29.

36. Richard E. Neustadt, *Presidential Power and the Modern Presidents: The Politics of Leadership from Roosevelt to Reagan* (New York: Free Press, 1990), xx, 37. These

quotes appeared in the 1960 edition read by Kennedy. For mention of Neustadt's plan to join the Kennedy White House, see Matthew Dickinson, "Rest in Peace Ted Sorensen," *Presidential Power with Matthew Dickinson*, October 31, 2010, https://sites .middlebury.edu/Presidentialpower/tag/john-f-kennedy/.

37. Sorensen, *Kennedy*, 283; Alan Brinkley, *John F. Kennedy* (New York: Times Books, 2012), 60; Knott, *Lost Soul of the American Presidency*, 164.

38. Giglio, *Presidency of John F. Kennedy*, 30; Brinkley, *John F. Kennedy*, 59; Knott, *Lost Soul of the American Presidency*, 164.

39. Brinkley, *John F. Kennedy*, 59–60; Knott, *Lost Soul of the American Presidency*, 164.

40. Dickinson and Neustadt, eds., *Guardian of the Presidency*, 60.

41. John F. Kennedy Presidential Library and Museum, "'The Presidency in 1960,' Address by Senator John F. Kennedy, January 14, 1960," https://www.jfklibrary.org /archives/other-resources/john-f-kennedy-speeches/presidency-in-1960–19600114.

42. John F. Kennedy Presidential Library and Museum, "'The Presidency in 1960.'"

43. Giglio, *Presidency of John F. Kennedy*, 29.

44. Brinkley, *John F. Kennedy*, 89.

45. Marilyn Geewax, "JFK's Lasting Economic Legacy: Lower Tax Rates," *National Public Radio*, November 14, 2013, https://www.npr.org/2013/11/12/244772593/jfks-last ing-economic-legacy-lower-tax-rates; James Hoopes, "When a Leader Overreaches: JFK's Pyrrhic Victory Over U.S. Steel," Babson College, https://www.babson.edu /academics/executive-education/babson-insight/leadership-and-management /when-a-leader-overreaches/.

46. Giglio, *Presidency of John F. Kennedy*, 130; James Hoopes, "When a Leader Overreaches."

47. John F. Kennedy Presidential Library and Museum, "News Conference #30, April 11, 1962," https://www.jfklibrary.org/archives/other-resources/john-f-kennedy -press-conferences/news-conference-30.

48. John F. Kennedy Presidential Library and Museum, "New Conference #30."

49. Giglio, *Presidency of John F. Kennedy*, 131–132.

50. Jeff Greenfield, "JFK's Dangerous Playbook for Trump," *Politico*, December 23, 2016, https://www.politico.com/magazine/story/2016/12/jfks-dangerous-play book-for-trump-214547.

51. Schlesinger quoted in Peggy Noonan, "Trump's Carrier Coup and a Lesson from JFK," *Wall Street Journal*, December 1, 2016, https://www.wsj.com/articles /trumps-carrier-coup-and-a-lesson-from-jfk-1480637967; Giglio, *Presidency of John F. Kennedy*, 132.

52. Simon, "See How Kennedy Created a Presidency."

53. Brinkley, *John F. Kennedy*, 50.

54. Brinkley, *John F. Kennedy*, 51–52; Giglio, *Presidency of John F. Kennedy*, 18.

55. Alexis C. Madrigal, "John F. Kennedy on Television's Political Impact," *Atlantic*, November 16, 2010, https://www.theatlantic.com/technology/archive/2010/11

/john-f-kennedy-on-televisions-political-impact/66644/; Knott, *Lost Soul of the American Presidency,* 172. Kennedy's 1960 presidential campaign was arguably the first to harness the power of primitive computer technology to package the candidate's message. See Jill Lepore, *If/Then: How the Simulatics Corporation Invented the Future* (New York: Liveright, 2020), ch. 6.

56. Madrigal, "John F. Kennedy on Television's Political Impact."

57. Jon Kelly, "Woodrow Wilson's Odd Early Press Conferences," *BBC News,* March 15, 2013, https://www.bbc.com/news/magazine-21761429.

58. John F. Kennedy Presidential Library and Museum, "John F. Kennedy and the Press," https://www.jfklibrary.org/learn/about-jfk/jfk-in-history/john-f-kennedy -and-the-press.

59. Knott, *Lost Soul of the American Presidency,* 108.

60. Knott, *Lost Soul of the American Presidency,* 155–156.

61. Simon, "See How Kennedy Created A Presidency"; John F. Kennedy Presidential Library and Museum, "Salinger, Pierre E.G., Oral History Interview—JFK #2," https://www.jfklibrary.org/asset-viewer/archives/JFKOH/Salinger%2C%20Pierre %20E.%20G/JFKOH-PES-02/JFKOH-PES-02.

62. John F. Kennedy Presidential Library and Museum, "John F. Kennedy and the Press."

63. John F. Kennedy Presidential Library and Museum, "Salinger, Pierre E.G."

64. Giglio, *Presidency of John F. Kennedy,* 260; Knott, *Lost Soul of the American Presidency,* 165.

65. Quoted in Max Holland, "The Truth Behind JFK's Assassination," *Newsweek,* November 20, 2014, https://www.newsweek.com/2014/11/28/truth-behind-jfks-assas sination-285653.html.

66. Kenneth T. Walsh, "Behind the Lens of History," *U.S. News and World Report,* October 11, 2017, https://www.usnews.com/news/the-report/articles/2017–10–11/white -house-photographers-are-the-ultimate-insiders.

67. "JFK's White House Photographer Cecil Stoughton, 88," *NPPA: The Voice of Visual Journalists,* November 5, 2008, https://nppa.org/news/1199; Amanda Hopkinson, "Cecil Stoughton," *Guardian,* November 19, 2008, https://www.theguardian .com/world/2008/nov/20/photographer-obituary-cecil-stoughton; Jackson Krule, "All the President's Photographers," *New Yorker,* February 17, 2012, https://www .newyorker.com/culture/photo-booth/all-the-Presidents-photographers.

68. Richard J. Tofel, *Sounding the Trumpet: The Making of John F. Kennedy's Inaugural Address* (Chicago: Ivan R. Dee, 2005), 171; John F. Kennedy Presidential Library and Museum, "Commencement Address at American University, Washington, D.C., June 10, 1963," https://www.jfklibrary.org/archives/other-resources /john-f-kennedy-speeches/american-university-19630610.

69. Thomas Frank, "The Maintenance Crew," *Harper's Magazine,* October 2012, https://harpers.org/archive/2012/10/the-maintenance-crew/.

70. "The Loneliest Job," *New York Times,* The New York Times Store, https:// store.nytimes.com/products/the-loneliest-job-john-f-kennedy. This image was, for

a time, prominently displayed at the Museum at the John F. Kennedy Library in Boston.

71. John F. Kennedy Presidential Library and Museum, "'The Presidency in 1960.'"

CHAPTER 2. THE HUNDRED YEARS' WAR

1. Frank Hobbs and Nicole Stoops, *Demographic Trends in the Twentieth Century: Census 2000 Special Reports* (Washington, DC: U.S. Department of Commerce, 2002), 93.

2. Sheldon M. Stern, "John F. Kennedy and the Politics of Race and Civil Rights," *Reviews in American History* 5 (2007): 118–125; Nick Bryant, *The Bystander: John F. Kennedy and the Struggle for Black Equality* (New York: Basic Books, 2006), ch. 1.

3. Ted Sorensen, *Counselor: A Life at the Edge of History* (New York: HarperCollins, 2008), 270–271.

4. For a discussion of Bowers and his influence on Franklin Roosevelt and mid-twentieth century scholarship, see Stephen F. Knott, *Alexander Hamilton and the Persistence of Myth* (Lawrence, KS: University Press of Kansas, 2002), 116–118.

5. Quoted in Stern, "Kennedy and the Politics of Race," 119.

6. Stanley Turkel, *Heroes of the American Reconstruction: Profiles of Sixteen Educators, Politicians and Activists* (Jefferson, NC: McFarland, 2005), 17.

7. Robert J. Cook, *Troubled Commemoration: The American Civil War Centennial, 1961–1965* (Baton Rouge: Louisiana State University Press, 2007), 96; David Pevear, "Ames Daughter Dogged JFK Over Characterization in 'Profiles,' *Lowell Sun*, July 2, 2008, https://www.lowellsun.com/2008/07/02/ames-daughter-dogged -jfk-over-characterization-in-profiles/.

8. Ted Sorensen appears to have done the bulk of the research and writing for this book. Craig Fehrman notes that "the book's structure, research, first draft and most of its second came from the aide [Ted Sorensen]. Even the book's idea came from him. Amid the thousands of pages of *Profiles* material at the Kennedy Presidential Library, one can find only a few examples of Kennedy's contributions— mostly from the handwritten notebooks and dictabelt recordings that include his attempts to make sense of the previous books on those senators, attempts Kennedy undertook only after Sorensen had read those very same books and written his first drafts." See Craig Fehrman, "I Would Rather Win a Pulitzer Than Be President," *Politico*, February 11, 2020, https://www.politico.com/news/magazine/2020/02/11 /john-f-kennedy-pulitzer-obsession-consumed-him-113452.

JFK biographer Fredrik Logevall differs with Fehrman, noting that the allegation that Kennedy did not write the book "was largely baseless. For one thing, Kennedy had a bigger role in the writing, and certainly in the conception and framing of the book, than many of these analysts suggested. . . . Friends who visited in Florida attested to his hard work on the manuscript, as did secretaries who took his dictation, as did, with great vehemence, Jackie Kennedy." Fredrik Logevall, *JFK: Coming of Age in the American Century, 1917–1956* (New York: Random House, 2020), 617.

9. Papers of John F. Kennedy. Personal Papers. Manuscripts: Profiles in Courage.

Part 3, Chapter 6: Edmund G. Ross: Item 6-mimeograph, https://www.jfklibrary.org
/asset-viewer/archives/JFKPP/028/JFKPP-028–043#folder_info.

10. John F. Kennedy, *Profiles in Courage: Inaugural Edition* (New York: Harper
& Row, 1961), ch. 7; Nicholas Lemann, *Redemption: The Last Battle of the Civil War*
(New York: Farrar, Straus, and Giroux, 2006), 151; Michael Newton, *The Ku Klux
Klan in Mississippi: A History* (Jefferson, NC: McFarland, 2010), 14.

11. Brook Thomas, *The Literature of Reconstruction* (Baltimore, MD: Johns Hopkins University Press, 2017), 6–7.

12. Alan Brinkley, *John F. Kennedy* (New York: Times Books, 2012), 107.

13. James N. Giglio, *The Presidency of John F. Kennedy* (Lawrence, KS: University
Press of Kansas, 1991), 176–177.

14. Quoted in *William Faulkner: Critical Assessments, volume 4*, ed. Henry Clar-
idge (East Sussex, UK: Helm Information, 1999), 105.

15. Cook, *Troubled Commemoration*, 42.

16. Cook, *Troubled Commemoration*, 84.

17. Cook, *Troubled Commemoration*, ch. 3.

18. *Public Papers of the Presidents of the United States, John F. Kennedy, 1961, January 20 to December 31, 1961* (Washington, DC.: U.S. Government Printing Office,
1962), 92.

19. Cook, *Troubled Commemoration*, 102–107.

20. Cook, *Troubled Commemoration*, 108.

21. Steven Levingston, *Kennedy and King: The President, The Pastor, and the Battle
Over Civil Rights* (New York: Hachette Books, 2017), 224–225; Herbert S. Parmet,
JFK: The Presidency of John F. Kennedy (New York: Penguin Books, 1983), 85.

22. Quoted in Parmet, *JFK*, 252.

23. Sean J. Savage, *JFK, LBJ, and the Democratic Party* (Albany, NY: State University Press of New York, 2004) 87–88.

24. Quoted in Carl M. Brauer, *John F. Kennedy and the Second Reconstruction*
(New York: Columbia University Press, 1977), 48.

25. Sorensen, *Counselor*, 272.

26. Papers of John F. Kennedy, Presidential Papers, White House Central File, Subject File, Martin Luther King, Jr., to Frank Reeves, Special Assistant to the President,
February 28, 1961, https://www.jfklibrary.org/asset-viewer/february-28–1961-letter.

27. Peter Grier, "Martin Luther King, Jr. and John F. Kennedy: Civil Rights
Wary Allies," *Christian Science Monitor*, January 20, 2014, https://www.csmonitor
.com/USA/Politics/DC-Decoder/2014/0120/Martin-Luther-King-Jr.-and-John-F.
-Kennedy-civil-rights-wary-allies.

28. Giglio, *Presidency of John F. Kennedy*, 272. In an oral history interview conducted by Arthur Schlesinger Jr. in 1964, Jacqueline Kennedy described Martin Luther King as "tricky" and "phony" and that she could not look at a photograph of
King "without thinking . . . that man's terrible." The former First Lady had been
told by her husband about King's extramarital affairs and by Robert Kennedy of de-
rogatory comments allegedly uttered by King while watching her husband's funeral.

These comments were recorded by the FBI and eagerly transmitted to Attorney General Robert Kennedy by FBI Director J. Edgar Hoover. Tim Mak, "Jackie O Not an MLK Fan," *Politico*, 9 September 2011, https://www.politico.com/story/2011/09 /jackie-o-not-an-mlk-fan-063078.

29. John F. Kennedy Oral History Collection, "Nicholas deBelleville Katzenbach, Oral History Interview—RFK #1," October 8, 1969, https://www.jfklibrary .org/asset-viewer/archives/RFKOH/Katzenbach%2C%20Nicholas%20deB/RFK OH-NDK-01/RFKOH-NDK-01.

30. David J. Garrow, "The F.B.I. and Martin Luther King," *Atlantic*, July/August 2002, https://www.theatlantic.com/magazine/archive/2002/07/the-fbi-and-martin -luther-king/302537/; Giglio, *Presidency of John F. Kennedy*, 184–185.

31. "JFK Assassination Records, Findings on MLK Assassination," National Archives, https://www.archives.gov/research/jfk/select-committee-report/part-2e.html #electronic.

32. King Encyclopedia, s.v. "Communism," https://kinginstitute.stanford.edu /encyclopedia/communism.

33. "Findings on MLK Assassination," JFK Assassination Records, National Archive, https://www.archives.gov/research/jfk/select-committee-report/part-2e.html #electronic.

34. JFK Assassination Records, "Findings on MLK Assassination."

35. King Encyclopedia, s.v. "Levison, Stanley," https://kinginstitute.stanford.edu /encyclopedia/levison-stanley-david; King Encyclopedia, s.v. "O'Dell, Hunter Pitts 'Jack,'" https://kinginstitute.stanford.edu/encyclopedia/odell-hunter-pitts-jack.

36. Encyclopedia of Alabama, s.v. "James L. Baggett, Eugene 'Bull' Connor," http://www.encyclopediaofalabama.org/article/h-1091.

37. Papers of John F. Kennedy. Pre-Presidential Papers. Presidential Campaign Files, 1960, Alabama, Political, A-C, https://www.jfklibrary.org/asset-viewer/archives /JFKCAMP1960/0925/JFKCAMP1960–0925–008.

38. John F. Kennedy Oral History Collection, "Patterson, John M.: Oral History Interview—JFK #1, 5/26/1967," https://www.jfklibrary.org/asset-viewer/archives/JFK OH/Patterson%2C%20John%20M/JFKOH-JMP-01/JFKOH-JMP-01.

39. Sean Trende, "Did JFK Lose the Popular Vote?" *Real Clear Politics*, October 19, 2012, https://www.realclearpolitics.com/articles/2012/10/19/did_jfk_lose_the_popu lar_vote_115833-full.html. Trende argues that Kennedy did not win the popular vote in the 1960 presidential election due to Alabama's convoluted election system. Voters were given a choice to select up to eleven electors, the total electoral vote possessed by the state in the electoral college. Of the eleven electors who won their races, five were pledged to Kennedy and six to Dixiecrat Harry Byrd. But while six Byrd electors were chosen by the voters, none of the popular vote is awarded to Byrd in most accounts of the election. The popular votes for each of these electors, whether they voted for Byrd or Kennedy, was ultimately given to Kennedy, even though many Byrd supporters were unlikely to favor Kennedy. *Congressional Quarterly* initially proclaimed Nixon the winner of the popular vote in Alabama by approximately 60,000 votes,

using a mathematical equation that allocated the popular vote for electors between Kennedy, Byrd, and Nixon. This would also translate into Nixon winning the popular vote nationwide.

On a separate note, there was an effort made by electors from Mississippi and Alabama in 1960 to persuade their fellow electors to deny Kennedy the presidency in the electoral college. Various schemes were put forward by Governor Ross Barnett of Mississippi and other southern Democrats. These schemes included a proposal to "reverse the position of the candidates," with Lyndon Johnson selected as president and Kennedy as vice president. Another option involved persuading Republican electors from all fifty states to meet in Chicago and select a president from a "list of 'outstanding southern men.'" Richard Nixon was not involved in these efforts. Ronald G. Shafer, "Hijacking the Electoral College: The Plot to Deny JFK the Presidency 60 Years Ago," *Washington Post,* December 13, 2020, https://www.washingtonpost .com/history/2020/12/13/electoral-college-jfk-trump/.

40. Gerald Strober, *Let Us Begin Anew: An Oral History of the Kennedy Presidency* (New York: HarperCollins, 1993), ch. 13; Harris Wofford, *Of Kennedys and Kings: Making Sense of the Sixties* (Pittsburgh, PA: The University Press of Pittsburgh, 1992), 157–158.

41. John F. Kennedy Oral History Collection, "Farmer, James L.: Oral History Interview—JFK #2, 4/25/1979," https://www.jfklibrary.org/asset-viewer/archives/JFK OH/Farmer%2C%20James%20L/JFKOH-JLF-02/JFKOH-JLF-02.

42. John F. Kennedy Oral History Collection, "Farmer, James L.: Oral History Interview—JFK #2."

43. James Farmer, Letter to President John F. Kennedy, 4/26/1961, https://www .jfklibrary.org/learn/education/students/leaders-in-the-struggle-for-civil-rights /james-farmer.

44. For an in-depth look at the impact of race relations on Kennedy's foreign policy see Thomas Borstelmann, *The Cold War and the Color Line: American Race Relations in the Global Arena* (Cambridge, MA: Harvard University Press, 2003); Brenda Gayle Plummer, *Window on Freedom: Race, Civil Rights, and Foreign Affairs, 1945–1988* (Chapel Hill, NC: University of North Carolina Press, 2003); and Mary Dudziak, *Cold War Civil Rights: Race and the Image of American Democracy* (Princeton, NJ: Princeton University Press, 2011).

45. Raymond Arsenault, *Freedom Riders: 1961 and the Struggle for Racial Justice* (Oxford, UK: Oxford University Press, 2006), 133.

46. Arsenault, *Freedom Riders,* 137.

47. Arsenault, *Freedom Riders,* 108.

48. David Niven, *The Politics of Injustice: The Kennedys, the Freedom Rides, and the Electoral Consequences of a Moral Compromise* (Knoxville, TN: University of Tennessee Press, 2003), 96.

49. Brauer, *Kennedy and the Second Reconstruction,* 100.

50. Brinkley, *John F. Kennedy,* 99–101; Robert Dallek, *Camelot's Court: Inside the Kennedy White House* (New York: HarperCollins, 2013), 175–176.

51. Robert F. Kennedy, "Law Day Address at the University of Georgia Law School," May 6, 1961, https://americanrhetoric.com/speeches/rfkgeorgialawschool .htm.

52. *Public Papers of the Presidents of the United States, John F. Kennedy, 1961,* 391.

53. John F. Kennedy Oral History Collection, "Farmer, James L.: Oral History Interview—JFK #1, 3/10/1967," https://www.jfklibrary.org/asset-viewer/archives/JFK OH/Farmer%2C%20James%20L/JFKOH-JLF-01/JFKOH-JLF-01.

54. *The Papers of Martin Luther King, Jr., To Save the Soul of America, January 1961-August 1962,* eds. Clayborne Carson and Tenisha Armstrong (Oakland, CA: University of California Press, 2014), 368n1; King Encyclopedia, s.v. "Voter Education Project" (VEP), https://kinginstitute.stanford.edu/encyclopedia/voter-educa tion-project-vep.

55. John F. Kennedy Presidential Library and Museum, "Voter Registration, 1961–1963," Burke Marshall Personal Papers, https://www.jfklibrary.org/asset-viewer/ar chives/BMPP/034/BMPP-034-013

56. Giglio, *Presidency of John F. Kennedy,* 173–176.

57. William Doyle, *An American Insurrection: James Meredith and the Battle of Oxford, Mississippi, 1962* (New York: Anchor Books, 2001), 111–112.

58. Michael Newton, *White Robes and Burning Crosses: A History of the Ku Klux Klan from 1866* (Jefferson, NC: McFarland, 2014), 132; Doyle, *American Insurrection,* 162–163.

59. Charles W. Eagles, *The Price of Defiance: James Meredith and the Integration of Old Miss* (Chapel Hill, NC: University of North Carolina Press, 2009), 336.

60. Yasuhiro Katagiri, *The Mississippi State Sovereignty Commission: Civil Rights and States' Rights* (Jackson, MS: University Press of Mississippi, 2001), 61.

61. Giglio, *Presidency of John F. Kennedy,* 176; "Nicholas Katzenbach Dead at 90," *Politico,* May 9, 2012, https://www.politico.com/story/2012/05/nicholas-katzen bach-dead-at-90–076118.

62. Brauer, *Kennedy and the Second Reconstruction,* 200–201.

63. Wofford, *Of Kennedys and Kings,* 168; John F. Kennedy Presidential Library and Museum, "Integrating Ole Miss: A Civil Rights Milestone," https://microsites .jfklibrary.org/olemiss/meredith/.

64. John F. Kennedy Presidential Library and Museum, "Integrating Ole Miss: A Civil Rights Milestone, Public Opinion: Bumper Stickers from the Period, Collected by Walter Lord," https://microsites.jfklibrary.org/olemiss/meredith/.

65. Brinkley, *John F, Kennedy,* 106–107.

66. Emily Charnock, "The Second Emancipation Proclamation," *Virginia Quarterly Review Online,* August 28, 2013, https://www.vqronline.org/history/second -emancipation-proclamation; Karen Grigsby Bates, "1963 Emancipation Proclamation Party Lacked A Key Guest," *National Public Radio,* February 12, 2013 https:// www.npr.org/sections/codeswitch/2013/02/12/171815620/1963-Emancipation-Procla mation-Party-Lacked-A-Key-Guest; Taylor Branch and Haley Sweetland Edwards,

"A Second Emancipation," *Washington Monthly,* January/February 2013, https://washingtonmonthly.com/magazine/janfeb-2013/a-second-emancipation/.

67. William Faulkner, *Novels: 1942–1954, Go Down Moses, Intruder in the Dust, Requiem for a Nun, A Fable* (New York: Literary Classics of the United States, 1994), 535.

68. John F. Kennedy Presidential Library and Museum, "Remarks of Senator John F. Kennedy, New York Coliseum, New York, New York, November 5, 1960," https://www.jfklibrary.org/archives/other-resources/john-f-kennedy-speeches/new-york-ny-coliseum-19601105; John F. Kennedy Presidential Library and Museum, "News Conference 45, November 20, 1962," https://www.jfklibrary.org/archives/other-resources/john-f-kennedy-press-conferences/news-conference-45.

69. I am indebted to the anonymous reviewer of this manuscript who suggested the inclusion of these observations.

CHAPTER 3. FINDING HIS VOICE: "WE FACE . . . A MORAL CRISIS AS A COUNTRY"

1. Frederick Douglass, "Oration in Memory of Abraham Lincoln," April 14, 1876, https://teachingamericanhistory.org/library/document/oration-in-memory-of-abraham-lincoln/.

2. Devon Link, "Fact Check: A 1964 Conspiracy Theory Misrepresents Lincoln and Kennedy's Similarities," *USA TODAY,* June 6, 2020, https://www.usatoday.com/story/news/factcheck/2020/06/06/fact-check-1964-lincoln-kennedy-comparisons-only-partly-accurate/5311926002/.

3. Gabrielle Emanuel, "The Story of the Reverse Freedom Rides," *NPR,* January 1, 2020, https://www.npr.org/2020/01/01/792916566/the-story-of-the-reverse-freedom-rides.

4. John F. Kennedy Presidential Library and Museum, "Integrating Ole Miss: A Civil Rights Milestone," https://microsites.jfklibrary.org/olemiss/meredith/.

5. The Martin Luther King, Jr. Research and Education Institute, "Birmingham Campaign,"https://kinginstitute.stanford.edu/liberation-curriculum/create-your-own-classroom-activity/birmingham-campaign.

6. Martin Luther King. Jr., "Letter from aa Birmingham Jail," The Martin Luther King, Jr. Research and Education Institute, https://kinginstitute.stanford.edu/king-papers/documents/letter-birmingham-jail.

7. Jonathan Rieder, "The Day President Kennedy Embraced Civil Rights—And the Story Behind it," *Atlantic,* June 11, 2013, https://www.theatlantic.com/national/archive/2013/06/the-day-President-kennedy-embraced-civil-rights-and-the-story-behind-it/276749/.

8. Rieder, "The Day President Kennedy Embraced Civil Rights,"; John F. Kennedy Presidential Library and Museum, "Meetings, Tape 85, Americans for Democratic Action, 4 May 1963," https://www.jfklibrary.org/asset-viewer/archives/JFKPOF/MTG/JFKPOF-MTG-085–002/JFKPOF-MTG-085–002.

9. Steven Levingston, *Kennedy and King: The President, The Pastor, and the Battle Over Civil Rights* (New York: Hachette Books, 2017), 325–329, 331.

10. Philip A. Goduti, Jr., *Robert F. Kennedy and the Shaping of Civil Rights* (Jefferson, NC: McFarland, 2013), 194; Jeremy Gray, "As Confederate Flag Flew Over Capitol, Robert Kennedy, George Wallace, Met in Montgomery," AL.com, April 25, 2013, https://www.al.com/birmingham-news-stories/2013/04/as_confederate_flag_flew_over.html.

11. John F. Kennedy Presidential Library and Museum, "Civil Rights: Alabama, 1963: 17 May–10 October," https://www.jfklibrary.org/asset-viewer/archives/JFKPOF/096/JFKPOF-096-018

12. John F. Kennedy Presidential Library and Museum, "Wallace, George C.: Oral History Interview—JFK-1, 5/25/1967," https://www.jfklibrary.org/asset-viewer/archives/JFKOH/Wallace%2C%20George%20C/JFKOH-GCW-01/JFKOH-GCW-01.

13. "Governor George C. Wallace's School House Door Speech," Alabama Department of Archives and History, https://archives.alabama.gov/govs_list/schooldoor.html.

14. Andrew Cohen, *Two Days in June: John F. Kennedy and the 48 Hours That Made History* (New York: Signal, 2016), 260; Allison Graham, *Framing the South: Hollywood, Television, and Race During the Civil Rights Struggle* (Baltimore, MD: The Johns Hopkins University Press, 2003), 136.

15. Big Think, "Nicholas Katzenbach on John Lewis, George Wallace, and the 2008 Election," YouTube, April 23, 2012, https://www.youtube.com/watch?v=TWoS8VgRAyE.

16. Dan T. Carter, *The Politics of Rage: George Wallace, The Origins of the New Conservatism, and the Transformation of American Politics* (Baton Rouge, LA: Louisiana State University Press, 2000), 149–150.

17. John F. Kennedy Presidential Library and Museum, Kennedy Library Forums, "A Civil Rights Milestone," January 21, 2008, https://www.jfklibrary.org/events-and-awards/forums/past-forums/transcripts/a-civil-rights-milestone.

18. Levingston, *Kennedy and King*, 399–402; Ted Sorensen, *Counselor: A Life at the Edge of History* (New York: HarperCollins, 2008), 278–282; Richard Aldous, *Schlesinger: The Imperial Historian* (New York: W.W. Norton, 2017), 304.

19. John F. Kennedy Presidential Library and Museum, "Radio and Television Report to the American People on Civil Rights, June 11, 1963," https://www.jfklibrary.org/archives/other-resources/john-f-kennedy-speeches/civil-rights-radio-and-television-report-19630611.

20. Robert Schlesinger, "The Story Behind JFK's 1963 Landmark Civil Rights Speech," *U.S. News and World Report*, June 11, 2013, https://www.usnews.com/opinion/blogs/robert-schlesinger/2013/06/11/the-story-behind-jfks-1963-landmark-civil-rights-speech.

21. James N. Giglio, *The Presidency of John F. Kennedy* (Lawrence, KS: University Press of Kansas, 1991), 180; Sorensen, *Counselor*, 282.

22. Stephen F. Knott, *The Lost Soul of the American Presidency: The Decline into*

Demagoguery and the Prospects for Renewal (Lawrence, KS: University Press of Kansas, 2019), 221–222.

23. *Public Papers of the Presidents of the United States, John F. Kennedy, January 1 to November 22, 1963* (Washington, D.C.: U.S. Government Printing Office, 1964), 493–494.

24. Sorensen, *Counselor*, 282–283; Giglio, *Presidency of John F. Kennedy*, 182–183.

25. Andrew Kohut, "From the Archives: JFK's America," July 5, 2019, https://www.pewresearch.org/fact-tank/2019/07/05/jfks-america/.

26. Giglio, *Presidency of John F. Kennedy*, 187.

27. John F. Kennedy Presidential Library and Museum, "News Conference 61, September 12, 1963," https://www.jfklibrary.org/archives/other-resources/john-f-kennedy-press-conferences/news-conference-61

28. For a terrific account of the creation of the myth of Kennedy as a martyr for civil rights and other liberal causes, see James Piereson, *Camelot and the Cultural Revolution: How the Assassination of John F. Kennedy Shattered American Liberalism* (New York: Encounter Books, 2007).

29. Debbie Elliott, "Fifty Years After Medgar Evers Killing, The Scars Remain," *National Public Radio*, June 5, 2013, https://www.npr.org/sections/codes witch/2013/06/05/188727790/fifty-years-after-medgar-evers-killing-the-scars-remain.

30. Andrew Glass, "Medgar Evers Laid to Rest, June 19, 1963," *Politico*, June 19, 2014, https://www.politico.com/story/2014/06/medgar-evers-la-108023; John F. Kennedy Library, Instagram Post, June 16, 2021, https://www.instagram.com/p/CQMP70SLpjX/.

31. Stephan Lesher, *George Wallace: American Populist* (Cambridge, MA: Perseus, 1994), 248.

32. John F. Kennedy Presidential Library and Museum, "Martin Luther King, Jr., Telegram, September 15, 1963," https://www.jfklibrary.org/asset-viewer/september-15-1963-telegram

33. *Public Papers of the Presidents of the United States, John F. Kennedy, 1963*, 681; "1963 Church Bombing Fast Facts," CNN.com, https://www.cnn.com/2013/06/13/us/1963-birmingham-church-bombing-fast-facts/index.html.

34. "The Malcom X Interview: A Playboy Classic, Alex Haley Interviews Malcolm X," https://www.unix-ag.uni-kl.de/~moritz/Archive/malcolmx/malcolmx.playboy.pdf; "Malcolm X Scores U.S. and Kennedy: Likens Slaying to 'Chickens Coming Home to Roost," *New York Times*, December 2, 1963, https://www.nytimes.com/1963/12/02/archives/malcolm-x-scores-us-and-kennedy-likens-slaying-to-chickens-coming.html.

35. "Transcript: John Lewis on the March on Washington," *Washington Post*, August 22, 2013, https://www.washingtonpost.com/lifestyle/style/transcript-john-lewis-on-the-march-on-washington/2013/08/22/f6ee9968–0a8d-11e3–8974-f97ab3b3c677_story.html.

36. John F. Kennedy Presidential Library and Museum, Lewis, "John R.: Oral History

Interview—JFK #1, 3/19/2004," https://www.jfklibrary.org/asset-viewer/archives/ JFK OH/Lewis%2C%20John%20R/JFKOH-JRL-01/JFKOH-JRL-01; Lauren Feeney, "Two Versions of John Lewis' Speech," BillMoyers.com, July 24, 2013, https://www.goo gle.com/search?q=john+lewis+speech+on+the+march+on+washington&rlz=1C 1CHBF_enUS761US761&oq=john+lewis+speech+on+the+march+on+washington &aqs=chrome..69i57j0i2.7566j1j4&sourceid=chrome&ie=UTF-8.

37. "Rep. John Lewis on the Legacy of President John F. Kennedy," November 22, 2013, https://johnlewis.house.gov/media-center/press-releases/rep-john-lewis-legacy -President-john-f-kennedy.

38. Giglio, *Presidency of John F. Kennedy*, 186.

39. Dan T. Carter, *From George Wallace to Newt Gingrich: Race in the Conservative Counterrevolution, 1963–1994* (Baton Rouge, LA: Louisiana State University Press, 1999), xii.

40. Ronald P. Formisano, *Boston Against Busing: Race, Class, and Ethnicity in the 1960s and 1970s* (Durham, NC: University of North Carolina Press, 2004),76–77, 139; John Kifner, "Large Wallace Vote Reflects Depth of Anti-busing Sentiments in Boston's Working-Class Neighborhoods," *New York Times,* March 8, 1976, https://www .nytimes.com/1976/03/08/archives/large-wallace-vote-reflects-depth-of-anti-busing -sentiment-in.html.

CHAPTER 4. CUBA: THE SINS OF WILLIAM MCKINLEY

1. I am grateful to Patrick LaCroix for this observation.

2. Sheldon M. Stern, *The Cuban Missile Crisis in American Memory: Myths versus Reality* (Stanford, CA: Stanford University Press, 2012), 3–4, 11, 19, 52–53; Stephen F. Knott, "Legends of the Fall," *Review of Politics* 75, no. 3 (Summer 2013), 486.

3. Stephen F. Knott, *Secret and Sanctioned: Covert Operations and the American Presidency* (New York: Oxford University Press, 1996), 88; Thomas Jefferson to James Monroe, June 11, 1823, Founders Online, https://founders.archives.gov/documents /Jefferson/98–01–02–3559.

4. James N. Giglio, *The Presidency of John F. Kennedy* (Lawrence, KS: University Press of Kansas, 1991), 49.

5. The Commission on Presidential Debates, "The Fourth Kennedy-Nixon Presidential Debate, 21 October 1960 Debate Transcript," www.debates.org/index .php?page=october-21–1960-debate-transcript; "Excerpts of Remarks by Senator John F. Kennedy, Johnstown, PA, October 15, 1960," http://www.presidency.ucsb .edu/ws/index.php?pid=74041; Stephen F. Knott, *The Lost Soul of the American Presidency: The Decline into Demagoguery and the Prospects for Renewal* (Lawrence, KS: The University Press of Kansas, 2019), 163.

6. Knott, "Legends of the Fall," 484–487.

7. Giglio, *Presidency of John F. Kennedy*, 49.

8. Naftali and Kornbluth claimed that Kennedy had not been briefed during a panel discussion at the John F. Kennedy Presidential Library and Museum in 2011. John F. Kennedy Presidential Library and Museum, "50th Anniversary of the Bay of

Pigs Invasion," https://www.jfklibrary.org/events-and-awards/forums/past-forums/transcripts/50th-anniversary-of-the-bay-of-pigs-invasion.

9. Howard Jones, interview with John Patterson, "The Bay of Pigs—Alabama's Involvement," 2013, https://vimeo.com/70699318.

10. Alexander Fursenko and Timothy Naftali, *"One Hell of a Gamble": Khrushchev, Castro, and Kennedy, 1958–1964* (New York: W.W. Norton, 1997), 71.

11. Fursenko and Naftali, *"One Hell of a Gamble,"* 99.

12. Alexander Fursenko and Timothy Naftali, *Khrushchev's Cold War: The Inside Story of an American Adversary* (New York: W.W. Norton, 2006), 295.

13. Fursenko and Naftali, *"One Hell of a Gamble,"* 71.

14. I am indebted to Timothy Naftali for this observation. See John F. Kennedy Presidential Library and Museum, "50th Anniversary of the Bay of Pigs Invasion."

15. For an interesting account of Kennedy's shift toward a more nuanced and tolerant approach toward the nonaligned world, especially India, the Congo, Indonesia, Guinea, Egypt, and Tanzania, see Robert B. Rakove, *Kennedy, Johnson, and the Nonaligned World* (Cambridge, UK: Cambridge University Press, 2012). According to Rakove, this approach was abandoned under President Johnson. See pp. xxv, 218, 256–257. I am indebted to the anonymous reviewer of this manuscript for some of the observations included in this paragraph.

16. Trumbull Higgins, *The Perfect Failure: Kennedy, Eisenhower, and the CIA at the Bay of Pigs* (New York: W.W. Norton, 1987).

17. *Public Papers of the Presidents of the United States, John F. Kennedy, 1961,* 1–3.

18. Mike Reed, "Howard Zinn Discusses Cold War Myths," *The Amherst Student,* November 8, 2000, https://amherststudent-archive.amherst.edu/current/news/view.php%3Fyear=2000–2001&issue=09&section=news&article=08.html; Howard Zinn, *A People's History of the United States* (New York: Harper, 2017), 440–441.

19. Giglio, *Presidency of John F. Kennedy,* 58–59.

20. Michael Burleigh, *Small Wars, Faraway Places: Global Insurrection and the Making of the Modern World, 1945–1965* (New York: Penguin Books, 2013), 436; Knott, "Legends of the Fall," 484–487.

21. Giglio, *Presidency of John F. Kennedy,* 56–58; Herbert S. Parmet, *JFK: The Presidency of John F. Kennedy* (New York: Penguin Books, 1983), 168–170. The three most impressive accounts of the Bay of Pigs operation are Howard Jones, *The Bay of Pigs* (New York: Oxford University Press, 2008); Peter Wyden, *Bay of Pigs: The Untold Story* (New York: Simon & Schuster, 1979); and Jim Rasenberger, *The Brilliant Disaster: JFK, Castro, and America's Doomed Invasion of Cuba's Bay of Pigs* (New York: Scribner, 2011).

22. Vernon Loeb, "Soviets Knew Date of Cuban Attack," *Washington Post,* April 29, 2000, https://www.washingtonpost.com/archive/politics/2000/04/29/soviets-knew-date-of-cuba-attack/805b049c-4073-4b24-aefe-d0409695cbd6/. I am indebted to the anonymous reviewer of this manuscript for some of the observations included in this paragraph.

23. John F. Kennedy Presidential Library and Museum, "50th Anniversary."

24. Stephen Kinzer, *The Brothers: John Foster Dulles, Allen Dulles, and Their Secret World War* (New York: Times Books, 2013), 303.

25. John F. Kennedy Presidential Library and Museum, "Recollecting JFK," October 22, 2003, https://www.jfklibrary.org/events-and-awards/forums/past-forums/transcripts/recollecting-jfk. See also Robert Dallek, *Camelot's Court: Inside the Kennedy White House* (New York: HarperCollins, 2013), ch. 4, "Never Rely on the Experts." Privately, Kennedy expressed a visceral contempt for the advice he had received from the CIA and the military. Regarding the latter's propensity to adorn their uniforms with ribbons and medals, Kennedy remarked, "Those sons of bitches with all the fruit salad just sat there nodding, saying it would work." Quoted in Dallek, 149.

26. The author was told by former Kennedy aide David F. Powers that the taping system was installed as a consequence of the self-serving accounts given to the media by some advisors after the Bay of Pigs. However, it should be noted that the system was installed fifteen months after that event, raising questions about the president's motive.

27. Stephen F. Knott, "What Might Have Been," *Review of Politics*, 76, no. 4 (Fall 2014): 661–670; Knott, "Legends of the Fall," 484–487.

28. Evan Thomas, *Robert Kennedy: His Life* (New York: Simon & Schuster, 2000), 154–159, 171; Jeff Shesol, *Mutual Contempt: Lyndon Johnson, Robert Kennedy, and the Feud that Defined a Decade* (New York: W.W. Norton, 1997), 129; Knott, *Secret and Sanctioned*, 170; Knott, "What Might Have Been."

29. Sheldon M. Stern, *Averting "The Final Failure": John F. Kennedy and the Secret Cuban Missile Crisis Meetings* (Stanford, CA: Stanford University Press, 2003), 15; Knott, "What Might Have Been"; Knott, "Legends of the Fall," 487; I am indebted to the anonymous reviewer of this manuscript for some of the observations included in this paragraph.

30. Gene Miller, "Bay of Pigs Banner Returned to Brigade," *Miami Herald*, April 16, 1976, http://latinamericanstudies.org/bay-of-pigs/2506banner.htm.

31. Knott, "What Might Have Been"; Knott, "Legends of the Fall."

32. Knott, *Secret and Sanctioned*, 171.

33. Quoted in Brent Durbin, *The CIA and the Politics of U.S. Intelligence Reform* (Cambridge, UK: Cambridge University Press, 2017), 263.

34. Quoted in Loch K. Johnson, *Strategic Intelligence: Understanding the Hidden Side of Government* (Westport, CT: Praeger Security International, 2007), xv.

35. Knott, *Secret and Sanctioned*, 171.

36. Knott, *Secret and Sanctioned*, 172.

37. Arthur Schlesinger Jr., *Journals, 1952–2000*, eds. Andrew Schlesinger and Stephen Schlesinger (New York: Penguin Press, 2007), 675; Knott, "What Might Have Been," 664.

38. Ted Sorensen, *Counselor: A Life at the Edge of History* (New York: HarperCollins, 2008), 319; Knott, "What Might Have Been," 665.

39. Christopher Andrew, *For the President's Eyes Only: Secret Intelligence and the*

American Presidency from Washington to Bush (New York: HarperCollins, 1995), 275–276; Knott, "What Might Have Been," 664–665.

40. Abram N. Shulsky and Gary J. Schmitt, *Silent Warfare: Understanding the World of Intelligence* (Dulles, VA: Potomac Books, 2002), 223n.4; Knott, "What Might Have Been," 665.

41. I am deeply indebted to the anonymous reviewer of this manuscript for some of the observations included in this paragraph.

42. Stern, *Cuban Missile Crisis*, 4, 68–71, 133, 148–153; Knott, "What Might Have Been," 667; Knott, "Legends of the Fall," 485.

43. Stern, *Cuban Missile Crisis*, 52, 137, 149, 153; Knott, "Legends of the Fall," 485.

44. Stern, *Cuban Missile Crisis*, 32–33, 52; Knott, "Legends of the Fall," 485. Robert Kennedy's fictional account of the missile crisis remains remarkably resilient. In March 2020, Jon Meacham, a popular historian, wrote an op-ed for the *New York Times* that relied on RFK's account. See Jon Meacham, "Great Leadership in a Time of Crisis," *New York Times*, March 24, 2020, https://www.nytimes.com/2020/03/24/books/review/great-leadership-in-a-time-of-crisis.html.

45. Benjamin Schwarz, "The Real Cuban Missile Crisis: Everything You Think You Know about Those 13 Days is Wrong," *Atlantic*, January-February 2013, https://www.theatlantic.com/magazine/archive/2013/01/the-real-cuban-missile-crisis/309190/; Stern, *Cuban Missile Crisis*, 4.

46. Stern, *Cuban Missile Crisis*, 158.

47. Stern, *Cuban Missile Crisis*, 16–17, 88–89, 146.

48. Jason Zorbas, *Diefenbaker and Latin America: The Pursuit of Canadian Autonomy* (Newcastle upon Tyne, UK: 2011), 139.

49. Sergei Khrushchev, "How My Father and President Kennedy Saved the World," *American Heritage*, October 2002, https://www.americanheritage.com/how-my-father-and-President-kennedy-saved-world.

50. Khrushchev, "My Father and President Kennedy."

51. James G. Blight and Janet M. Lang, "How Castro Held the World Hostage," *New York Times*, October 25, 2012, https://www.nytimes.com/2012/10/26/opinion/how-castro-held-the-world-hostage.

52. Khrushchev, "My Father and President Kennedy."

53. For a full account of Castro's lobbying for a first strike and his attempt to retain tactical nuclear weapons, see Sergo Mikoyan, *The Soviet Cuban Missile Crisis: Castro, Mikoyan, Kennedy, Khrushchev and the Missiles of November*, ed. Svetlana Savranskaya, (Stanford, CA: Stanford University Press, 2012); Juan O. Tamayo, "The Untold Story of the Cuban Missile Crisis," *Miami Herald*, October 15, 2012, https://www.mcclatchydc.com/news/nation-world/world/article24738718.html; "Cuban Missile Crisis' Untold Story: Castro Almost Kept Nuclear Warheads on the Island," *Huffington Post*, October 15, 2012, https://www.huffpost.com/entry/cuban-missile-crisis-unto_n_1967544.

54. See William Taubman, *Khrushchev: The Man and His Era* (New York: W.W. Norton, 2003), 487–488.

55. The Fulbright quote is from Arthur M. Schlesinger, Jr., *A Thousand Days: John F. Kennedy in the White House* (Boston: Houghton Miffline Company, 2002), 251. I am indebted to the anonymous reviewer of this manuscript for some of the observations included in this paragraph, and in the previous paragraph as well.

56. See Michael Beschloss, "When JFK Secretly Reached Out to Castro," *New York Times,* December 18, 2014, https://www.nytimes.com/2014/12/18/upshot/when-jfk -secretly-reached-out-to-castro.html; William Attwood, *The Twilight Struggle: Tales of the Cold War* (New York: Harper and Row, 1987), 259–263.

57. John F. Kennedy Presidency Library and Museum, "William H. Attwood, Oral History Statement, November 8, 1965," https://www.jfklibrary.org/asset-viewer/ar chives/JFKOH/Attwood%2C%20William%20H/JFKOH-WHA-01/JFKOH -WHA-01.

58. Beschloss, "When JFK Secretly Reached Out to Castro"; Attwood, *Twilight Struggle,* 259–263.

CHAPTER 5. KHRUSHCHEV, KENNEDY, AND THE "NUCLEAR SWORD OF DAMOCLES"

1. John F. Kennedy Presidential Library and Museum, "Remarks of Senator John F. Kennedy in the United States Senate, Monday, February 29, 1960," https://www .jfklibrary.org/archives/other-resources/john-f-kennedy-speeches/unite-states-sen ate-national-defense-19600229; John F. Kennedy Presidential Library and Museum, "50th Anniversary of the Missile Gap Controversy," September 26, 2011, https://www .jfklibrary.org/events-and-awards/forums/past-forums/transcripts/50th-anniversary -of-the-missile-gap-controversy.

2. Richard Reeves, *President Kennedy: Profile of Power* (New York: Simon & Schuster, 1993), 59n.

3. John L. Helgerson, *Getting to Know the President: Intelligence Briefings of Presidential Candidates, 1952–2004* (Washington, DC: Government Printing Office, 2001), 39.

4. Greg Thielmann, "The Missile Gap Myth and Its Progeny," Arms Control Association, https://www.armscontrol.org/act/2011–05/missile-gap-myth-its-progeny.

5. John F. Kennedy Presidential Library and Museum, "Missile Gap Controversy."

6. John F. Kennedy Presidential Library and Museum, "Wheeler, Earle G.: Oral History Interview—JFK #1, 1964," https://www.jfklibrary.org/asset-viewer/archives /JFKOH/Wheeler%2C%20Earle%20G/JFKOH-ERGW-01/JFKOH-ERGW-01.

7. John F. Kennedy Presidential Library and Museum, "Missile Gap Controversy"; Thielmann, "Missile Gap Myth"; National Geospatial-Intelligence Agency, "Corona Program," https://www.nga.mil/About/History/NGAinHistory/Pages/CO RONAProgram.aspx.

8. John F. Kennedy Presidential Library and Museum, "Brown, Harold, Oral History Interview—JFK #1, July 7, 1964," https://www.jfklibrary.org/asset-viewer /archives/JFKOH/Brown%2C%20Harold/JFKOH-HAB-01/JFKOH-HAB-01.

9. John F. Kennedy Presidential Library and Museum, "Brown, Harold, Oral History Interview."

10. Reeves, *President Kennedy*, 33.

11. Thielmann, "Missile Gap Myth."

12. Reeves, *President Kennedy*, 58–59.

13. "Full Text of 'Roswell Gilpatric Speech Before the Business Council,'" Internet Archive, https://archive.org/stream/RoswellGilpatricSpeechBeforeTheBusiness Council/ELS000–010_djvu.txt.

14. John F. Kennedy Presidential Library and Museum, "News Conference 18, November 8, 1961," https://www.jfklibrary.org/archives/other-resources/john-f-ken nedy-press-conferences/news-conference-18.

15. Max Frankel, *High Noon in the Cold War: Kennedy, Khrushchev, and the Cuban Missile Crisis* (New York: Presidio, 2005), 54–55.

16. Alan Brinkley, *John F. Kennedy* (New York: Times Books, 2012), 79; Reeves, *President Kennedy*, 162.

17. For Kennedy's attitude toward Diefenbaker, see Denis Smith, *Rogue Tory: The Life and Legend of John Diefenbaker* (Toronto: Macfarlane, Walter & Ross, 1995), 457.

18. Reeves, *President Kennedy*, 147.

19. For a full discussion of Kennedy's medical challenges, see Robert Dallek, *An Unfinished Life: John F. Kennedy, 1917–1963* (New York: Back Bay Books, 2004), 27, 33–35, 73–77; James N. Giglio, "Growing Up Kennedy: The Role of Medical Ailments in the Life of JFK, 1920–1957," *Journal of Family History*, 31, no. 4 (October 1, 2006) https://doi.org/10.1177%2F0363199006291659.

20. Peter Carlson, "How Doctor Feelgood Almost Drove John F. Kennedy to the Brink of Disaster," *HistoryNet*, June 2011, https://www.historynet.com/jack-kennedy -dr-feelgood.htm; Frederick Kempe, "Berlin 1961: Kennedy's 'Dr. Feelgood,' *Atlantic Council*, May 26, 2011, https://atlanticcouncil.org/content-series/thinking-global /berlin-1961-kennedy-s-dr-feelgood/; Giglio, *Presidency of John F. Kennedy*, 263–264; Brinkley, *John F. Kennedy*, 93–94.

21. Michael Dobbs, *One Minute to Midnight: Kennedy, Khrushchev, and Castro on the Brink of Nuclear War* (New York: Vintage Books, 2009), 215.

22. Robert Dallek, *John F. Kennedy* (New York: Oxford University Press, 2011), 37; John F. Kennedy Presidential Library and Museum, "Missile Gap Controversy."

23. John F. Kennedy Presidential Library and Museum, "U.S.S.R.: Vienna Meeting: Memos of Conversation, June, 1961: Drafts," https://www.jfklibrary.org /asset-viewer/archives/JFKPOF/126a/JFKPOF-126a-001.

24. Quoted in Dobbs, *One Minute to Midnight*, 36.

25. Reeves, *President Kennedy*, 171.

26. Reeves, *President Kennedy*, 172; Andrew Glass, "JFK and Khrushchev Met in Vienna June 3, 1961," *Politico*, June 2, 2017, https://www.politico.com/story/2017/06/02 /jfk-and-khrushchev-meet-in-vienna-june-3–1961–238979

27. John F. Kennedy Presidential Library and Museum, "Bohlen, Charles E.: Oral

History Interview—JFK #1, May 21, 1964," https://www.jfklibrary.org/asset-viewer /archives/JFKOH/Bohlen%2C%20Charles%20E/JFKOH-CEB-01/JFKOH-CEB-01.

28. John F. Kennedy Presidential Library and Museum, "Radio and Television Report to the American People on the Berlin Crisis, July 25, 1961," https://www.jfkli brary.org/archives/other-resources/john-f-kennedy-speeches/berlin-crisis-19610725.

29. Giglio, *Presidency of John F. Kennedy*, 81–82.

30. Nina Khrushcheva, "The Case of Khrushchev's Shoe," *New Statesman America*, October 2, 2000, https://www.newstatesman.com/politics/politics/2014/04/case -khrushchevs-shoe

31. Giglio, *Presidency of John F. Kennedy*, 78.

32. Frederick Kempe, *Berlin 1961: Kennedy, Khrushchev, and the Most Dangerous Place on Earth* (New York: G. P. Putnam's Sons, 2011), 6.

33. Rusk quoted in Thomas W. Zeller, *Dean Rusk: Defending the American Mission Abroad* (Wilmington, DE: Scholarly Resources, 2000), 48. I am indebted to the anonymous reviewer of this manuscript for some of the observations included in this paragraph.

34. John Bainbridge, "Die Mauer: The Early Days of the Berlin Wall," *New Yorker*, October 27, 1962, https://www.newyorker.com/magazine/1962/10/27/die-mauer; "Why Did the GDR Build the Berlin Wall," Germany in the USA, German Embassy Washington, August 18, 2019, https://germanyinusa.com/2019/08/18/why-did-the-gdr -build-the-berlin-wall/.

35. W.R. Smyser, *Kennedy and the Berlin Wall: "A Hell of a Lot Better Than a War"* (Lanham, MD: Rowman & Littlefield, 2009), 115.

36. Kempe, *Berlin 1961*, 12, 129, 324, 327.

37. Smyser, *Kennedy and the Berlin Wall*, 106.

38. Raymond L. Garthoff, "Berlin 1961: The Record Corrected," *Foreign Policy* 84 (Autumn 1991), 155.

39. Jean Edward Smith, *Lucius D. Clay: An American Life* (New York: Henry Holt, 1990), 657, 662.

40. Garthoff, "Berlin 1961," 142–156.

41. Giglio, *Presidency of John F. Kennedy*, 76.

42. Smyser, *Kennedy and the Berlin Wall*, ch. 7; Giglio, *Presidency of John F. Kennedy*, 84.

43. See Ben Zimmer, "'Ich Bin Ein Berliner': JFK Got it Right—He was No Jelly Donut," The *Wall Street Journal*, November 7, 2019, https://www.wsj.com/articles/ich -bin-ein-berliner-jfk-got-it-righthe-was-no-jelly-doughnut-11573152244; Len Dighton, *Berlin Game* (New York: Alfred A. Knopf, 1983), 85.

44. Thomas Putnam, "The Real Meaning of *Ich Bin Ein Berliner*," *Atlantic*, September 18, 2013, https://www.theatlantic.com/magazine/archive/2013/08/the-real -meaning-of-ich-bin-ein-berliner/309500/; Stephen Evans, "John F. Kennedy: "How 'Ich Bin Ein Berliner' Gave a City Hope," *BBC News Magazine*, June 25, 2013, https:// www.bbc.com/news/magazine-23029697.

45. Dallek, *John F. Kennedy*, 52–53.

46. Brinkley, *John F. Kennedy*, 86.

47. "Soviet Nuclear Test Summary," Nuclear Weapon Archive, October 7, 1997, https://nuclearweaponarchive.org/Russia/Sovtestsum.html.

48. John F. Kennedy Presidential Library and Museum, "Historic Speeches, Address to the United Nations General Assembly," September 25, 1961, https://www.jfklibrary.org/learn/about-jfk/historic-speeches/address-to-the-united-nations-general-assembly.

49. Stephen Dowling, "The Monster Bomb That was Too Big to Use," *BBC.com*, August 16, 2017, https://www.bbc.com/future/article/20170816-the-monster-atomic-bomb-that-was-too-big-to-use; Amy Tikkanen, *Encyclopedia Britannica*, s.v. "Tsar Bomba," https://www.britannica.com/topic/Tsar-Bomba.

50. John F. Kennedy Presidential Library and Museum, "Radio and Television Address to the American People: 'Nuclear Testing and Disarmament,' March 2, 1962, https://www.jfklibrary.org/asset-viewer/archives/JFKPOF/037/JFKPOF-037-023.

51. John F. Kennedy Presidential Library and Museum, "Brown, Harold, Oral History Interview, JFK—#1."

52. Walter A. Rosenblith, ed., *Jerry Wiesner, Scientist, Statesman, Humanist: Memories and Memoirs* (Cambridge, MA: MIT Press, 2003), 178.

53. James E. Goodby, "The U.S. Arms Control and Disarmament Agency 1961–63: A Study in Governance," Hoover Institution, https://www.hoover.org/sites/default/files/research/docs/goodby_the_us_arms_control.pdf; John F. Kennedy Presidential Library and Museum, "Nuclear Test Ban Treaty," https://www.jfklibrary.org/learn/about-jfk/jfk-in-history/nuclear-test-ban-treaty.

54. Goodby, "U.S. Arms Control and Disarmament Agency."

55. John F. Kennedy Presidential Library and Museum, "Foster, William C.: Oral History Interview—JFK #1, August 5, 1964," https://www.jfklibrary.org/asset-viewer/archives/JFKOH/Foster%2C%20William%20C/JFKOH-WCF-01/JFKOH-WCF-01.

56. John F. Kennedy Presidential Library and Museum, "Foster, William C.: Oral History Interview—JFK #1, August 5, 1964."

57. Sheldon M. Stern, *The Cuban Missile Crisis in American Memory: Myths versus Reality* (Stanford, CA: Stanford University Press, 2012), 15.

58. Stern, *Cuban Missile Crisis*, 12–13.

59. Stern, *Cuban Missile Crisis*, 13–14.

60. Stern, *Cuban Missile Crisis*, 14–15.

61. John F. Kennedy Presidential Library and Museum, "Bohlen, Charles E.: Oral History Interview—JFK #1, May 21, 1964"; Stern, *Cuban Missile Crisis*, 15.

62. Stern, *Cuban Missile Crisis*, 15.

63. Stern, *Cuban Missile Crisis*, 15

64. Quoted in Sheldon M. Stern, "Reflections on Fredrik Logevall's 'JFK: Coming of Age in the American Century, 1917–1956,'" *History News Network*, December 13, 2020, https://historynewsnetwork.org/article/178486.

65. John F. Kennedy Presidential Library and Museum, "Remarks of Senator John F. Kennedy, American Association of School Administrators Convention, Atlantic

City Auditorium, Atlantic City, New Jersey, February 19, 1957," https://www.jfklibrary
.org/archives/other-resources/john-f-kennedy-speeches/atlantic-city-nj-19570219.

66. Stern, *Cuban Missile Crisis*, 16–17; 161–163; 167–170.

67. Robert Dallek, "JFK vs. the Military," *Atlantic*, September 10, 2013, https://
www.theatlantic.com/magazine/archive/2013/08/jfk-vs-the-military/309496/.

68. The "umbrella man" is clearly visible in the Zapruder film and in multiple
photographs taken in Dealey Plaza on November 22, 1963, and became the subject
of countless conspiracy theories regarding Kennedy's assassination. The "umbrella
man" was later identified as Louie Steven Witt of Dallas. Witt testified before the
House Assassination Committee in 1978 that he brought the umbrella to Dealey
Plaza to "heckle" the president. The umbrella was an accoutrement carried by British Prime Minister Neville Chamberlain whose policy of territorial concessions toward Nazi Germany was supported at the time by United States Ambassador Joseph
P. Kennedy. Chamberlain and his umbrella came to symbolize appeasement, and
President Kennedy was seen as an appeaser by many right-wing extremists. Witt's
umbrella was presented as evidence before the committee and its members determined that it did not contain a weapon of any kind, contrary to the speculation
of a number of conspiracy theorists. George Lardner, Jr., "Umbrella Man at JFK
Killing was Heckling," *Washington Post*, September 26, 1978. https://www.washing
tonpost.com/archive/politics/1978/09/26/umbrella-man-at-jfk-killing-was-heckling
/d66ea324-e6ad-409a-b1ee-c01e69c6d4e8/

69. Quoted in Arthur M. Schlesinger, Jr., *A Thousand Days: John F. Kennedy in the
White House* (Boston: Houghton Mifflin Company, 2002), 88.

70. Andreas Wenger, *Living with Peril: Eisenhower, Kennedy, and Nuclear Weapons* (Lanham, MD; Rowman and Littlefield, 1997), 259.

71. John F. Kennedy Presidential Library and Museum, "Seaborg, Glenn T.: Oral
History—JFK #1, Circa 1965," https://www.jfklibrary.org/asset-viewer/archives/JFK
OH/Seaborg%2C%20Glenn%20T/JFKOH-GTS-01/JFKOH-GTS-01.

72. Wenger, *Living With Peril*, 261–263.

73. "Comprehensive Test Ban Treaty Chronology," Federation of American Scientists, https://fas.org/nuke/control/ctbt/chron1.htm.

74. John F. Kennedy Presidential Library and Museum, "New Conference 52,
March 21, 1963," https://www.jfklibrary.org/archives/other-resources/john-f-kenne
dy-press-conferences/news-conference-52.

75. Ted Sorensen, *Counselor: A Life at the Edge of History* (New York: HarperCollins, 2008), 327.

76. John F. Kennedy Presidential Library and Museum, "Commencement Address at American University, June 10, 1963," https://www.jfklibrary.org/archives
/other-resources/john-f-kennedy-speeches/american-university-19630610.

77. Sorensen, *Counselor*, 327.

78. Glenn T. Seaborg with Eric Seaborg, *Adventures in the Atomic Age: From Watts
to Washington* (New York: Farrar, Straus, and Giroux, 2001), 192–193, 198, 211; John F.
Kennedy Presidential Library and Museum, "Nuclear Test Ban Treaty."

79. Vojtech Mastny, "The 1963 Nuclear Test Ban Treaty: A Missed Opportunity for Détente?" *Journal of Cold War Studies* 10, no. 1 (Winter 2008): 8; Seaborg, *Adventures in the Atomic Age,* 192–193, 198, 295; John F. Kennedy Presidential Library and Museum, "Nuclear Test Ban Treaty."

80. John F. Kennedy Presidential Library and Museum, "Aiken, George: Oral History Interview—JFK #1, April 25, 1964," https://www.jfklibrary.org/asset-viewer /archives/JFKOH/Aiken%2C%20George/JFKOH-GA-01/JFKOH-GA-01.

81. Goodby, "U.S. Arms Control and Disarmament Agency,"; Seaborg, *Adventures in the Atomic Age,* 192–193, 198, 295; John F. Kennedy Presidential Library and Museum, "Nuclear Test Ban Treaty."

82. John F. Kennedy Presidential Library and Museum, "Foster, William C.: Oral History Interview"; John F. Kennedy Presidential Library and Museum, "Bohlen, Charles E.: Oral History Interview."

83. I am indebted to the anonymous reviewer of this manuscript for some of the observations included in this paragraph.

84. Garry Wills, "Did Kennedy Cause the Crisis?" *Atlantic,* February 1982, https:// www.theatlantic.com/magazine/archive/2013/08/did-kennedy-cause-the-crisis/3094 88/. This piece was reissued in 2013.

85. Robert D. Dean, *Imperial Brotherhood: Gender and the Making of Cold War Foreign Policy* (Amherst, MA: University of Massachusetts Press, 2003). See, for instance, pp. 7, 182, 243.

CHAPTER 6. "IN THE FINAL ANALYSIS, IT IS THEIR WAR"

1. Quoted in Sheldon M. Stern, "Reflections on Fredrik Logevall's 'JFK: Coming of Age in the American Century, 1917-1956,'" *History News Network,* December 13, 2020, https://historynewsnetwork.org/article/178486.

2. Tom Wicker, *Dwight D. Eisenhower* (New York: Times Books, 2002), 33.

3. John F. Kennedy, *Why England Slept* (London: Hutchinson, 1940), 157, 184. For a comprehensive account of Kennedy's experience in writing, publishing, and promoting his senior college thesis, see Fredrik Logevall, *JFK: Coming of Age in the American Century, 1917-1956* (New York: Random House, 2020), 250–276.

4. James N. Giglio, *The Presidency of John F. Kennedy* (Lawrence, KS: University Press of Kansas, 1991), 221–223; Anna Kasten Nelson, "President Kennedy's National Security Policy: A Reconsideration," *Reviews in American History* 19, no. 1 (March 1991): 7–8, 10.

5. John F. Kennedy Presidential Library and Museum, "Gullion, Edmund A., Oral History Interview—JFK #1," July 17, 1964, https://www.jfklibrary.org/asset-viewer /archives/JFKOH/Gullion%2C%20Edmund%20A/JFKOH-EDAG-01/JFK OH-EDAG -01.

6. Daniel Ellsberg, *Secrets: A Memoir of Vietnam and the Pentagon Papers* (New York: Penguin Books, 2003), 197.

7. Susan Kelley, "Logevall: Despite Doubts, Presidents Stoked Vietnam War," *Cornell Chronicle,* June 10, 2013, https://news.cornell.edu/stories/2013/06/logevall-despite

-doubts-Presidents-stoked-vietnam-war; John T. Shaw, *JFK in the Senate: Pathway to the Presidency* (New York: St. Martin's, 2013), 92.

8. Robert Mann, *A Grand Delusion: America's Descent into Vietnam* (New York: Basic Books, 2001), 85.

9. Quoted in John F. Kennedy Presidential Library and Museum, "Remarks of Senator John F. Kennedy on Indochina Before the Senate, Washington, D.C., April 6,1954," https://www.jfklibrary.org/archives/other-resources/john-f-kennedy-speeches /united-states-senate-indochina-19540406.

10. Herbert S. Parmet, *Jack: The Struggles of John F. Kennedy* (New York: Dial Press, 1980), 227–228.

11. Shaw, *JFK in the Senate*, 94.

12. John F. Kennedy Presidential Library and Museum, "Kennedy on Indochina."

13. Shaw, *JFK in the Senate*, 97–98; John F. Kennedy Presidential Library and Museum, "Partial Remarks of Senator John F. Kennedy Before the Executives Club, Chicago, Illinois, May 28, 1954," https://www.jfklibrary.org/archives/other-resources /john-f-kennedy-speeches/chicago-il-executives-club-19540528.

14. Fisher, "The Second Catholic President," 130.

15. Shaw, *JFK in the Senate*, 99.

16. John F. Kennedy Presidential Library and Museum, "Remark of Senator John F. Kennedy at the Conference on Vietnam Luncheon in the Hotel Willard, Washington D.C., June 1, 1956," https://www.jfklibrary.org/archives/other-resources/john-f -kennedy-speeches/vietnam-conference-washington-dc-19560601; James T. Patterson, *Grand Expectations: The United States, 1945-1974* (New York: Oxford University Press, 1996), 430.

17. David L. Anderson, "J. Lawton Collins, John Foster Dulles, and the Eisenhower Administration's 'Point of No Return' in Vietnam," *Diplomatic History* 12, no. 2 Spring 1988): 146. See also George C. Herring, *From Colony to Superpower: U.S. Foreign Relations Since 1776* (New York: Oxford University Press, 2008), 661–662, 726; Jean Edward Smith, *Eisenhower in War and Peace* (New York: Random House, 2012), 615; William J. Rust, *Kennedy in Vietnam: American Vietnam Policy 1960–63* (New York: Scribner, 1985), xiii—xvii.

18. John F. Kennedy Presidential Library and Museum, "Kennedy at the Conference on Vietnam Luncheon."

19. John F. Kennedy Presidential Library and Museum, "Kennedy at the Conference on Vietnam Luncheon."

20. Quoted in Arthur M. Schlesinger, Jr., *A Thousand Days: John F. Kennedy in the White House* (Boston: Houghton Mifflin Company, 2002), 311.

21. John Hellman, "Vietnam as Symbolic Landscape: The Ugly American and the New Frontier," *Peace and Change* 9, nos. 2–3 (July 1983): 40; Edward Miller, *Misalliance: Ngo Dinh Diem, the United States, and the Fate of South Vietnam* (Cambridge, MA: Harvard University Press, 2013), 70.

22. Steven Watts, "When JFK Endorsed the Ugly American," *History Reader,*

November 18, 2016, https://www.thehistoryreader.com/contemporary-history/ugly
-american-jfk/

23. Watts, "When JFK Endorsed the Ugly American."

24. Commission on Presidential Debates, October 7, 1960 Debate Transcript,
https://www.debates.org/voter-education/debate-transcripts/october-7–1960-de
bate-transcript/; Commission on Presidential Debates, October 13, 1960, https://www
.debates.org/voter-education/debate-transcripts/october-13–1960-debate-transcript/.

25. John Prados, *Safe for Democracy: The Secret Wars of the CIA* (Chicago: Ivan R.
Dee, 2006), 338.

26. John M. Newman, *JFK and Vietnam: Deception, Intrigue, and the Vietnam War*
(North Charleston, SC: Create Space Independent Publishing Platform, 2017), 53.

27. Office of the Secretary of Defense, Historical Office, "Roswell L. Gilpatric,"
https://history.defense.gov/DOD-History/Deputy-Secretaries-of-Defense/Article
-View/Article/585241/roswell-1 -gilpatric/; Prados, *Safe for Democracy*, 338.

28. Leslie H. Gelb, *The Irony of Vietnam: The System Worked* (Washington, D.C.:
Brookings Institution, 1979), 87n56; Peter Kross, "General Maxwell Taylor's Mission
to Vietnam," *HistoryNet*, https://www.historynet.com/general-maxwell-taylors-mis
sion-to-vietnam.htm.

29. Rust, *Kennedy in Vietnam*, 34.

30. James S. Olsen and Randy W. Roberts, *Where the Domino Fell: American and
Vietnam, 1945 to 2010* (Hoboken, NJ: Wiley-Blackwell, 2013) 172.

31. John F. Kennedy Presidential Library and Museum, "News Conference #17,
October 11, 1961," https://www.jfklibrary.org/archives/other-resources/john-f-ken
nedy-press-conferences/news-conference-17.

32. "Analysis of the Khrushchev Speech of January 6, 1961," Central Intelligence
Agency, June 16, 1961, https://www.cia.gov/library/readingroom/docs/1961–06–16
.pdf.

33. David L. Anderson, *The Columbia Guide to the Vietnam War* (New York; Columbia University Press, 2002), 118; Patterson, *Grand Expectations*, 510; Giglio, *Presidency of John F. Kennedy*, 243.

34. Giglio, *Presidency of John F. Kennedy*, 243; Alan Brinkley, *John F. Kennedy*
(New York: Times Books, 2012), 135–136.

35. Patterson, *Grand Expectations*, 511; Brinkley, *John F. Kennedy*, 136.

36. Robert D. Schulzinger, *A Time for War: The United States and Vietnam, 1941–
1975* (New York: Oxford University Press, 1997), 108.

37. Robert Dallek, *An Unfinished Life: John F. Kennedy, 1917-1963* (New York: Back
Bay Books, 2004), 450, 452.

38. Schulzinger, *Time for War*, 110–113.

39. Evelyn Frances Krache Morris, "Into the Wind: The Kennedy Administration and the Use of Herbicides in South Vietnam," (doctoral dissertation, Georgetown University, 2012), https://repository.library.georgetown.edu/bitstream/handle
/10822/557621/KracheMorris_georgetown_0076D_11888.pdf?sequ.

40. John F. Kennedy Presidential Library and Museum, "Taylor, Maxwell D.: Oral History Interview—RFK #2, 11/13/1969, https://www.jfklibrary.org/asset-viewer /archives/RFKOH/Taylor%2C%20Maxwell%20D/RFKOH-MDT-02/RFKOH -MDT-02.

41. Dallek, *Unfinished Life,* 450.

42. Schulzinger, *Time for War,* 110.

43. Dallek, *Unfinished Life,* 527.

44. I am indebted to the anonymous reviewer of this manuscript for the observations included in this paragraph.

45. For a discussion of Kennedy and Laos, see Rust, *Kennedy in Vietnam,* 28–33, 70–77, 87–90; Timothy N. Castle, *At War in the Shadow of Vietnam: U.S. Military Aid to the Royal Lao Government, 1955–1975* (New York: Columbia University Press, 1993), 26–29, 32–34, 40–42, 45–49, 130–131; Robert S. McNamara with Brian VanDe-Mark, *In Retrospect: The Tragedy and Lessons of Vietnam* (New York: Vintage Books, 1996, 35—37, 62.

46. Robert Dallek, "JFK vs. the Military," *The Atlantic,* September 10, 2013, https:// www.theatlantic.com/magazine/archive/2013/08/jfk-vs-the-military/309496/.

47. Chester J. Pach and Elmo Richardson, *The Presidency of Dwight D. Eisenhower* (Lawrence, KS: University Press of Kansas, 1999), 95–98. See also David L. Anderson, *Trapped by Success: The Eisenhower Administration and Vietnam, 1953–1961* (New York: Columbia University Press, 1991) 121–199.

48. Brinkley, *John F. Kennedy,* 137.

49. William Prochnau, *Once Upon a Distant War: David Halberstam, Neil Sheehan, Peter Arnett—Young War Correspondents and Their Early Vietnam Battles* (New York: Random House, 1995), 42; John F. Kennedy Presidential Library and Museum, "Mansfield, Mike, April 1962-September 1963," https://www.jfklibrary.org/asset-view er/archives/JFKPOF/031/JFKPOF-031–023.

50. Charles DeBenedetti, *An American Ordeal: The Antiwar Movement of the Vietnam Era* (Syracuse, NY: Syracuse University Press, 1990), 84.

51. John F. Kennedy Presidential Library and Museum, "Address at U.S. Military Academy, West Point, NY, 6 June 1962," https://www.jfklibrary.org/asset-viewer /archives/JFKPOF/038/JFKPOF-038–035.

52. Rust, *Kennedy in Vietnam,* 64–67.

53. Giglio, *Presidency of John F. Kennedy,* 244–245.

54. "Paper Prepared by the President's Military Representative (Taylor), September 20, 1962," United States Department of State, Office of the Historian, Foreign Relations of the United States, 1961–1963, vol. 2, Vietnam, 1962, https://history.state.gov/histori caldocuments/frus1961–63v02/d288.

55. Dallek, *Unfinished Life,* 525–526.

56. Gregory A. Olsen, *Mansfield and Vietnam: A Study in Rhetorical Adaptation* (East Lansing, MI: Michigan State University Press, 1995111–113; John F. Kennedy Presidential Library and Museum, "Mansfield, Michael Joseph: Oral History

Interview—JFK #1, 6/23/1964," https://www.jfklibrary.org/asset-viewer/archives/JFK OH/Mansfield%2C%20Michael%20Joseph/JFKOH-MJM-01/JFKOH-MJM-01.

57. Olsen, *Mansfield and Vietnam,* 111–113 John F. Kennedy Presidential Library and Museum, "Mansfield, Michael Joseph: Oral History Interview."

58. Rod Paschell, "Prescient at the Creation," HistoryNet, https://www.history net.com/prescient-at-the-creation.htm. Paschell offers a spirited defense of General Harkins' conduct as MACV commander, noting that if his advocacy of a patient approach toward the ARVN and his support for President Diem had been followed, the course of events in Vietnam would likely have unfolded differently.

59. Richard Reeves, *President Kennedy: Profile of Power* (New York: Simon & Schuster, 1993), 445–447.

60. "Editorial Note," United States Department of State, Office of the Historian, *Foreign Relations of the United States, 1961–1963,* vol. 3, Vietnam, January-August 1963, https://history.state.gov/historicaldocuments/frus1961–63v03/d1.

61. Thomas E. Ricks, "Gen. Harkins Explains Why We Lost the Vietnam War: Halberstam was Jewish," *Foreign Policy,* March 24, 2011, https://foreignpolicy.com/2011 /03/24/gen-harkins-explains-why-we-lost-the-vietnam-war-halberstam-was-jewish/.

62. For Kennedy's definition of victory, see Newman, *JFK and Vietnam,* 426.

63. Orrin Schwab, *Defending the Free World: John F. Kennedy, Lyndon Johnson, and the Vietnam War, 1961–1963* (Westport, CT: Praeger, 1998), 44.

64. The seminal account of Vann's life can be found in Neil Sheehan, *A Bright Shining Lie: John Paul Vann and America in Vietnam* (New York: Random House, 1988). See also Richard Holbrooke, "Front Man," *New Republic,* October 24, 1988, https://newrepublic.com/article/75890/front-man; Peter Kross, "John Paul Vann: Man and Legend," HistoryNet, https://www.historynet.com/john-paul-vann-man -and-legend.htm.

65. Giglio, *Presidency of John F. Kennedy,* 247–248.

66. Miller, *Misalliance,* 302–311; Joseph Gregory, "Madame Nhu, Vietnam War Lightning Rod, Dies," *New York Times,* April 26, 2011, https://www.nytimes.com /2011/04/27/world/asia/27nhu.html; Brinkley, *John F. Kennedy,* 140.

67. McNamara, *In* Retrospect, 51; Reeves, *President Kennedy,* 559.

68. Brinkley, *John F. Kennedy,* 140–141.

69. Reeves, *President Kennedy,* 561–563.

70. "The Diem Coup," Miller Center of Public Affairs, University of Virginia, https://millercenter.org/the-presidency/educational-resources/diem-coup.

71. Giglio, *Presidency of John F. Kennedy,* 250–251.

72. Reeves, *President Kennedy,* 552–553; Johanna Crosby, "Camelot's Last Summer," *Barnstable Patriot,* June 6, 2013, https://www.barnstablepatriot.com/article /20130606/news/306069941.

73. John F. Kennedy Presidential Library and Museum, "Transcript of CBS Broadcast with Walter Cronkite, 2 September 1963," https://www.jfklibrary.org/asset -viewer/archives/JFKPOF/046/JFKPOF-046-025.

74. Rufus C. Phillips, III, *Why Vietnam Matters: An Eyewitness Account of Lessons*

Not Learned (Annapolis, MD: Naval Institute Press, 2008), ch. 13; "Tapes Give New Voice to JFK's Vietnam Doubt," History.net, June 2012, https://www.historynet.com /tapes-give-new-voice-to-jfks-vietnam-doubt.htm; *Foreign Relations of the United States, 1961–1963, Volume 4, Vietnam, August–December 1963, 83, Memorandum of Conversation, September 10, 1963,* https://history.state.gov/historicaldocuments/frus 1961–63v04/d83.

75. Quoted in Reeves, *President Kennedy*, 602.

76. *The Pentagon Papers, The Defense Department History of United States Decision Making on Vietnam, Senator Mike Gravel Edition*, vol. 2 (Boston, MA: Beacon Press, 1971), 206.

77. Reeves, *President Kennedy*, 602, 607–615.

78. James K. Galbraith, "Exit Strategy: In 1963 JFK Ordered a Complete Withdrawal from Vietnam," *Boston Review*, September 1, 2003, http://bostonreview.net /us/galbraith-exit-strategy-vietnam.

79. See Newman, *JFK and Vietnam*, 404–409; and Howard Jones, *Death of a Generation: How the Assassinations of Diem and JFK Prolonged the Vietnam War* (New York: Oxford University Press, 2004), 219, 238, 257–258, 377–378, 440–442, 452–453.

80. See Noam Chomsky and James K. Galbraith, "Letters from Chomsky and Galbraith on Vietnam," *Boston Review*, December 1, 2003, https://bostonreview.net /world/chomsky-galbraith-letters-vietnam-jfk-kennedy.

81. Galbraith, "Exit Strategy."

82. Newman, *JFK and Vietnam*, 407; Galbraith, "Exit Strategy."

83. Howard Jones, "JFK Wanted Out of Vietnam," *History News Network*, February 14, 2004, https://historynewsnetwork.org/article/3446; Newman, *JFK and Vietnam*, 427.

84. Reeves, *President Kennedy*, 641.

85. Reeves, *President Kennedy*, 643.

86. *The Pentagon Papers, The Defense Department History of United States Decision Making on Vietnam*, vol. 2, 201–232; Reeves, *President Kennedy*, 648–649, 653.

87. Brinkley, *John F. Kennedy*, 141–142.

88. Galbraith, "Exit Strategy."

89. John F. Kennedy Presidential Library and Museum, "Ball, George W.: Oral History Interview—JFK #3, 2/16/1968," https://www.jfklibrary.org/asset-viewer/ar chives /JFKOH/Ball%2C%20George%20W/JFKOH-GWB-03/JFKOH-GWB-03.

90. Galbraith, "Exit Strategy."

91. Cited in John McAdams, "Unspeakably Awful," *Washington Decoded*, December 11, 2009, https://www.washingtondecoded.com/site/2009/12/unspeakably-awful .html.

92. One of President Kennedy's lovers, Mimi Alford, referred to Kennedy as "the Great Compartmentalizer." Mimi Alford, *Once Upon a Secret: My Affair with President John F. Kennedy and its Aftermath* (New York: Random House, 2012), 95.

93. See for instance Newman, *JFK and Vietnam*, 219, regarding the effort to deny certain aspects of the expanding American involvement in Vietnam.

94. *JFK and Vietnam*, 423–427.

95. Stern, "Reflections on Fredrik Logevall's 'JFK: Coming of Age in the American Century, 1917–1956.'"

CHAPTER 7. NO ASSASSINS TO THE LEFT

1. Art Swift, "Majority in U.S. Still Believe JFK Killed in a Conspiracy: Mafia, Federal Government Top List of Potential Conspirators," *Gallup*, November 15, 2013. https://news.gallup.com/poll/165893/majority-believe-jfk-killed-conspiracy.aspx

2. Vincent Bugliosi, *Reclaiming History: The Assassination of President John F. Kennedy* (New York: W.W. Norton, 2007), xliii.

3. John F. Kennedy Presidential Library and Museum, "Address at California Democratic Party Dinner, Los Angeles, California, November 18, 1961," https://www.jfklibrary.org/asset-viewer/archives/JFKPOF/036/JFKPOF-036-020.

4. Karen Olsson, "Right Twisted: How Texas Became the Vanguard of Conservative Revolt," *Bookforum*, September–November 2015, https://www.bookforum.com/print/2203/how-texas-became-the-vanguard-of-conservative-revolt-14963.

5. Max Holland, "Images from an Assassination," The Kansas City Public Library, YouTube, November 13, 2013, https://www.youtube.com/watch?v=gro5L19U0BI.

6. Dante Chinni, "The One Thing All Americans Agree On: JFK Conspiracy," *NBC News*, October 29, 2017, https://www.nbcnews.com/storyline/jfk-assassination-files/one-thing-all-americans-agree-jfk-conspiracy-n815371.

7. Frances Folsom Cleveland was twenty-one years old when she married President Grover Cleveland in the White House, becoming the nation's youngest First Lady.

8. Stephen Knott, review of *Breach of Trust: How the Warren Commission Failed the Nation and Why* by Gerald D. McKnight, *History: Reviews of New Books* 53, no. 1 (2006): 26.

9. Quoted in Sheldon M. Stern, "Review: A Prosecutor Takes on the JFK Assassination," *Reviews in American History* 36, no. 1 (March 2008): 148.

10. Steven M. Gillon, "Why the Public Stopped Believing the Government About JFK's Murder," History, October 30, 2017, https://www.history.com/news/why-the-public-stopped-believing-the-government-about-jfks-murder.

11. Cited in Max Holland, "After Thirty Years: Making Sense of the Assassination," *Reviews in American History* 22, no. 2 (June 1994): 192.

12. JFK Assassination Records, "Findings," National Archives, https://www.archives.gov/research/jfk/select-committee-report/part-1c.html#anticastro.

13. Connie Gentry, "Arrest of Lee Harvey Oswald: August 9, 1963," New Orleans Historical Organization, https://neworleanshistorical.org/items/show/1471; Assassination Archives and Research Center, *Warren Commission Hearings*, vol. 10, 32–42, http://www.aarclibrary.org/publib/jfk/wc/wcvols/wh10/html/WC_V0110_0021b.htm.

14. Michael R. Beschloss, *Taking Charge: The Johnson White House Tapes, 1963–1964* (New York: Touchstone Books, 1997), 69.

15. Bugliosi, *Reclaiming History*, 1282.

16. JFK Assassination Records, Warren Commission Report, Chapter 6, "Investigation of Possible Conspiracy," National Archives, https://www.archives.gov/research/jfk/warren-commission-report/chapter-6.html; James Piereson, *Camelot and the Cultural Revolution: How the Assassination of John F. Kennedy Shattered American Liberalism* (New York: Encounter Books, 2007), 161.

17. Philip Shenon, *A Cruel and Shocking Act: The Secret History of the Kennedy Assassination* (New York: Henry Holt, 2013), 155–157; Shenon, "What Was Lee Harvey Oswald Doing in Mexico?" *Politico*, March 18, 2015, https://www.politico.com/magazine/story/2015/03/jfk-assassination-lee-harvey-oswald-mexico-116195; Deb Riechmann and Alanna Durkin Richer, "Latest JFK Files Say No Evidence Found of CIA Link to Oswald," AP News, November 4, 2017, https://apnews.com/39ba5448cbea4e349d796b998af1a68a.

18. Holland, "After Thirty Years," 197.

19. Jeffrey Goldberg, "Castro: Oswald Could Not Have Been the One Who Killed Kennedy," *Atlantic*, November 20, 2013, https://www.theatlantic.com/international/archive/2013/11/castro-oswald-could-not-have-been-the-one-who-killed-kennedy/281674/.

20. Brian Latell, *Castro's Secrets: Cuban Intelligence, The CIA, and the Assassination of John F. Kennedy* (New York: St. Martin's Griffin, 2013), 215–216; Richard Luscombe, "Fidel Castro May Have Known of Oswald Plan to Kill JFK, Book Claims," *Guardian*, March 18, 2012, https://www.theguardian.com/world/2012/mar/18/fidel-castro-oswald-jfk-book.

21. Shenon, *Cruel and Shocking Act*, 5–9, 503–508, 527–529, 534, 546–547, 551–556; Ron Rosenbaum, "Why'd Oswald Do It?" *Slate*, November 21, 2013, https://slate.com/news-and-politics/2013/11/philip-shenons-a-cruel-and-shocking-act-stunning-reporting-in-new-book-may-reveal-why-oswald-shot-john-f-kennedy.html.

22. Quoted in Goldberg, "Castro."

23. Ron Rosenbaum, "Why'd Oswald Do It?" *Slate*, November 21, 2013, https://slate.com/news-and-politics/2013/11/philip-shenons-a-cruel-and-shocking-act-stunning-reporting-in-new-book-may-reveal-why-oswald-shot-john-f-kennedy.html.

24. Goldberg, "Castro."

25. Piereson, *Camelot and the Cultural Revolution*, 130.

26. Thomas Mallon, "Dead Reckoning," *Columbia Journalism Review*, May/June 2009, https://archives.cjr.org/second_read/dead_reckoning_1.php.

27. Quoted in Richard D. Mahoney, *Sons & Brothers: The Days of Jack and Bobby Kennedy* (New York: Arcade Publishing, 1999), 87.

28. Arthur M. Schlesinger Jr., *Robert Kennedy and His Times* (Boston, MA: Houghton Mifflin , 1978), 494–495.

29. Thomas Maier, "Inside the CIA's Plot to Kill Fidel Castro—With Mafia Help," *Politico*, February 24, 2018, https://www.politico.com/magazine/story/2018/02/24/fidel-castro-cia-mafia-plot-216977.

30. David Kaiser, *The Road to Dallas: The Assassination of John F. Kennedy* (Cambridge, MA: Belknap Press, 2009), 3–6.

31. Jeffrey A. Frank, "The Sins of the Godfather?: Mob Lawyer Frank Ragano Says He Knows Who Killed JFK," *Washington Post*, June 21, 1994, https://www.washingtonpost.com/archive/lifestyle/1994/06/21/the-sins-of-the-godfather-mob-lawyer-frank-ragano-says-he-knows-who-killed-jfk/1ce335b6–23f0–4386-b371-e6990ebbd820/.

32. JFK Assassination Records, "Summary of Findings," National Archives, https://www.archives.gov/research/jfk/select-committee-report/part-1c.html

33. Gerald Posner, *Case Closed: Lee Harvey Oswald and the Assassination of President Kennedy* (New York: Anchor Books, 1994), 238–241.

34. Posner, *Case Closed*, 238–241.

35. Tim Cloward, "Conspiracy A-Go-Go: Dallas at the Fiftieth Anniversary of the Assassination," *Southwest Review* 98, issue 4 (Fall 2013): 407–436

36. Cloward, "Conspiracy A-Go-Go," 407–436.

37. Jim Naughton, "Don DeLillo, Caught in History's Trap," *Washington Post*, August 24, 1988, https://www.washingtonpost.com/archive/lifestyle/1988/08/24/don-delillo-caught-in-historys-trap/48a5b0b1–8bd9–412f-8426–843a405896fe/.

38. Thomas DePietro, ed., *Conversations with Don DeLillo* (Jackson, MS: University Press of Mississippi, 2005), 124.

39. Jim Naughton, "Don DeLillo."

40. Don DeLillo, "*Libra* Readers Guide," Penguin Random House, https://www.penguinrandomhouse.com/books/298769/libra-by-don-delillo/9781101042175/readers-guide/.

41. Cloward, "Conspiracy A-Go-Go."

42. Cloward, "Conspiracy A-Go-Go; Jonathan Kay, *Among the Truthers: A Journey Through America's Growing Conspiracist Underground* (New York: HarperCollins, 2011), 51; Jim Marrs, *The Terror Conspiracy: Deception, 9/11 and the Loss of Liberty* (New York: Disinformation Company, 2006), 399.

43. E. J. Dickson, "QAnon Followers Think JFK. Jr., is Coming Back on the 4th of July," *Rolling Stone*, July 3, 2019, https://www.rollingstone.com/culture/culture-features/qanon-jfk-jr-conspiracy-theory-854938/.

44. Jim Marrs, *Crossfire: The Plot that Killed Kennedy* (New York: Basic Books, 2013), xviii; Cloward, "Conspiracy A-Go-Go."

45. Quoted in Holland, "After Thirty Years," 192.

46. Holland, "After Thirty Years," 192–193.

47. For a more complete account of this event, which was not revealed until 2016, see my "JFK: A Motorcade. A Rifle. But This Wasn't Dallas." *History News Network*, April 24, 2016, https://historynewsnetwork.org/article/162604 and "The Assassination That Could Have Sparked World War III," *Washington Post*, November 23, 2018, https://www.washingtonpost.com/outlook/2018/11/23/assassination-that-couldve-sparked-world-war-iii/. American assassins tend to run young. John Wilkes Booth

was twenty-six when he killed President Lincoln; Leon Czolgosz was twenty-eight when he murdered President McKinley; Robert Kennedy's assassin, Sirhan Sirhan, was twenty-four.

48. John F. Kennedy Presidential Library and Museum, "Protecting Jacqueline Kennedy, Clint Hill" Kennedy Library Forums, https://www.jfklibrary.org/events -and-awards/forums/past-forums/transcripts/protecting-jacqueline-kennedy; Donald E. Wilkes, Jr., "Intriguing Mystery—The Secret Service and the JFK Assassination," School of Law, University of Georgia, Popular Media, September 5, 2012, https:// digitalcommons.law.uga.edu/cgi/viewcontent.cgi?article=1174&context=fac_pm.

49. Wilkes, "Intriguing Mystery." On November 7, 1962, President Kennedy called John Connally to discuss the latter's recent victory in his campaign for governor of Texas. Much of this four-minute conversation focused on the difficulties faced by Democratic candidates in Dallas, a city Connally described as composed of "junior executives and society gals." Connally lost Dallas rather convincingly, adding, "they just murdered all of us." John F. Kennedy Presidential Library and Museum, Telephone Recordings, Dictation Belt 6A, https://www.jfklibrary.org/asset-viewer/ar chives/JFKPOF/TPH/JFKPOF-TPH-06A/JFKPOF-TPH-06A.

50. Holland, "Truth Behind JFK's Assassination."

51. JFK Assassination Records, "Summary of Findings," National Archives.

52. JFK Assassination Records, "Summary of Findings," National Archives.

53. Posner, *Case Closed*, 241.

54. Bill Rockwood, "Twenty-Four Years," PBS, Frontline, November 19, 2013, https://www.pbs.org/wgbh/frontline/article/twenty-four-years/.

55. Holland, "Truth Behind JFK's Assassination."

56. Ted Gioia, "The Most Important Film of All Time," *The Daily Beast*, November 22, 2015, https://www.thedailybeast.com/the-most-important-film-of-all -time-266-seconds-by-abraham-zapruder; Alexandra Zapruder, *Twenty Six Seconds: A Personal History of the Zapruder Film* (New York: Twelve, 2016), 241–243; Dennis McLellan, "Charles Berlitz, 90; Linguist and Author on the Paranormal," *Los Angeles Times*, January 1, 2004, https://www.latimes.com/archives/la-xpm-2004-jan-01-me -berlitz1-story.html.

57. Edward Jay Epstein, *The JFK Assassination Diary: My Search for Answer to the Mystery of the Century* (New York: FastTrack Press, EJE Publications, 2014), 92–94.

58. Holland, "After Thirty Years," 203, 208.

59. Harrison Smith, "Priscilla Johnson McMillan, Historian who knew both JFK and Oswald, Dies at 92," *Washington Post*, July 9, 2021, https://www.washingtonpost .com/local/obituaries/priscilla-johnson-mcmillan-dead/2021/07/09/fbf09894-e0bd -11eb-9f54-7eee10b5fcd2_story.html.

CHAPTER 8. LEGACY

1. John F. Kennedy Presidential Library and Museum, "Remarks at Amherst College, Amherst, Massachusetts, October 26, 1963," https://www.jfklibrary.org/ar chives/other-resources/john-f-kennedy-speeches/amherst-college-19631026.

2. Stephen F. Knott, "John F. Kennedy: Prince of American Progressivism," *Blue Review*, March 31, 2017, https://thebluereview.org/john-f-kennedy/; Frank Newport, "Americans Say Reagan is the Greatest U.S. President," *Gallup*, February 18, 2011, https://news.gallup.com/poll/146183/americans-say-reagan-greatest-President.aspx; Gene Healy, "John F. Kennedy was No National Treasure," *Reason*, November 5, 2013, https://reason.com/2013/11/05/getting-past-the-john-f-kennedy-mytholog/.

3. Andrew Dugan and Frank Newport, "Americans Rate JFK Among Top Modern Presidents," *Gallup*, November 15, 2013, https://news.gallup.com/poll/165902/americans-rate-jfk-top-modern-President.aspx.

4. "Presidential Historians Survey, 2021," C-SPAN, June 30, 2021, https://www.c-span.org/presidentsurvey2021/?personid=2419.

5. The best account of Jacqueline Kennedy's control over her husband's funeral arrangements can be found in Michael J. Hogan, *The Afterlife of John Fitzgerald Kennedy: A Biography* (Cambridge: Cambridge University Press, 2017), ch. 4. See also David M. Lubin, "How Jackie Kennedy Orchestrated the Perfect Funeral," *Business Insider*, November 25, 2013, https://www.businessinsider.com/jfk-funeral-arrangement-2013–11; "John F. Kennedy Funeral, November 25, 1963," White House Historical Association, https://www.whitehousehistory.org/john-f-kennedy-funeral; Meghan O'Rourke, "How Jackie Mourned," *Slate*, November 21, 2013, https://slate.com/human-interest/2013/11/jfk-assassination-jacqueline-kennedy-mourned-in-public-with-grace-purpose-and-blood-on-her-suit.html.

6. Glen Johnson, "JFK Library Releases Full Text of Jackie's Interview After the Assassination," *Associated Press*, May 26, 1995, https://apnews.com/c2e19819ac56794b17c87325f1641a91.

7. Sally Bedell Smith, "Grace and Power," *New York Times*, July 24, 2004, https://www.nytimes.com/2004/07/25/books/chapters/grace-and-power.html; Madison Jones, "Jackie Kennedy: The Public Diplomacy of Camelot," *CPD Blog*, University of Southern California Center on Public Diplomacy, November 22, 2016, https://www.uscpublicdiplomacy.org/blog/jackie-kennedy-public-diplomacy-camelot.

8. James Piereson, *Camelot and the Cultural Revolution: How the Assassination of John F. Kennedy Shattered American Liberalism*, (New York: Encounter Books, 2007), 187–189; Mark White, *Kennedy: A Cultural History of an American Icon* (New York: Bloomsbury Academic, 2013), 89.

9. Barbie Zelizer, *Covering the Body: The Kennedy Assassination, the Media, and the Shaping of Collective Memory* (Chicago: University of Chicago Press, 1992), 102; Piereson, *Camelot and the Cultural Revolution*, 187.

10. Sam Kashner, "A Clash of Camelots," *Vanity Fair*, October 2009, https://www.vanityfair.com/news/2009/10/death-of-a-President200910; Thomas Mallon, "Dead Reckoning," *Columbia Journalism Review*, May/June 2009, https://archives.cjr.org/second_read/dead_reckoning_1.php.

11. Kashner, "A Clash of Camelots"; Richard Reeves, *President Kennedy: Profile of Power* (New York: Simon & Schuster, 1993), 669n44.

12. Michael J. Hogan, *Afterlife of John Fitzgerald Kennedy*, 278n13; Jill Abramson, "Kennedy, the Elusive President," *The New York Times*, October 22, 2013, https://www.nytimes.com/2013/10/27/books/review/the-elusive-president.html ; Alex Beam, "Intruder Scales the Walls of Camelot But Not the Fence Around JFK Library," South Florida Sun Sentinel, February 1, 1993, https://www.sun-sentinel.com/news/fl-xpm-1993–02–01–9301070044-story.html.

13. Ted Sorensen, *Counselor: A Life at the Edge of History* (New York: Harper, 2008), 407.

14. John F. Kennedy Presidential Library and Museum, "Fay, Paul B.: Oral History Interview—JFK#1, 11/9/1970"; Reeves, *President Kennedy*, 669n44; Evan Thomas, *Robert Kennedy, His Life* (New York: Simon & Schuster, 2000), 330; Andy Logan, "JFK: The Stained Glass Image," *American Heritage*, August 1967, vol. 18, no. 5, https://www.americanheritage.com/jfk-stained-glass-image. Richard Reeves puts the deleted word count from Fay's book at two thousand words.

15. Richard Reeves, "My Six Years with JFK," *American Heritage*, November 1993, vol. 44, no. 7, https://www.americanheritage.com/my-six-years-jfk#2.

16. Portions of this passage originally appeared in Stephen F. Knott, "What Might Have Been," *Review of Politics*, 76, no. 4 (Fall 2014): 661–670; Richard Reeves, "My Six Years with JFK."

17. Arthur Schlesinger, Jr., "On the Writing of Contemporary History," *Atlantic*, March 1967, https://www.theatlantic.com/magazine/archive/1967/03/on-the-writing-of-contemporary-history/305731/; John F. Kennedy Presidential Library and Museum, "Fay, Paul B.: Oral History Interview."

18. Arthur M. Schlesinger, Jr., *Journals: 1952–2000* (New York: Penguin Press, 2000), 280, 387, 415. Portions of this passage originally appeared in Knott, "What Might Have Been."

19. Schlesinger, *Journals: 1952–2000*, 432–433, 710, 745. Portions of this passage originally appeared in Knott, "What Might Have Been."

20. Schlesinger, *Journals: 1952–2000*, 432, 675; *The Letters of Arthur Schlesinger Jr.*, eds. Andrew Schlesinger and Stephen Schlesinger (New York: Random House, 2013), 488; Knott, "What Might Have Been," 663–665.

21. Schlesinger, *Letters*, 488–489; Sorensen, *Counselor*, 319; Schlesinger, *Journals: 1952–2000*, 558; Knott, "What Might Have Been," 663–665.

22. Robert Dallek, *An Unfinished Life: John F. Kennedy, 1917-1963* (New York: Back Bay Books, 2004), 476.

23. "Q & A With Robert Dallek," C-SPAN, January 2, 2014, https://www.c-span.org/video/?316974–1/qa-robert-dallek.

24. "President Kennedy: Profile of Power," C-SPAN, October 14, 1993, https://www.c-span.org/video/?52460–1/President-kennedy-profile-power; Paula Span, "Monumental Ambition," *Washington Post*, February 17, 2002, https://www.washingtonpost.com/archive/lifestyle/magazine/2002/02/17/monumental-ambition/e61fbd91–0e31–4f4f-af6c-a12f98e3d10b/.

25. Paula Span, "Monumental Ambition."

26. Hogan, *Afterlife of John Fitzgerald Kennedy*, 207, 274n56; Paula Span, "Monumental Ambition."

27. Hogan, *Afterlife of John Fitzgerald Kennedy*, 175–178.

28. John Meroney, "'The Kennedys' Creator Defends His Controversial New Series," *Atlantic*, March 31, 2011, https://www.theatlantic.com/entertainment/archive/2011/03/the-kennedys-creator-defends-his-controversial-new-series/73210/; Joan Vennochi, "Kennedys Still Writing Their Own Script," *Boston Globe*, January 13, 2011, http://archive.boston.com/bostonglobe/editorial_opinion/oped/articles/2011/01/13/kennedys_still_writing_their_own_script/.

29. Larry Sabato, "John F. Kennedy's Final Days Reveal a Man Who Craved Excitement," *Forbes*, October 16, 2013, https://www.forbes.com/sites/realspin/2013/10/16/john-f-kennedys-final-days-reveal-a-man-who-craved-excitement/?sh=51a9e8617a9.

30. Billings quoted in Fred I. Greenstein, *The Presidential Difference: Leadership Style from FDR to Barack Obama* (Princeton, NJ: Princeton University Press, 2009), 72.

31. Janny Scott, "In Tapes, Candid Talk by Young Kennedy Widow," *New York Times*, September 11, 2001, https://www.nytimes.com/2011/09/12/us/12jackie.html?; Barbara Leaming, "The Winter of Her Despair," *Vanity Fair*, October, 2014, https://www.vanityfair.com/style/society/2014/10/jacqueline-kennedy-jfk-assassination-depression.

32. Liesl Schillinger, "JFK's Intern," *New York Times*, February 11, 2012, https://www.nytimes.com/2012/02/12/opinion/sunday/jfks-intern.html; Sorensen, *Counselor*, 122.

33. Sorensen, *Counselor*, 118; portions of this passage originally appeared in Knott, "What Might Have Been."

34. Sorensen, *Counselor*, 118, 122–123.

35. Sorensen, *Counselor*, 121; 123. Portions of this passage originally appeared in Knott, "What Might Have Been."

36. Sabato, *The Kennedy Half-Century*, 129. Portions of this passage originally appeared in Knott, "What Might Have Been."

37. Seymour M. Hersh, *The Dark Side of Camelot* (Boston: Back Bay Books, 1998), 243–246.

38. The John F. Kennedy Library in Boston has a copy of a sad poem written by Jacqueline Kennedy entitled "A Secret Reflection," written after the president's murder, acknowledging the many women in his life (whom she claims he never loved) but noting that she had always remained special to him.

39. Author Taylor Branch argues that there was something of a quid pro quo between Robert Kennedy and J. Edgar Hoover, where Hoover, "without ever saying, 'you've got to do this for that,'" essentially blackmailed Robert Kennedy into authorizing the wiretapping of King in exchange for keeping the lid on President Kennedy's extramarital affairs. See Taylor Branch, *Parting the Waters: America in the King Years, 1954–63* (New York: Simon & Schuster, 1988), 904–914; C-SPAN, Booknotes, "Interview with Taylor Branch," April 12, 1998, http://www.booknotes.org/Watch/100454–1/Taylor-Branch.

40. Benjamin Hufbauer, *Presidential Temples: How Memorials and Libraries Shape Public Memory* (Lawrence, KS: University Press of Kansas, 2005), 71–72.

41. Jon Ward, *Camelot's End: The Democrats' Last Great Civil War* (New York: Twelve, 2019), 152, 154. Regarding Jacqueline Kennedy's "ostentatious" "flinch"— President Carter had already kissed Mrs. Kennedy when he first arrived at the library. He then went for a tour of the museum and then appeared on stage where he attempted to repeat the act for a televised audience.

42. John F. Kennedy Presidential Library and Museum, "1979 Dedication Remarks by Senator Edward M. Kennedy," https://www.jfklibrary.org/about-us/about -the-jfk-library/history/1979-dedication-remarks-by-senator-kennedy.

43. Ward, *Camelot's End*, ch. 10; Jonathan Martin, "Mudd: Kennedy Recollection a 'Fantasy,'" *Politico*, September 18, 2009, https://www.politico.com/story/2009/09 /mudd-kennedy-recollection-a-fantasy-027316.

44. Barbara A. Perry, *Edward M. Kennedy: An Oral History* (New York: Oxford University Press, 2019), 227.

45. John B. Judis, "This Book was the First to Spill JFK's Secrets. So Why has it Been Totally Forgotten?" *New Republic*, October 28, 2013, https://newrepublic.com /article/115383/very-good-jfk-biography-why-has-search-jfk-been-forgotten; John M. Murphy, *John F. Kennedy and the Liberal Persuasion* (East Lansing, MI: Michigan State University Press, 2019) 312n129; Thomas C. Reeves, *A Question of Character: A Life of John F. Kennedy* (New York: Prima Publishing, 1997), 8.

46. Peter Collier and David Horowitz, *The Kennedys: An American Drama* (New York: Summit Books, 1984).

47. Christopher Lehmann-Haupt, "Books of the Times," *New York Times*, June 13, 1984, https://www.nytimes.com/1984/06/13/books/books-of-the-times-256806.html.

48. Thomas C. Reeves, *A Question of Character: A Life of John F. Kennedy* (New York: Prima Publishing, 1997), 8, 106.

49. Reeves, *Question of Character*, 118.

50. Reeves, *Question of Character*, 278.

51. Nancy Gager Clinch, *The Kennedy Neurosis: A Psychological Portrait of an American Dynasty* (New York: Grosset & Dunlap, 1973).

52. William E. Leuchtenberg, "John F Kennedy: Twenty Years Later," *American Heritage*, December 1983, vol. 35, issue 1, https://www.americanheritage.com /john-f-kennedy-twenty-years-later#5.

53. Thomas G. Paterson, *Kennedy's Quest for Victory: American Foreign Policy, 1961–1963* (New York: Oxford University Press, 1989).

54. Paterson, *Kennedy's Quest for Victory: American Foreign Policy, 1961–1963* (New York: Oxford University Press, 1989), 5, 7, 19, 20; Thomas G. Paterson, "Bearing the Burden: A Critical Look at JFK's Foreign Policy," *Virginia Quarterly Review*, Spring 1978, vol. 54, no. 2, https://www.vqronline.org/essay/bearing-burden-critical -look-jfk%E2%80%99s-foreign-policy; Sheldon M. Stern, *The Cuban Missile Crisis in American Memory: Myths versus Reality*, (Stanford, CA: Stanford University Press, 2012), 155–156.

55. "Christopher Hitchens Liked Guys, Hated JFK," *New York Post,* May 2, 2010, https://pagesix.com/2010/05/02/christopher-hitchens-liked-guys-hated-jfk/; Christopher Hitchens, "Feckless Youth: What Kennedy Magic?" *Atlantic,* September 2006, https://www.theatlantic.com/magazine/archive/2006/09/feckless-youth/305095/.

56. Garry Wills, "Did Kennedy Cause the Crisis?"; Wills quoted in Thomas E. Cronin, *On the Presidency: Teacher, Soldier, Shaman, Pol* (New York: Routledge, 2009), 111.

57. Quoted in Cronin, *On the Presidency,* 112.

58. Bruce Miroff, *Icons of Democracy: American Leaders as Heroes, Aristocrats, Dissenters, and Democrats* (Lawrence, KS: University Press of Kansas, 2000), 402n36; Bruce Miroff, *Pragmatic Illusions: The Presidential Politics of John F. Kennedy* (New York: David McKay, 1976), 96–100; Ronald E. Powaski, *American Presidential Statecraft: During the Cold War and After* (New York: Palgrave MacMillan, 2017), 15.

59. Kallina contends that the Daley machine's primary concern was the local Cook County elections, not the presidential race. He dismisses many of the main talking points about the "stolen" election, including the timing of the release of the Cook County votes and the false claim that there was never a recount in Cook County (there were two). Edmund F. Kallina Jr., *Courthouse over White House: Chicago and the Presidential Election of 1960* (Gainesville, FL: University Press of Florida, 1988); Edmund F. Kallina Jr., *Kennedy v. Nixon: The Presidential Election of 1960* (Gainesville, FL: University Press of Florida, 2010); Paul Von Hippel, "Here's a Voter Fraud Myth: Richard Daley 'Stole' Illinois for John Kennedy in the 1960 Election," *Washington Post,* August 8, 2017, https://www.washingtonpost.com/news/monkey-cage/wp/2017/08/08/heres-a-voter-fraud-myth-richard-daley-stole-illinois-for-john-kennedy-in-the-1960-election/.

60. Hersh, *Dark Side of Camelot,* xii, 2–3, 4–5, 100, 131, 140, 167, 168, 244–245, 295–296, 324, 439; Edward J. Epstein, "The Dark Side of Camelot," *Los Angeles Times,* December 28, 1997, https://www.latimes.com/archives/la-xpm-1997-dec-28-bk-3242-story.html.

61. Garry Wills, "A Second Assassination," *New York Review of Books,* December 18, 1997, https://www.nybooks.com/articles/1997/12/18/a-second-assassination/; Barry Bearak, "Book Portrays JFK as Reckless and Immoral," *New York Times,* November 9, 1997, https://www.nytimes.com/1997/11/09/us/book-portrays-jfk-as-reckless-and-immoral.html; Glenn Frankel, "Major Scoops and Controversies of a Storied Investigative Journalist," *Washington Post,* June 15, 2018, https://www.washingtonpost.com/outlook/major-scoops-and-controversies-of-a-storied-investigative-journalist/2018/06/15/f7439398–5937–11e8–8836-a4a123c359ab_story.html.

62. Hersh, *Dark Side of Camelot,* 1–2; Epstein, "Dark Side of Camelot."

63. Epstein, "Dark Side of Camelot."

64. Bearak, "Book Portrays JFK as Reckless and Immoral."

65. Seymour Hersh won a Pulitzer for his reporting on the My Lai Massacre, and other awards for his coverage of Vietnam and Watergate. His later investigative reporting consistently emphasized the conspiratorial nature of every action of

the United States government. He appeared on Alex Jones' *Infowars* program, and his work was frequently cited on the Russian network *RT*. In 2015 he published a thinly sourced piece questioning almost every element of the Obama administration's account of the killing of Osama Bin Laden: "The White House's story might have been written by Lewis Carroll." He also flirted with the conspiracy theory that a staffer for the Democratic National Committee who was murdered in 2016 was the source of a leak of embarrassing emails related to Hillary Clinton. Additionally, Hersh accepted the denials of the Assad government in Syria that they had not used chemical weapons against their own people, abandoning the skeptical approach he routinely practiced with the American government. Seymour M. Hersh, "The Killing of Osama Bin Laden," *London Review of Books*, May 21, 2015, vol. 37, no. 10, https://www.lrb.co.uk/the-paper/v37/n10/seymour-m.-hersh/the-killing-of-osama-bin-laden; Paul Farhi, "The Ever-iconoclastic, Never-to-be-ignored, Muckraking Seymour Hersh," *Washington Post*, May 15, 2015, https://www.washingtonpost.com/lifestyle/style/the-ever-iconoclastic-never-to-be-ignored-muckraking-seymour-hersh/2015/05/15/4eb1195a-f9a2-11e4-9ef4-1bb7ce3b3fb7_story.html; Steve Bloomfield, "Whatever Happened to Seymour Hersh," *Prospect*, July 17, 2018, https://www.prospectmagazine.co.uk/magazine/whatever-happened-to-seymour-hersh.

66. Timothy Noah, "JFK, Monster," *New Republic*, February 8, 2012, https://newrepublic.com/article/100566/jfk-monster; Leslie Bennetts, "JFK Intern-Mistress Mimi Alford Confesses, 'I Did Love Him,'" *Daily Beast*, February 9, 2012, https://www.thedailybeast.com/jfks-intern-mistress-mimi-alford-confesses-i-did-love-him; Liesl Schillinger, "JFK's Intern," *New York Times*, February 11, 2012, https://www.nytimes.com/2012/02/12/opinion/sunday/jfks-intern.html.

67. Reeves, "My Six Years With JFK."

68. *JFK: Intimate Memories of an Icon*, directed by Susan Bellows (Boston: American Experience Films, Public Broadcasting System, 2013), https://www.pbs.org/wgbh/americanexperience/features/jfk-intimate-memories-icon/.

69. Christopher Matthews, *Jack Kennedy: Elusive Hero* (New York: Simon & Schuster, 2011), 44, 404.

70. "John F. Kennedy and PT-109," John F. Kennedy Presidential Library and Museum, https://www.jfklibrary.org/learn/about-jfk/jfk-in-history/john-f-kennedy-and-pt-109; Schlesinger, *Journals: 1952–2000*, 120–121.

71. "Robert S. McNamara, Architect of a Futile War, Dies at 93," *New York Times*, July 6, 2009, https://www.nytimes.com/2009/07/07/us/07mcnamara.html.

72. Kenneth P. O'Donnell and David F. Powers, *Johnny We Hardly Knew Ye: Memories of John Fitzgerald Kennedy* (Boston: Little, Brown, and Company, 1970), 262.

73. Ted Sorensen, *Kennedy: The Classic Biography* (New York: Harper Perennial Modern Classics, 2013), 63.

74. Dan Glickman, "Kennedy's Wit and Humor: A Legacy for Political Leadership," *The Hill*, November 11, 2013, https://thehill.com/blogs/congress-blog/politics/190791-kennedys-wit-and-humor-a-legacy-for-political-leadership.

75. Quoted in Stephen Hess, *America's Political Dynasties* (New York: Routledge, 2017), 520.

76. Quoted in Robert J. Dole, *Great Presidential Wit (I Wish I Was in This Book): A Collection of Humorous Anecdotes and Quotations* (New York: Scribner, 2001), 16–17.

77. Robert J. Dole, *Great Political Wit: Laughing (Almost) All the Way to the White House* (New York: Broadway Books, 1998), 23.

78. Lloyd Grove, "Barry Goldwater's Left Turn," *Washington Post,* July 28, 1994, https://www.washingtonpost.com/wp-srv/politics/daily/may98/goldwater072894 .htm.

79. Arthur M. Schlesinger, Jr., *A Thousand Days: John F. Kennedy in the White House* (Boston: Houghton Mifflin Company, 2002), 577.

80. Scott Simon, "JFK had the Wit to Lampoon Himself," *National Public Radio,* November 23, 2013, https://www.npr.org/templates/story/story.php?storyId=246872435.

81. "Dave Powers: First Museum Curator," John F. Kennedy Presidential Library and Museum, https://www.jfklibrary.org/about-us/about-the-jfk-library/history/dave -powers-first-museum-curator.

82. John F. Kennedy Presidential Library and Museum, "Cushing, Richard Cardinal, Oral History Interview—JFK #1, 1966," https://www.jfklibrary.org/asset-viewer /archives/JFKOH/Cushing%2C%20%20Richard%20Cardinal/JFKOH-RCC-01/JFK OH-RCC-01; Thomas Meier, *The Kennedys: America's Emerald Kings* (New York: Basic Books, 2003), 229.

83. Meier, *The Kennedys,* 229.

84. Reeves, "My Six Years with JFK."

85. John F. Kennedy Presidential Library and Museum, "Fay, Paul B.: Oral History Interview."

86. John F. Kennedy Presidential Library and Museum, "Address at Rice University on the Nation's Space Effort, September 12, 1962," https://www.jfklibrary .org/archives/other-resources/john-f-kennedy-speeches/rice-university-19620912; John F. Kennedy Presidential Library and Museum, "Remarks at the Dedication of the Aerospace Medical Health Center, San Antonio, Texas, November 21, 1963," https://www.jfklibrary.org/archives/other-resources/john-f-kennedy-speeches/san -antonio-tx-19631121.

87. Quoted in Joshua Lawson, "The Apollo 11 Moon Landing was a Triumph of American Exceptionalism," *Federalist,* July 18, 2019, https://thefederalist.com/2019 /07/18/apollo-11-moon-landing-triumph-american-exceptionalism/.

88. Andrew Glass, "JFK Proposes Joint Lunar Expedition with Soviets, September 20, 1963," *Politico,* September 20, 2017, https://www.politico.com/story/2017/09/20 /jfk-proposes-joint-lunar-expedition-with-soviets-sept-20–1963–242843.

89. John F. Kennedy Presidential Library and Museum, "Special Message to Congress on Urgent National Needs," May 25, 1961," https://www.jfklibrary.org /asset-viewer/archives/JFKPOF/034/JFKPOF-034-030; Sorensen, *Counselor,* 337; Charles Fishman, "The Race to the Moon was so Unpopular at One Point, President

Eisenhower Called JFK 'Nuts,'" *Fast Company*, July 14, 2019, https://www.fastcom
pany.com/90375432/the-race-to-the-moon-was-so-unpopular-at-one-point-Presi
dent-eisenhower-called-jfk-nuts.

90. Charles Fishman, *One Giant Leap: The Impossible Mission That Flew Us to the Moon* (New York: Simon & Schuster, 2019), 6, 17.

91. Fishman, *One Giant Leap*, 5.

92. Fishman, *One Giant Leap*, 34–35, 39; Lawson, "The Apollo 11 Moon Landing Was a Triumph of American Exceptionalism"; Fishman, "The Race to the Moon."

93. Charles Fishman, "If President Kennedy Hadn't Been Killed, Would We Have Landed on the Moon on July 20, 1969? It Seems Unlikely," *Fast Company*, July 17, 2019, https://www.fastcompany.com/90376962/if-President-kennedy-hadnt-been
-killed-would-we-have-landed-on-the-moon-on-july-20–1969-it-seems-unlikely.
Fishman argues that Kennedy was experiencing "creeping doubt" about the moon landing goal, doubts that were magnified when NASA Director James Webb informed him that the goal would not be achieved by the end of Kennedy's second term. Fishman speculates that "if Kennedy himself wasn't 100% behind it, Apollo might well have lost momentum."

94. John F. Kennedy Presidential Library and Museum, "Address at Rice University on the Nation's Space Effort, September 12, 1962."

95. Douglas Brinkley, *American Moonshot: John F. Kennedy and the Great Space Race* (New York: HarperCollins, 2019), 359–364; Abigail Malangone, "The JFK Library Archives: An Inside Look, We Choose to go to the Moon: The 55th Anniversary of the Rice University Speech," National Archives, September 12, 2017, https://jfk
.blogs.archives.gov/2017/09/12/we-choose-to-go-to-the-moon-the-55th-anniversary
-of-the-rice-university-speech/.

96. "Transcript of Presidential Meeting in the Cabinet Room of the White House, Topic: Supplemental appropriations for the National Aeronautics and Space Administration (NASA), November 21, 1962," https://history.nasa.gov/JFK-Webbconv
/pages/transcript.pdf.

97. John F. Kennedy Presidential Library and Museum, "Remarks at the Dedication of the Aerospace Medical Health Center, San Antonio, Texas, November 21, 1963"; Andrew Lynch, "Nation in Shock at News of JFK's Assassination," *Independent.ie*, March 5, 2017, https://www.independent.ie/irish-news/nation-in-shock
-at-news-of-jfks-assassination-35497969.html; Barbara A. Perry, "Catholics and the Supreme Court," in *Catholics and Politics: The Dynamic Tension Between Faith and Power*, eds. Kristen E. Heyer, Mark J. Rozell, Michael A, Genovese (Washington: Georgetown University Press, 2008), 156; Julian Barnes, ed., *The Best of Frank O'Connor*, (New York: Everyman's Library, 2009), 480.

98. Brinkley, *American Moonshot*, 367, 453; Fishman, "The Race to the Moon." The final cost for the entire Apollo program was in the $25 to $28 billion range.

99. John F. Kennedy Presidential Library and Museum, "News Conference 53, April 3, 1963," https://www.jfklibrary.org/archives/other-resources/john-f-kennedy
-press-conferences/news-conference-53.

100. "Reagan is Laid to Rest," *CNN*, June 11, 2004, https://www.cnn.com/2004/ALLPOLITICS/06/11/reagan.friday2/index.html.

101. John F. Kennedy Presidential Library and Museum, "1985 Tribute by President Reagan," June 24, 1985, https://www.jfklibrary.org/about-us/about-the-jfk-library/history/1985-tribute-by-President-reagan.

102. Christopher J. Matthews, "Your Host, Ronald Reagan," *New Republic*, March 26, 1984, https://newrepublic.com/article/132690/host-ronald-reagan.

103. Stephen F. Knott, *The Lost Soul of the American Presidency* (Lawrence, KS: The University Press of Kansas, 2019), 160; Yuval Levin, "Burke, Paine, and Reagan," *National Review*, December 4, 2013, https://www.nationalreview.com/corner/burke-paine-and-reagan-yuval-levin/.

104. Scott Farris, *Kennedy and Reagan: Why Their Legacies Endure* (Guilford, CT: Lyons Press, 2013), viii, 90; "Kennedy and Reagan: Why Their Legacies Endure," *Kirkus Reviews*, October 20, 2013, https://www.kirkusreviews.com/book-reviews/scott-farris/kennedy-and-reagan/.

105. "A City Upon a Hill: JFK Cribs from John Winthrop," *New England Historical Society*, https://www.newenglandhistoricalsociety.com/city-upon-hill-sermon-good-speech/; Daniel T. Rodgers, "What We Get Wrong About 'A City On A Hill," *Washington Post*, November 13, 2018, https://www.washingtonpost.com/outlook/2018/11/13/what-we-get-wrong-about-city-hill/.

106. John F. Kennedy Presidential Library and Museum, "1985 Tribute by President Reagan."